OUT OF THE CHANNEL

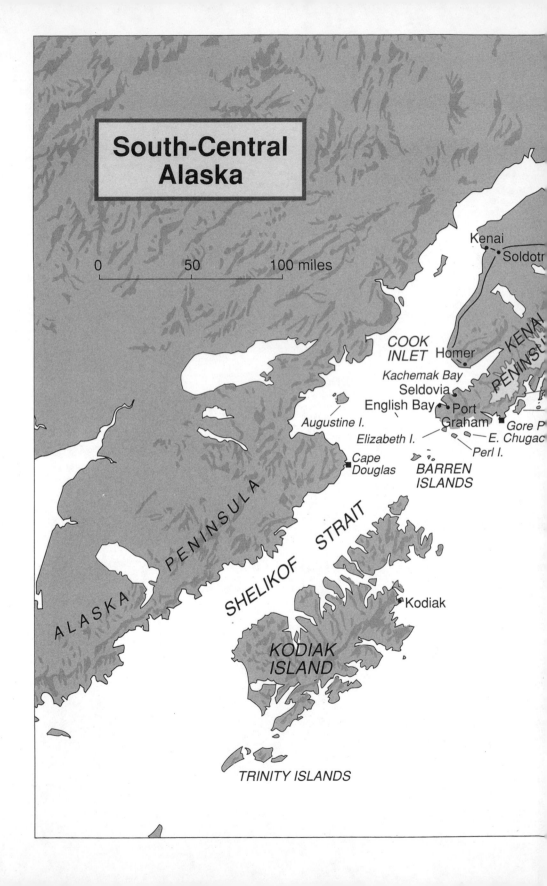

South-Central Alaska

0　　　　50　　　　100 miles

Kenai

Soldotr

COOK
INLET　Homer

KENAI

PENINSU

Kachemak Bay

Seldovia

English Bay　　Port
　　　　　　　　Graham

Augustine I.

Gore P

E. Chugac

Elizabeth I.

Perl I.

Cape
Douglas

BARREN
ISLANDS

SHELIKOF　STRAIT

ALASKA　PENINSULA

Kodiak

KODIAK
ISLAND

TRINITY ISLANDS

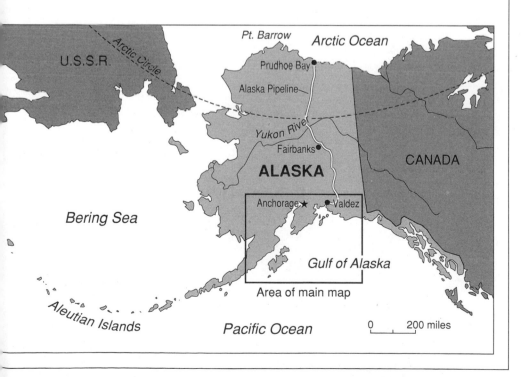

Glennallen
Glenn Highway
Copper R.
Richardson Highway
Prince William Sound
Columbia Glacier
Valdez
Alaska Pipeline
Glacier I.
Anchorage
Ellamar
Tatitlek
Whittier
Esther I.
Perry I.
Orca Bay
Cordova
Naked I.
Bligh I.
Hawkins I.
Port Nellie Juan
Smith I.
Knight Island Passage
Hinchinbrook I.
Chenega
Knight I.
Cape Hinchinbrook
Seward
Green I.
Evans I.
Montague I.
Resurrection Bay
Bainbridge I.
Cape St. Elias
Cape Resurrection
Latouche I.
Elrington I.
Kenai Fjords National Park
a I.

GULF OF ALASKA

Pt. Barrow
Arctic Ocean
Arctic Circle
U.S.S.R.
Prudhoe Bay
Alaska Pipeline
Yukon River
Fairbanks
ALASKA
CANADA
Bering Sea
Anchorage ★
Valdez
Gulf of Alaska
Area of main map
Aleutian Islands
Pacific Ocean
0   200 miles

OUT OF THE CHANNEL

The Exxon Valdez
Oil Spill in
Prince William Sound

JOHN KEEBLE

■ HarperCollins*Publishers*

Portions of this book appeared in different form in the *Village Voice*, May 16, 1989; and in *Season of Dead Waters*, edited by Helen Frost (Breitenbush Books, 1990).

FIRST EDITION

Designed by Helene Berinsky

Library of Congress Cataloging-in-Publication Data

Keeble, John, 1944–
   Out of the channel : the Exxon *Valdez* oil spill in Prince William
Sound / by John Keeble.
     p.   cm.
   Includes bibliographical references.
   ISBN 0-06-016334-8
   1. Oil spills—Environmental aspects—Alaska—Prince William Sound
Region. 2. Oil spills—Economic aspects—Alaska—Prince William
Sound Region. 3. Tankers—Accidents—Environmental aspects—Alaska—
Prince William Sound Region. 4. Exxon *Valdez* (Ship) 5. Alyeska
Pipeline Service Company. I. Title.
TD427.P4K38 1991
363.73'82'097983—dc20   89-46513

91 92 93 94 95   AC/MP   10 9 8 7 6 5 4 3 2 1

To individuals of these, and more, to all of them, snagged in the channel . . .

Phalacrocorax pelagicus, Oceanodroma furcata, Charadrius semipalmatus, Brachyramphus marmoratus, Uria aalge, Cepphus columba, Lunda cirrhata, Haliaeetus leucocephalus, Ursus arctos, Odocoileus hemionus, Enhydra lustris, Phoca vitulina, Megaptera novaeangliae, Orcinus orca, Oncorhynchus gorbuscha, Hippoglossus stenolepsis, Katharina tunicata, Musculus niger, Saxidomus giganteus, Pycnopodia helianthoides, Solaster dawsoni, Zostera marina, Chlorophycophyta, Anonyx . . .

In Memoriam.

CONTENTS

II MONEY

ACKNOWLEDGMENTS

With the exception of industry and government officials, and eventually of members of the scientific community who for one reason and another were not permitted to speak to the press, it was rare to find people in and out of Alaska who were not willing to share freely their insights and experiences with the Alaskan and other oil spills. Many, but not all, of those who spoke to me are mentioned in the pages that follow. I am grateful to each of them. Others took it upon themselves to inform me to a degree well beyond the immediate requirements. Among these were Charles Jurasz, Peter Jurasz, Lynn Schooler, Hild Sandstede, Mei Mei Evans, Richard Newman, Riki Ott, Kathy Conlan, Dan Reed, Bruce Stewart, Gordon Robilliard, Nancy Bird, Ken Adams, Gerald McCune, Marilyn Leland, and Rick Steiner. I am also indebted to the Exxon Corporation for information provided to me, to Arco Oil for support in the form of a tour of North Slope facilities, to the office of my congressman, Thomas J. Foley, for documents and advice speedily given, and especially to the editors of the *Village Voice*, who displayed their trust by first sending me to Valdez.

As I traveled, there were those who not only gave me the advantage of their knowledge but also offered their friendship, and the comfort of a meal, of a place to take a shower, or to sleep. Among these were Larry

Smith of Homer, and his mother, Louella Smith, Vivien and John Mickelson of Seldovia, Susan and Ron Chappell of Anchorage, Belle and Pete Mickelson, Heather and Max McCarty, Kelly Weaverling and Susan Ogle, and Brenda Guest, all of Cordova. John Oliver of Moss Landing Marine Institute and David Grimes of Cordova each added immeasurably to my understanding and made what would prove to be indispensable arrangements to put me in direct contact with the waters of Prince William Sound. I am grateful to my fellow writers, Tess Gallagher and Barry Lopez, for advice given at critical moments, and to my editor, Ted Solotaroff, for his enduring patience and care.

Despite her own busy schedule, my wife, Claire, helped to keep my ever-mounting stacks of documents organized and put in library time for me, and along with my three sons otherwise supported this unexpected obsession. More than that, she and my sons, and my parents, provided a backdrop of constancy and hope against which the events in Alaska came to be cast. The sense of my great good luck in having my life stitched together with their lives was a thing I carried with me always in my travels and my witnessing of the struggles of others to restore themselves in the disaster's aftermath. Many of them had been shaken to their roots and discovered that the very groundwork of the ties by which they had previously connected themselves to the world had been sundered.

I OIL

Chapter 1

INTRUDERS

> . . . the structure of every organic being is related, in the most essential yet often hidden manner, to that of all the other organic beings, with which it comes into competition for food or residence, or from which it has to escape, or on which it preys.
>
> —Charles Darwin, *The Origin of Species,* 1859

On June 15, 1989, 82 days after the grounding of the Exxon *Valdez,* I walked along a beach of coarse sand and pebbles with Peter Slattery of Moss Landing Marine Institute and Gordon Robilliard, vice president of Entrix, a private environmental consulting company based in San Diego. Both men are marine biologists. A semipalmated plover appeared in our path. It was a sandpiperlike bird, small, leggy, and colored to keep itself secret—tan on top and white beneath, with a black breast band. It limped in front of us, one outstretched wing dragging on the ground. The three of us stopped. The plover stumbled toward a narrow creek that drained into the sea, then disappeared over the edge of the bank.

When we changed our course to the left, it appeared again, chirping wildly. It flew toward us, landed, and limped off. Peter moved farther along and the plover straggled in his path. Gordon and I swung to the right. A second plover appeared with precisely the same infirmity as the first. It chirped at us. The plover near Peter chirped back. The sound they exchanged was like a very thin, hysterical cry. It was a decoy activity, we realized. The second plover stopped right in front of Gordon's boot and spread out one wing, placing itself in a position of extreme vulnerability.

3

I glanced over at Gordon. He is a large man, bearded, heavyset, and possessed of a sharp wit and at times an aggressive sense of irony. It was he who had introduced me to the phrase "the Bambi effect" as a description of the emotional and ideological turbulence awakened by the wholesale death of sea otters following the grounding of the Exxon *Valdez*. He gazed down at the plover and smiled faintly. In an instant of alarm, I thought he might step out and crush the bird.

I was wrong. He didn't move a muscle, and no doubt would never have considered harming the plover. On the contrary, the alarm was within myself, a tangle of feeling and instinct and sense that pleasured in the beauty of the bird, the pale brown and white, its delicacy of color and structure, the small, dark yellow bill with the black tip, and that at the same time was awakened to the curiosity of the bird's action, its apparent pliancy in the face of death. I found an ancient demon in myself, the killer who arose to salute the power in Gordon's position, but also another perhaps equally ancient thing, the taboo, the corrective sense to take a breath and simply watch and trust. Gordon took a step back. The bird darted off to our right and settled among the small stones. To the left, Peter stood still. There, the first bird limped along, dragging its wing. It disappeared back into the creek bed. It wished to lead Peter that way. The space of 30 square yards or so that we occupied in the company of the birds had grown radiant and taut like a drumhead. To our right, Gordon and I saw them then, the two plover chicks, no larger than my big toe and the same color exactly as the pebbles. Peter came to look. The second parent darted from one chick to the other and away. It feigned nesting activity among the pebbles, as if to distract us. Plovers make their shallow nests, or "scrapes," among the pebbles and right out in the open. It sat still for a moment, but then as if wrenched into desperation by our presence, it came back to its chicks, first to one, the other, and then away again.

The three of us moved off, down along the creek bed, across its mouth, and up a gravel bar that overlooked a broad estuary. The estuary, fed by two rivers, is called Useless Cove, probably because it is not deep enough to accommodate boats. We stopped when we saw a large brown bear in it, loping through the shallows. Its motion seemed effortless, and yet in a moment it had crossed to the tall grass on the far side directly opposite us, and then into the trees. Its flight scared up a flock of Canadian geese. They churned out of the water, flew seaward and then circled back toward the mountains. We could see water up there on the lower slopes, flashing in the sun. The geese dropped out of sight.

Chastened, we retraced our steps to where the creek met the sea. A quarter mile to our left the orange Zodiac (a fast, inflatable rubber boat) that had motored us here from our ship was beached, and not far from it I could see the figure of Kathy Conlan, a crustacean specialist from the Canadian National Museum of Natural Sciences. She was crouched and bent forward so that her face almost touched the ground. Her fingers were in the sea wrack, which she happily raided for just the sort of tiny littoral life plovers liked to eat, small crabs, amphipods, snails ... We were on the mainland, on a long, gently sloping beach between Long Point and Flent Point just west of the mouth of Columbia Bay. Back past Kathy and the Zodiac, past Flent Point, around the corner, and not visible to us but deep in the recesses of Columbia Bay, was the Columbia Glacier. Across the water before us was Glacier Island. Bits of ice had drifted to the shore where we stood, and large, blue-colored chunks of it floated out in the water. In the maritime trade the large chunks are called "growlers" after the sound they make when they rub against the hull of a ship. Similar chunks and even larger ones, called "bergy bits," floated free past Glacier Island toward the Valdez Arm. The bergy bits were the size of a train car or small house, big enough to wreak havoc with an oil tanker.

The water lapped against the shore. The booming sound of the glacier calving could be heard in the distance. It was like sporadic thunder, but a more self-contained sound without the ripping quality of thunder. The sound came from huge masses of ice shearing loose from the face of the ice flow and falling into the water. The glacier was retreating. It sloughed off huge quantities of ice, especially during the spring, summer, and fall. At the height of its activity, it could release 14 million tons of ice a day. Past the northern edge of Glacier Island, we could see the mouth of the long fjord called Valdez Arm, which was the tanker channel, and faintly the dark blue hump of Bligh Island, so named in 1794 by Captain George Vancouver, who at that time was still seeking the mythical Northwest Passage that would connect the Atlantic with the Pacific. As a young man, Vancouver had served with William Bligh under James Cook. In his search for the same passage, Cook had entered the waters of what he would call Prince William Sound in 1778.

Eighty-two days earlier, Gordon, Peter, and I might have been able to see the Exxon Valdez aground on Bligh Reef. There was no oil on this beach, nor in the water, not a trace of it, the first such place we'd seen in days. Northeastward along the arm some 40 miles from where we stood was Port Valdez and the city of Valdez itself.

Chapter 2

THE SCREENS ON
THE STAGE

The result of that brave setting out of the Pilgrims has been an atavism that thwarts and destroys. The agonized spirit, that has followed like an idiot with undeveloped brain, governs with its great muscles, babbling in a text of the dead years. Here souls perish miserably, or, escaping, are bent into grotesque designs of violence and despair. It is an added strength thrown to a continent already too powerful for men. One had not expected that this seed of England would come to impersonate, and to marry, the very primitive itself; to creep into the very intestines of the settlers and turn them against themselves, to befoul the New World.

It has become "the most lawless country in the civilized world," a panorama of murders, perversions, a terrific ungoverned strength, excusable only because of the horrid beauty of its great machines. To-day it is a generation of gross know-nothingism, of blackened churches where hymns groan like chants from stupefied jungles, a generation universally eager to barter permanent values (the hope of an aristocracy) in return for opportunist material advantages, a generation hating those whom it obeys.

What prevented the normal growth? Was it England, the northern strain, the soil they landed on? It was, of course, the whole weight of the wild continent that made their condition of mind advantageous, forcing it to reproduce its own likeness, and no more.

—William Carlos Williams, *In the American Grain*, 1925

The name is pronounced *Valdeez*. The place was first called Puerto Valdes, so named in 1790 by the Spanish explorer Salvador Fidalgo, in honor of Admiral Antonio Valdes, the commander of the Spanish Navy. The purpose of Fidalgo's voyage was to reassert the dominion of the fading Spanish empire over regions into which Russia was expanding. As it happened, Spain would hold nothing in Alaska, but Fidalgo's foray deep into the tricky waters of the sound was remarkable for the fact that it was done with a sailing vessel. The remnants of his appearance here are a few names—Valdez, Cordova, Port Gravina, Revillagigedo. Port Fidalgo, a bay just south and east of Bligh Island, was later named in honor of the Spanish explorer by Captain George Vancouver.

Valdez was not "settled" until 1898, and then mainly by Americans from the upper Midwest who had their own way of saying the word. It is suggested that since 1898 was the year of the Spanish American War, the current pronunciation was born of anti-Spanish sentiment. Valdez is situated in south-central Alaska at 61 degrees north, or at approximately the same latitude as Leningrad and the Shetland Islands. It is 375 miles south of the Arctic Circle. The average temperature is 38 degrees and the annual precipitation is near to 60 inches, much of that in the form of snow. The reason for the town's existence is the elongated, protected, and ice-free oval of water called Port Valdez. The town is built at sea level, although the mass of nearby mountains gives it the impression of elevation. Down at the docks, the open space across the bay provides a view of the Chugach Mountains, the jagged peaks backed endlessly by jagged peaks, the sheer rock faces, snow, the long fingers of ice and plunging, glaciated crevasses. At the back of town, the mountains come near. Within five miles several peaks rise to 5,000 feet. They give the sense of tremendous weight bearing straight down. Up there is the "wild," the cold, the heady contrast of dark stone and radiant ice.

On Good Friday in 1964, Valdez was destroyed by the tsunami, or seismic wave, that followed the Alaskan earthquake and swept up Valdez Arm to the Port of Valdez. Thirty-three people died, most of whom were taken by surprise on the pier. The port installations and 325 homes were destroyed. What remained of the old town was razed and a new one was rebuilt on another site, on what is referred to as "stable" ground—a somewhat higher habitat that the planners considered more secure from disruptive natural forces. The slate had been wiped clean. The new site was filled, graded, tamped down, and on it were placed buildings of the type known as "modular." The residential section is laid out on a grid. There and throughout the downtown, metal siding and sameness are preeminent, and the idiosyncrasies granted by the passage of time are held to a minimum. There has been talk lately of introducing a Swiss architectural theme for the sake of the tourist trade. But for now there remains a stripped-away look to the place, even in the summer . . . streets, poured concrete curbs, square houses, and bright patches of dirt, not even much in the way of weed and bramble poking up through the crevices.

Architecturally, the town seems to grant that it is merely transitional to yet another condition. Though comfortable enough within, insulated, well-equipped, and modern, the buildings are shelters only, or high-tech tents. Up the highway as it passes by the airport are more houses, more individuated and more responsive to the terrain, but here in town the buildings seem to acknowledge nothing quite so much as the flimsiness of their hold, the ephemerality of their purpose, and the much greater power of what lies beyond their walls.

Throughout recent history change has come to this town in rushes of irresistible, transformational force, both natural and commercial: following the Canadian Klondike strike of 1897, the Alaskan gold strikes for which the Port of Valdez served as an entryway; the completion of the Richardson Road to Fairbanks in 1919; the earthquake of 1964; the completion of the 800-mile Alaska pipeline and terminal in 1977; the 11 million-gallon oil spill from the Exxon *Valdez* in 1989.

By road, Valdez is 300 miles from Anchorage, close to 300 from Fairbanks, and nearly 3,000 from Seattle. Anchorage has become the economic center of Alaska, thanks to the military presence following World War II and the ensuing development of commercial air transport. It's a "mother city" with a vengeance. Its importance as a trading and financial center far exceed what its population of 250,000 would suggest. Due to ice floes and heavy sediment loads, the Anchorage harbor is intrinsically inferior to the natural harbors of both Valdez and Seward over on the Kenai Peninsula, but through improvements it has come to serve as Alaska's primary docking point for ships carrying goods and equipment. By sea on a route the oil tankers sometimes travel between Cook Inlet and Valdez, the distance to Anchorage is in the neighborhood of 500 miles.

The road from Valdez to Anchorage winds first northward along the drainages through the Chugach Range on the Richardson Highway, and then back southwesterly on the Glenn Highway. During the pipeline boom of the mid-1970s and the construction of the terminal in Valdez, the town abruptly swelled from about 1,000 to 8,000 residents. The stocks on the shelves of its stores grew sparse, and it was not uncommon for people to drive the hundred miles to Glennallen or even on to Anchorage to shop. Here and in the other small towns along the water, the people have continued out of need and desire to turn toward what is made available through one pipeline or another. There are fish canneries, but otherwise little is made here, not clothing, cans, or paper, almost nothing manufactured, and no food grown except in gardens cultivated by experts in the hazards of cold, short summers, and ponderous shade.

There is hunting, and there is the sea. Some in Valdez and, no doubt, a higher proportion of the people in what would prove to be the region affected by the oil spill—Prince William Sound, the Kenai Peninsula, and Kodiak Island—rely to some degree upon the sustenance nature provides. Some, such as the Native people of the villages, rely heavily upon hunting, gathering, and fishing. Many of the newcomers—white people, by and large—hunt and fish for some of their food, but they have nothing like the intricate and delicately balanced system of subsistence or the concomitant spiritual way of seeing that the Native people have formed over time. Most white people do not possess anything approaching the required knowledge of the natural world to sustain such a system. There are exceptions.

Since the passage of the Alaska Native Claims Settlement Act (ANCSA) in 1971, however, the relationship between Native and white people has come to be so filled with overlaps and ironies, particularly in matters of commerce, that at times the positions taken by the two groups turn common expectation on its head. The boards of Native Regional and Village Corporations, which ANCSA established, regularly seek resource development on their lands, and they have sometimes displayed a cavalier attitude toward despoilment. In response, and for reasons ranging from environmental concern to securing their own economic positions, certain contingents among the whites try to apply the brakes to Native development. Other white and Asian developers use Native ownership as a Trojan horse by which to advance their interests. The tradition of enmity between the peoples, which dates back to British and American overfishing and overhunting in the nineteenth and early twentieth centuries, and further back to forced labor and the wholesale movement of Native communities into what might be called penal colonies during the Russian fur trade of the early nineteenth century, sharpens the edgy entanglement of the present relationship.

For the moment, however, to describe the relationship as the dichotomy with which Americans are familiar, it can be said that for those Native people who follow what is called (in a strange dissonance of

sociological jargon) the "subsistence lifestyle,"* the exchange is immediate and wealth in the form of stores set against winter is measured in
the here and now: salmon, herring, clam, mussel, urchin, sea cucumber,
chiton, crab, roe, sea lion, seal, deer, bear, porcupine, duck, mink, berry,
wood . . . This way of life is followed fairly strictly in some villages and
by some Native people in the predominantly white towns. For the white
people, on the other hand, the measure of wealth has nearly always been
elsewhere: in the eighteenth and nineteenth centuries, the furs taken to
China to trade for silk and tea, and the goods of the Orient returned to
Europe, later, the gold traded on the basis of a rate of exchange set in
New York, and now the timber shipped to Japan, and the ore, and the
North Slope petroleum shipped to the West Coast of what Alaskans refer
to as the "lower forty-eight" and refined and sold there as a federally
mandated hedge against shortfalls in the international market.†

The people here, and especially the people of Valdez, whose economic lives since the seventies have been driven by the Trans-Alaska
Pipeline System (TAPS), have lived simultaneously in touch with two
worlds: the old world of the wilderness that presses close upon them, or
the persistent "idea," at least, of that old world sustained by echoes of
exchange in the here and now, and the new world out there where the
terms of exchange are placed in the hands of the powerful and seem to
be in a state of ceaseless revolution. The people depend upon all the

---

* Subsistence is also a legal and political question in Alaska. A federal law passed in 1980
established the subsistence use of fish and game as the highest-priority application of the
resource, and defines subsistence as "the customary and traditional uses by rural Alaska
residents of wild, renewable resources for direct personal or family consumption as food,
shelter, fuel, clothing, tools or transportation, for the making and selling of handicraft
articles out of nonedible byproducts of fish and wildlife resources taken for personal or
family consumption, and for the customary trade, barter or sharing for personal or family
consumption." State priority laws were passed in 1978 and 1986. The 1986 law establishes
that only rural residents can be considered subsistence users. The question reemerged in
1990 in the form of a proposed amendment to the Alaska State Constitution, following a
State Supreme Court decision to the effect that existing laws discriminated against urban
hunters and fishermen. The legislature deadlocked on the issue through two special sessions called by Governor Steve Cowper. The issue pitted tourism interests and outfitters
(professional hunters) against Native subsistence interests. Left unresolved, subsistence
management will return to the jurisdiction of the federal Department of Fish and Wildlife.
This raises the question of states' rights relative to federal management, which is a frequently occurring issue in Alaska that nearly always turns upon the disposition of resources. In a typically Alaskan twist, oil lobbyists, no doubt heeding the extent to which
Alaskan lands are owned by Native Corporations, supported the proposed amendment.

† Through the Trans-Alaska Pipeline System Authorization Act of 1973, Congress approved
the construction of the pipeline with the stipulation that North Slope crude oil production
be reserved for domestic use. This act has been reinforced in its substance by several
subsequent acts and amendments.

petroleum-powered pipelines, the air traffic to Anchorage, and the traffic by sea or land to Valdez to bring them their food, the computers and VCRs, books, microwaves, clothing, food, the toys for their children, the machinery with which to run their shops, the equipment with which to outfit their boats, the boats themselves, the modular components with which to construct their buildings. Shipping is a serious business here, and shipping crude oil out of Valdez is especially serious. The balance between the hardiness of life on an outpost and the reliance upon distant and powerful centers of commerce is presented in Valdez with particular clarity and force.

Alaska is a resource colony, or economic territory. From it are drawn ore, coal, timber, fish, and petroleum. At the same time, Alaska has been a state since 1959. The contrarieties of big externally financed and federally mandated industry on the one hand, and on the other, self-governance by a group of people strongly given to doing things their own way, whose small numbers (under 600,000) give them unusually ready access to state government and who, further, are divided among themselves between embracing what they have and capitalizing on the tailings of the industries of extraction, repeat the histories of all the western states. However, because the demand for raw materials has increased so dramatically in the twentieth century and the means for extracting them have grown so much more advanced, the replay tape is running at high speed. It's the last such tape the United States gets to play within its own boundaries.

As the images on the tape flicker by, the mythology of a nation heaps up ponderously in the background. The mythology is divided between what, on the one hand, was once the sense of the boundlessness of the wilderness to the west and north, the promise of engagement with that world, the rapture and terror and sense of right alignment that people experience when they allow their lives to join with the forces of nature, and on the other hand the material promise of the instruments of extraction, what William Carlos Williams called the "horrid beauty" of our "great machines." This contradiction was imbedded in nearly all the explorations of North America. James Cook, sailing for the British and seeking the illusory River of the West, was what Williams would call a great "voluptuary," a master seaman and proficient natural observer, a man of physical vigor, one who came to love where he was and what he found as he sailed the world, and yet who finally capitulated to weirdness at Hawaii. He became a complicitor by allowing his crews to extract bounty for themselves, the "white gods" of the ships, until at last the natives at Kealakekua Bay stabbed Cook from behind with a dagger, and then in their rage passed the dagger among themselves so as to share in the destruction of the fallen captain.

Lewis and Clark were voluptuaries in their quite differing ways. The one, Lewis, was an intellectual, and the other, Clark, a master practitioner, and they shared enough of each other's character to make a marriage ideal to the task of the journey from Saint Louis to the Pacific, and of doing that in a manner respectful of the place and the Indians who inhabited it, but they, too, followed the same overriding purpose of locating the illusory river. Failing to find it, they otherwise took hold of the west for the benefit of American interests, which would set about mending the loss of illusion by stitching in the paths to the Pacific—trails, rails, highways, air routes, and pipelines. Joseph Hazelwood, the captain of the tanker Exxon *Valdez*, though merely one among many captains in the shipping trade, carried the late-twentieth-century vestiges of this contradiction. At age 32, ten years after graduating from New York Maritime College, he became the youngest captain in Exxon's fleet, and he quickly gained a reputation in the industry for his seamanship, his *touch* or feel for the vessel, and his ability to extricate ships from dangerous situations. He is a man of intelligence and skill, who wanted mainly to be at sea, who despised the paperwork, the tailings of commercial bureaucracy that had come increasingly to be his obligation.

Two hundred eleven years after Cook set anchor at Snug Harbor Cove, just off what would be called Port Fidalgo, 199 years after Fidalgo plied the tricky waters of the Sound, and 184 years after Lewis and Clark reached the Coast of Oregon, Captain Hazelwood entered Prince William Sound the master of a great machine—Exxon Shipping's newest and most advanced tanker.* Whether or not it had anything to do with the grounding of the Exxon *Valdez*, Hazelwood had a weakness for alcohol, which would turn out to be the dagger passed through the news media so that the nation could share in his destruction. Hazelwood, too, bore the burden of what has become a fundamental American contradiction— in his case, the promise of engagement with what he loved, the sea, and the blunting of that promise by the oil delivery system he served. As it happens the balance at this time is tipped toward those who, as Williams (writing in New Jersey between the two world wars) put it, would compel the wilderness to fit their own image and nothing more. This, and the corollary economic and ethical questions attached to locating the line between necessary and excessive use of resources, make the central

---

* The fact that Hazelwood was given the command of this ship spoke of his company's regard for his abilities.

issue of the oil spill of March 24. The story of the spill is a parable for the future eventualities we must face.

The groups of people working one resource or another take on a character and a political stance. The fishermen,* of which Valdez has a significant number, may well be the quintessential Alaskans of the moment. They deal with live, replenishable things that swim at times willy-nilly in the water. They need to be attuned to the natural world. Their work is dangerous and requires intelligence and physical skill. Their catch is sold mainly to Japan. They are often deeply invested, but the most successful among them bring in six-figure incomes. Because of weak regulation and heavy, company-financed fishing during the territorial days of the first half of the twentieth century, the runs of salmon, which are the staple fish of the industry in south-central Alaska, had become dangerously depleted by the fifties and sixties. In response a cooperative effort was launched by the state, the fish processors, and most notably the fishermen themselves. There is now a flourishing salmon hatchery system, a marriage of science, technology, free enterprise, and nature, placed under the common proprietorship of the state and the fishermen. The system has so far accomplished two positive things. It helped to restore the salmon runs (by the eighties, returns of salmon from the hatcheries in Prince William Sound alone numbered in the tens of millions), and it strengthened the economic niche for a class of entrepreneurial fishermen, who are in some respects an economic throwback, harking to the Hamiltonian ideal of the independent producer.

The fishermen came into 1989 as aware as any other group of the need for the custodianship of resources, or of their resources, at least. The fishermen, too, are in touch with the two worlds, the old world of fish, the new world of aerial spotting and Japanese markets. They are articulate, aggressive, fiercely self-reliant, well-educated, and politically, if not the most powerful, as vigorous as any group in Alaska. They came out of 1989 even more aware of the frailty of resources, and more aggressive, and, finally, divided against themselves. Aside from the residents of the subsistence villages, the oil spill affected no group of people as tellingly as it affected the fishermen. They found themselves cast into a classic confrontation between their form of small, agrarian-based capitalism and big capitalism, to which power of the first rank belongs.

The petroleum industry is the Hudson Bay Fur Trading Company of

---

* There are many fisherwomen in Alaska. I was advised by several of them that they preferred to be called fishermen.

contemporary Alaska, or "superproprietor." Because of its power—the power to employ, to enrich the state treasury, the power to transform whatever it touches, to create its own science, to eclipse small and middle-sized businesses, the power of a constituency that consists of all gasoline-purchasing Americans, and the power of its ties to "national security"—avenues were left open to sloppiness, inattentiveness, profiteering, influence peddling, graft, and to the collaboration in word and deed among the producers, state and federal agencies, the Coast Guard, and both the Alaskan public and the public of the United States at large. All of this made the oil spill from the Exxon *Valdez* inescapable.

These, then, are some of the screens against which the oil spill was cast: the general use of Alaska as a resource colony, the needs of the fishing industry, and the politics, economics, and spirituality of the Native population. In addition, there are the ineffectiveness of federal regulatory agencies, especially the Environmental Protection Agency (EPA) and the Department of Fish and Wildlife (DFW), the ineffectiveness of state regulatory agencies, especially the Department of Environmental Conservation (DEC) and the Department of Fish and Game (DFG), and the compromise of information, especially of scientific information, the extent to which capital and the industries of extraction, especially the oil industry, drive public policy, and also the extent to which the American public through its own wastefulness allows itself to be held captive by oil. Culpability for what would be the largest oil tanker spill in the history of the United States, and arguably, the most destructive spill in the history of the world, is shared.*

A larger backdrop is the petroleum companies themselves. Beginning with the formation in the late nineteenth century of the Rockefeller Standard Oil trust (the ancestor of Exxon) and extending through World War I, the 1928 Redline Agreement which apportioned the resources of the Ottoman Empire among European and American interests, through World War II, the 1956 Suez War, the formation of the Organization of Petroleum Exporting Countries (OPEC)—which sought to restructure the world economic order—and the 1973 embargo, the petroleum in-

---

* Larger tanker spills, such as the 1967 *Torrey Canyon* spill (35 million gallons) off the Isles of Scilly at the mouth of the English Channel, and the more recent 1989 *Kharg 5* spill (37 million gallons) off the Moroccan coast, may cause less biological damage if the shorelines are less affected. Marine life at and near the shorelines is far denser than it is in open seas. Also, lighter oils, which evaporate more quickly, are less damaging. Even the 1978 Amoco *Cadiz* spill (close to 60 million gallons), which profoundly affected the shorelines of the French coast, seems to have caused less destruction than did the 11 million gallons from the Exxon *Valdez*. By way of example, estimates put bird mortality from the *Torrey Canyon* spill at 30,000, from the Amoco *Cadiz* at 20,000, and from the Exxon *Valdez* at somewhere between 90,000 and 300,000.

ternationals came to be involved as an agent in most of the critical world economic and political events of the twentieth century. These included battles, shooting and otherwise, over the oil resources of the various Middle Eastern countries, as well as, say, Angola, Venezuela, and Mexico. Petroleum is the primary energy source of industrialized societies, and it remains the principal fuel by which the machines of war are run. It is fundamental to strategic concerns, and because of the United States' early expertise in petroleum technology, it is directly tied to the U.S. domination during the twentieth century. The petroleum internationals regularly act in concert to set production rates and prices, and the distinction between their interests and the interests of their titular parent countries is extremely murky. In the case of the United States, foreign policy at times follows on the heels of oil interests. Sometimes, as with offshore and onshore oil exploration by Texaco, Mobil, and Exxon in South Africa, for example, the U.S. government has found itself backed into a political corner. The oil companies and the U.S. government would see the discovery of oil fields almost anywhere, including South Africa, as a means of relieving the dependency on Middle Eastern oil. At the same time, a substantial portion of the U.S. population was demanding an embargo against apartheid. This is but one typical and relatively well-defined example of the type of moral dilemma the international activity of the petroleum companies has consistently produced—mainly in the Middle East. Although the traditional major oil companies are products of the industrialized West, the complexity and extent of their international activities raises the question of whether or not they owe allegiance to any one country. From the perspective of an oil company like Exxon, the Alaskan oil spill had to be a minor, though surprisingly aggravating event in a history that includes leveraging heads of state and weathering African and Middle Eastern wars.

There are several very substantial edifices in Valdez: the elaborate and well-fitted community center just above the docks, the $11 million high school in town, and the Valdez grain terminal out beyond the edge of town. They're all tied to oil revenues, which comprise about 80 percent of the state treasury. The grain terminal was built in the early 1980s to facilitate export of products in accordance with the state of Alaska's agricultural plan. The plan for agricultural self-sufficiency failed, it is argued, because of a classic, state-supported boondoggle in which the farming practices of the northern Great Plains were foisted upon the Alaskan interior. Alaska had money to burn. Now, the towering silo stands empty just outside Valdez.

The strongest testimony by far to the presence of serious money in Valdez is the terminal operated by the Alyeska Pipeline Service Company, which along with the pipeline itself is owned by a consortium of oil companies, otherwise known as the Seven Sisters.* Built into a mountainside just across the bay from Valdez, the terminal has a Third Reich appearance. The egg-colored concrete holding tanks look like huge pillbox bunkers. There are 18 tanks in all, and each holds about a half-million barrels of crude oil.† Adding in smaller storage facilities, there is a total capacity at the terminal of 9.2 million barrels. There is an average flow through the pipeline from the North Slope drilling sites into the tanks at the terminal of 1.8 million barrels per day. This comes to over 650 million barrels a year. Even the numbers attached to Alaskan resources, both in the quantities of material and in dollars, tend to become so staggering that they veer toward incomprehensibility. A day's shutdown of the pipeline costs the oil industry millions of dollars. Between 1969 and 1987, the state took in an average of $1.5 billion a year in taxes, and the federal government close to $2 billion. During the same period, the oil industry made on average $2.4 billion in profit from Alaskan production and transportation. These facts, together with the fact that the bargain struck in Congress sends a portion of Alaskan oil revenues into a permanent fund whose principal is expected to reach $10 billion by 1991, and from which every Alaskan—man, woman, and child—receives an annual dividend check from the fund of between $800 and $1,000 explain the pressure to keep the oil flowing. When the question of dividends comes up, some Alaskans will quickly explain that their checks are put toward their children's education, or donated to an environmental cause, but the permanent fund has nevertheless turned into a persuasive device for the oil interests. By it, Alaskans are kept constantly aware that the money tap is trickling in their kitchen, too.

Built at a cost of over $8 billion, the pipeline and terminal were at the time the largest private construction project in the history of the United States. The Prudhoe Bay Oil Field is now one of several North Slope fields that feed into TAPS. It was the first field to be put into production, the twelfth largest field in the world, and the largest to be discovered in North America. It accounts for 25 percent of the total domestic U.S. production and one-eighth of U.S. consumption. Since startup in 1977,

---

* BP Exploration, Incorporated (a British-based international), 50.01 percent; ARCO Pipeline Company, 21.35 percent; Exxon Pipeline Company, 20.34 percent; Mobil Alaska Pipeline Company, 4.08 percent; Amerada Hess Pipeline Corporation, 1.5 percent; Phillips Alaska Pipeline Company, 1.36 percent; and Union Alaska Pipeline Company, 1.36 percent.

† One barrel equals 42 gallons.

more than 6 billion barrels have been shipped from Prudhoe Bay, and over 700 wells have been drilled to the field. At this time, about 9.4 billion barrels of oil are expected to be recovered from the 23.5 billion barrels that remain in place.* The reserves are declining, however, and there is strong pressure from the industry to explore for new fields and to develop additional known fields, particularly fields such as those in the Arctic National Wildlife Refuge (ANWR), which might be tied into the existing pipeline system.

The purpose of the terminal is simple. It's a big bladder at the end of the pipeline. Its storage tanks are reservoirs that hold crude oil for the tankers that come to carry the oil away to the lower West Coast. The obligation for managing the terminal and the pipeline fell to the Alyeska Pipeline Service Company. Alyeska had been formed precisely in order to centralize, first, the construction of the pipeline and terminal, and later, the operating and cleanup capabilities. Certain requirements were attached to terminal construction and its operations as conditions to the approval Congress granted to build the pipeline in 1971. These included incinerators to burn off sludge and toxic vapors, gauging the amount of oil and other toxins in ballast dumped into the harbor, and a state-of-the-art oil spill contingency plan. As the years passed, however, Alyeska junked many safeguards and never built others.

It never built 14 of the storage tanks that had been called for. It never built the incinerator to destroy toxic sludge produced by the terminal's operations. Contrary to its promises, it used less-expensive carbon steel rather than stainless steel on the miles of pipe in the vapor recovery system intended to draw off the poisonous crude oil gases that collect in the tops of the storage tanks. At the end of the vapor recovery system are incinerators that are intended to destroy the hydrocarbons in the vapors by burning them at high temperatures (1,400 degrees Fahrenheit). The pipe in the vapor recovery system sprang dozens of leaks and the incinerators regularly operated below the required temperatures, with the result that ever more vapors were released into the atmosphere and the incinerators fell ever more deeply into disrepair. Between 1980 and 1985, the vapor recovery system was shut down an average of one in every five days.

Besides that, the state of Alaska has estimated that as many as 1,000 tons of hydrocarbons a week enter the air through vents on the decks of the tankers, but Alyeska—taking a position that presaged its role in the cleanup of the Exxon *Valdez* spill—has argued that emissions from tank-

* Advances in recovery technology, price increases, or both would raise the amount of recoverable oil.

ers were not its responsibility. In this regard, it is important to remember that this is not just a matter of general environmental principle, but that there are workers on the premises and a town just across the way. Responsibility for tanker emissions apparently fell through a large crack, and it becomes apparent in this as in many other failures either of omission or commission that what was originally an attempt to centralize and streamline accountability on the part of the oil companies within Alyeska had resulted in the deflection of scrutiny.

Alyeska had promised that there would be a fleet of double-hulled tankers coming into the Port of Valdez, but virtually all the ships that have called here, including the Exxon *Valdez*, were single-hulled. It was also expected that the terminal would enlarge its capacity as the volume of crude oil "through-put" increased. The volume has increased fourfold since the startup of the plant, but the terminal itself is the same size as when it was constructed in 1977.

As oil prices began to fall in the early eighties, due to the oil glut, the owners of Alyeska (the oil companies) ordered deep cost-cutting measures. James Woodle, who had been the Coast Guard Commander for the Port of Valdez and then an Alyeska Marine Superintendent, saw his budget cut by a third just when he assumed his new duties. Woodle, who has since resigned his post, has said, "Based on my experience with Alyeska, the only surprise is that disaster didn't strike sooner. There was an overall attitude of petty cheapness. I was shocked at the shabbiness of the operation."

The matter of water quality in the Port of Valdez has been a point of contention for years, particularly as it pertains to the treatment of ballast water. The tankers must carry ballast as they travel to the Alyeska terminal; without it, they would be unstable. On the ships, ballast water is stored in the same tanks that will be filled with oil, and when pumped out the ballast carries an oil residue. It is Alyeska's obligation to clean the ballast water in its ballast treatment plant before discharging it into the Port of Valdez, but Alyeska never installed the planned system for continuous monitoring of the water released into the harbor, and it dismantled heaters designed to separate oil from the water because the heaters were difficult to maintain. Alyeska initially had a permit to dump water containing highly toxic hydrocarbons in quantities of as high as nine parts per million, which is a dangerous level. Upon expiration of the permit in 1983, state and federal regulators required that new permits reduce the limits by as much as 85 percent, but Alyeska continued to dump out high levels of hydrocarbons while tying up the EPA in administrative wrangles.

In 1985, regulators charged Alyeska with releasing sludge from the holding tanks through the ballast water system and discharging it into the water together with the ballast water. While internal Alyeska records showed that in 1980 Alyeska was seeking ways to dispose of 4,200 cubic yards of sludge, George Nelson, the Alyeska president, stated that the terminal had only produced 480 cubic yards of sludge in nine years of operation. Alyeska then at first refused to comply with an EPA subpoena for an investigation of water quality, and following an EPA suit, Nelson, according to EPA attorneys, avoided appointments with the EPA, although his deposition was eventually taken. Alyeska has continued to fight state and federal regulators' demands to cut discharge of toxic hydrocarbons.

Alyeska employees have given accounts not simply of sloppy operations but also of deliberate falsification of test results. Steve Eward, a technician from 1977 to 1980, reported that he was frequently ordered to disconnect the meter that measured how much treated ballast water was being flushed into the harbor. James Woodle said that Alyeska avoided meeting EPA standards for treated ballast water by sending samples to Seattle for testing so that by the time it was tested some of the pollutants would have decayed. Erline Blake, a technician in Alyeska's testing laboratory from 1977 to 1983, said that it was "standard operating procedure" to doctor test results.

Finally, the advanced system, or contingency plan, for dealing with oil spills went through a similar evolution—from a bright promise to virtually nothing at all. Testifying on behalf of Alyeska and the oil companies for the approval of the pipeline in 1971, a senior petroleum specialist for British Petroleum, L. R. Beynon, stated at Department of Interior hearings that Alyeska's contingency plan would "detail methods for dealing promptly and effectively with any oil spill which may occur, so that its effects on the environment will be minimal. We have adequate knowledge for dealing with oil spills and improvements in techniques and equipment are continuing to become available through worldwide research. The best equipment, materials and expertise, which will be made available as part of the oil spill contingency plan, will make operations in Port of Valdez and Prince William Sound the safest in the world." Eighteen years later, following the Exxon *Valdez* spill, the chief of the EPA, William Reilly, would say, "One of the things that impressed me in Alaska was how inadequate is the technology that we have to deal with these spills, how relatively primitive it all is, skimmers that collect five hundred gallons an hour in the face of ten million [gallons spilled], dispersants that have a lot of toxicity. . . ."

Often, the drills conducted in order to maintain readiness for oil spills dissolved into comedy. During a drill in the early 1980s, a boat carrying the top Alyeska manager and a group of oil industry executives ran aground. In 1982, Alyeska dismantled the crew that had been devoted to oil spill response and either reassigned or laid off the workers. The response equipment began to fall into disrepair. In 1984, a drill generally beset with confusion had to be canceled when a containment boom sank. In a report to his superiors, a state inspector, Tom McCarty, wrote that Alyeska's spill response capability had "regressed to a dangerous level." In 1985, an Alyeska official declined to practice deploying a hose during a sloppily run drill because "it would be too much trouble to roll it up again."

A former oil spill coordinator for Alyeska, Jerry Nebel, said, "We knew exactly what was coming, where we were supposed to be, and we still messed it up. Drills were a farce, comic opera." In March of 1988, Alyeska conducted an inventory of cleanup equipment but could find only half of the emergency lights. The other half, it was later discovered, were being readied for use in Valdez's winter carnival. Half the required length of six-inch hose was missing, and so was some 3,700 feet of boom,* nearly 15 percent of the required amount, and eight of ten blinking barricades listed in the contingency plan were nowhere to be found. Duane Thompson, who worked from 1985 to 1989 for Alyeska and for Earthmovers, a company that had a maintenance contract with Alyeska, told me that the cleanup personnel took only a verbal test to prepare for spills, and that because personnel were constantly being shifted into other duties, there were at any one time very few people on duty who even knew how to run the equipment. The oil spill drills, Thompson said, "were a joke." State drills would be announced as long as three months ahead of time. "And then," Thompson said, "they'd drop oranges in the water because an orange has about the same buoyancy as a tar ball. We'd get out there on the day of the drill, sit around, and eat oranges."

Another aspect of the Alyeska situation is the role played by the agency charged with the primary regulatory duties, Alaska's Department of Environmental Conservation. The DEC acquired this role as a result of a

---

* Boom, a staple of oil spill cleanup equipment, is a floating fence. It comes in various grades and sizes and may be linked together in sections to make a chain hundreds of yards long. It may include oil-absorbent material. From a distance, it looks like a long hose laid out on the water. Although it is most effective for containing small spills in calm waters, it may also be heavily constructed and come with skirts attached to its bottom and splash shields attached to its top for use in rough waters. Its usefulness decreases dramatically with large spills and in open, heavy waters.

land exchange between the federal and state governments prior to the construction of the terminal, which allowed the U.S. Department of Interior to abandon its regulatory capacity. In the days and months following the Exxon *Valdez* spill, the DEC became deeply involved as the principle arm of the state government, and DEC Commissioner Dennis Kelso became widely admired for his willingness to stand up to the oil industry. But for years the state agency had been seriously underfunded and had devolved into the second smallest agency in state government. The lack of funding and the tendency of middle- and upper-level DEC officials to overlook Alyeska transgressions bespoke the ability of oil interests to influence state government. Before the spill, Kelso had not read the oil spill contingency plan, and the largest of a handful of fines levied against Alyeska was $10,000 for a 1986 air-pollution conviction. Bills to increase the budget of the DEC and to increase the agency's monitoring capabilities consistently died in the legislature. The original staff of three full-time inspectors assigned to Alyeska had been reduced to one part-time inspector.

The ultimate penalty to Alyeska's repeated violations, or what Bob LaResche, Alaska's oil spill coordinator after the spill, would call "the Nuke," was simply to shut down the pipeline. Of course, this was never considered by either the state or federal government. There was far too much money at stake, and the infrastructure that had been formed between oil interests and state government was too dense and too heavy to move. A shutdown, which technically speaking the state had the power to apply, would have been tantamount to declaring war on itself. LaResche would say, ". . . if we didn't like Alyeska's contingency plan, we could shut down the pipeline, and that would last five or six hours until the National Guard arrived."

For ten years, the DEC representative in Valdez had been Dan Lawn. A big, bearded man, rather given to bluster, Lawn was regarded by some of his own colleagues as a troublemaker, and he was disliked by Alyeska officials. At one point in 1986 Alyeska officials threw him off Alyeska premises while he was videotaping operations. After the Exxon *Valdez* spill, other Alaskans would come to regard Lawn as a kind of outlaw hero within the government bureaucracy.

In 1982, Lawn had reported to his supervisor that the Alyeska contingency plan was "superficial at best." Lawn went on to say that "all our experience with Alyeska oil spill recovery rates indicates that the recovery rates listed [by Alyeska] are eighty percent too high." In 1984, Lawn reported that there had "taken place a general disemboweling of the Alyeska Valdez terminal operational plan. . . . Most knowledgeable and competently trained individuals have either quit, been terminated, or transferred up the line." Regarding his role as a DEC monitor, Lawn wrote, the department was too "underbudgeted and understaffed to adequately inspect the terminal and keep in touch with Alyeska's day-to-day operations. . . . Unfortunately, this has been a signal to Alyeska that the state is no longer interested in the Trans-Alaska Pipeline project. Alyeska has consistently broken promises made to the state of Alaska and the federal government prior to our granting permission to build the terminal. We can no longer ignore the routine monitoring of Alyeska, unless we do not care whether a major catastrophic event occurs." The extent to which the oil industry and state government were enmeshed with one another is attested to by the tendency of officials to treat Lawn as if he were a "whistleblower," even though his assignment was designed to be adversarial. His job was to report violations. He was an inspector for the state government, and yet he found himself left outside the very channel that employed him.

Each month, 80 ships—or between two and three of them a day—are loaded at the terminal before setting out across Prince William Sound toward the Gulf of Alaska, and thence to ports on the lower West Coast. Alyeska and oil industry officials point to the fact that prior to the Exxon *Valdez* spill, over 8,000 ships had passed in and out of the Port of Valdez "without incident." In fact, there had been numerous near misses, including one as early as 1979 when the supertanker *Prince William Sound* lost power and steering in high winds. The tanker was within half an hour of foundering on the rocks when a wind shift moved it back into deeper waters and it regained power. There were also common occurrences of small spills within the Port of Valdez.

The condition of the Valdez fleet generally has been subject to question, and this comprises yet another of the screens against which the Exxon *Valdez* grounding should be cast. During the 1970s tankers were replaced as a matter of course, but during the 1980s—again, because of declining petroleum prices—the oil companies cut back sharply on purchases of new tankers. United States law requires that American-built tankers be used to transport Alaskan crude, but no American shipyard has built a supertanker in recent years. On average, the age of the ships in the Alaskan fleet is 15 years greater than that of the U.S. fleet otherwise. The Gulf of Alaska is also the roughest water any U.S. tanker will have to travel. Because of their size and the weight they carry, the tankers are designed to flex in heavy seas so as to avoid breaking apart. One can stand at the stern of a tanker and see the bow swing and the tensile hull literally rippling under the force of waves. It's an unnerving sight, and yet because of the size of the tanker and the weight of its load, it's also utterly necessary for the ship to give. One result of the extreme twisting and heaving of hulls as the ships negotiate the Gulf of Alaska is metal fatigue and cracking, and the greatest fear has been that a cracked tanker would simply break apart at sea, or ground and then break apart, as the Amoco Cadiz did.

An analysis by the U.S. Coast Guard, the Marine Structural Casualty Study, compiled between 1984 and 1986 and released in 1988, finds that the rate of structural failures among tankers traveling Alaskan waters is unusually high. Although tankers of the Alaskan fleet represented only about one-eighth of the large ships in the survey, they suffered more than half the cracks and other structural failures. Commander Tom Purtell of the Coast Guard's Marine Investigation Division observed that 44 structural fractures were found in 30 tankers and 8 freighters included in the study, which surveyed a total of 445 ships of more than 10,000 tons. All of the ships with multiple fractures were Alaska-fleet tankers. "It seemed relevant to us," Purtell said, "that thirteen percent of the population suffered fifty-two percent of the casualties."

In January 1989, the tanker Thompson Pass leaked 72,000 gallons of oil into Port Valdez. This was the largest spill up to that time in Prince William Sound. The Thompson Pass, a British Petroleum tanker, had been observed to be leaking in San Francisco, but company officials there decided to send it on to Alaska for one more load before repairing it. In the Port of Valdez, the boom that had been placed around the tanker was left unwatched and before long the oil leaking from the ship rode the water, overwhelmed the boom, and spilled over its top. It took the Alyeska cleanup crew 15 days to recover the oil. Two weeks after the Thompson Pass spill, another tanker, the Cove Leader, spilled an additional 2,500 gallons into Port Valdez.

The fishermen based in Prince William Sound are represented by Cordova District Fishermen United (CDFU). When I talked in April 1989 with Ken Adams, a member of the CDFU board of directors, he was careful to make clear to me that CDFU was not a union but something akin to a lobby that was willing to take legal action on behalf of its membership. Based in Cordova, a fishing community some 70 miles east of Valdez, CDFU's 600 members represent well over half of the fishing permit holders in what is termed the Area E fishery—Prince William Sound. CDFU had opposed the construction of the pipeline from the start and then had fought to have the pipeline extended down through Canada to the lower forty-eight. At the very time pipeline construction was about to begin, the fishermen were initiating the salmon hatchery system in Prince William Sound. CDFU filed suit against the Secretary of the Interior's approval of pipeline and terminal construction. In 1973 the suit, by then consolidated with suits from environmental and Native groups, received a favorable ruling in a Federal District Court. The decision was subsequently upheld by the Supreme Court, but pipeline proponents turned to Congress and late in 1973 legislation was introduced to circumvent the court rulings and to foreclose all court challenges to pipeline construction on environmental grounds. In the Senate, a tie vote on the legislation was broken by Vice President Spiro Agnew.

In 1985, and in conjunction with Charles Hamel, an oil broker, CDFU filed a notice of intent to sue again over mismanagement of the ballast water treatment plant at the terminal and the discharge of toxic pollutants into the Port of Valdez. This notice was followed by the joint compliance order issued by the EPA and the DEC, requesting Alyeska to build a system to monitor, remove, and dispose of sludge. The response to this compliance order remains spotty. Throughout the time since the construction of the pipeline and terminal, CDFU, believing that the hatchery system and the fisheries generally were under threat, has had an extremely rocky relationship with Alyeska. In 1987, CDFU entered into the heated debate over whether or not to open the Arctic National Wilderness Refuge (ANWR) to oil exploration. CDFU hoped that this controversy would awaken national attention to the pollution problems in the Port of Valdez and to the oil industry's generally poor record of self-evaluation and performance.

When word of the *Thompson Pass* spill reached John Devens, the mayor of Valdez, he set about forming a committee to investigate safety problems at Alyeska. What he learned about Alyeska and water and air pollution alarmed him—rather surprisingly at that late date. A town meeting was called for Thursday evening, March 23. Alyeska declined the invitation to send a representative, and Devens invited Riki Ott instead to travel to Valdez from her home in Cordova to give a presentation on the Alyeska terminal and marine transport of oil. Ott is a member of the CDFU board of directors. An energetic young woman with a reputation for speaking her mind, she holds a master's degree in oil pollution and a Ph.D. in sediment toxicology as well as an Area E salmon drift gillnet permit. As it happened, bad weather grounded the flights from Cordova to Valdez, but the Valdez people arranged to hear Ott's presentation by teleconference. These were the two worlds of Alaska again—the old world of the outpost in which natural forces had the power to shut things down, set against the new world of communications. The people were willing to accommodate themselves to both.

Ott rode her bicycle into Cordova and at 7:00 P.M. gave her talk, speaking for two hours into a teleconference microphone. She spoke of oil revenues and Alaskan politics, of unauthorized design changes in the Alyeska terminal, of its overloaded pollution control systems, of its failure to live up to its promises, of the fact that the entire terminal was monitored by only one part-time DEC employee (Dan Lawn), of the condition of the tanker fleet. Like many of the fishermen, she believed that it was not a question of whether or not a major oil spill would happen, but of when it would happen. She spoke of the petroleum consortium's increasing incapability to clean up and contain a major spill. She said, "Given the high frequency of tankers into Port Valdez, the increasing age and size of that tanker fleet, and the inability to quickly contain and clean up an oil spill in the open water of Alaska, fishermen feel that we are playing a game of Russian roulette.

"When, not if," she went on, "The Big One does occur and much or all of the income from a fishing season is lost, compensation for processors, support industries and local communities will be difficult if not impossible to obtain. . . ."

Afterwards, Riki was pleased with the questions her talk had provoked. Little did she know that at the time she spoke, her prophecy on behalf of fishermen was in the process of being fulfilled. She went home, stoked her fire, and turned in. In less than 12 hours she awoke to hear acting CDFU president Jack Lamb banging on her door and found herself cast into the vanguard of the grassroots response to an 11-million-gallon spill.

Chapter 3

THE CHANNEL

The Gulf of Alaska extends southeasterly toward the Alexander Archipelago and southwesterly toward Kodiak Island. It is the threshold to the Pacific from south-central Alaska. As the crow flies, the edge of the gulf is about 60 miles from Valdez. By ship—because narrows, shallows, and islands must be negotiated—it is farther.

Roughly 30 by 75 miles and cast between the gulf and Valdez rather in the shape of a trapezoid is Prince William Sound, which the Exxon *Valdez* was scheduled to traverse. Port Valdez lies at the upper, northeastern corner of the trapezoid, dug into the mainland and pitched off eastward from the Valdez Arm. Once a tanker leaves the terminal, negotiates the Valdez Narrows and the Valdez Arm, and passes between Bligh Island and Glacier Island, the target becomes the Hinchinbrook entrance, which lies between Hinchinbrook and Montague islands.

The contours of the sound are most strongly characterized by the radical irregularity of its shorelines. No rendering will accurately capture the detail of the shoreline. Because the geological formations are recent, relatively speaking, much of the shoreline in sound is indented with countless tiny coves and inlets into which small craft might be drawn, and the shorelines themselves and the reefs are rocky. The beaches are far from flat. They're frequently bounded by sheer, heavily striated rock faces. They are often composed of cobbled stone. Sometimes they're coarsely sanded, as was the beach off Flent Point that Peter Slattery, Gordon Robilliard, Kathy Conlan, and I walked. The irregularity of the formation further increases the surface exposed to the water, to the tides which run at a rate up to two and a half knots and ebb and flow between a low of minus three feet to a high of 16 feet. A thumbnail accounting of shoreline surface area is 1,800 miles of mainland shoreline and 1,200 miles of shoreline along rocks and islands.

On and in these irregular surfaces, in all the cracks and crevices of the tidepools and estuaries, the near shore, the intertidal zone, live a host of creatures: amphipods, copepods, sea worms, clams, crabs, mussels, periwinkles, starfish, shrimp, urchins . . . Here, too, is the plant life, the algae, kelp, fucus, and eel grass which the creatures may colonize and upon which they feed. From deeper waters come fish and ten species of marine mammals—seals, sea lions, whales, porpoises, and between 10,000 and 12,000 sea otters. From shore come over 30 species of land mammals, including bear, mountain goat, fox, wolf, lynx, deer, beaver, mink, river otter, marten, porcupine, and human beings. There are the seabirds, more than 200 species of them, some of which are permanent residents and others of which are migratory. Great concentrations of migratory birds arrive between March and June, sometimes in flocks of hundreds of thousands. The total numbers of birds that pass through the sound are in the millions. There are 3,000 bald eagles. Each of these creatures, the amphipod, the crab, the mussel, the seal, the otter, the killer whale, the Sitka blacktailed deer, the semipalmated plover, murrelet, pelagic cormorant, tern, scoter, goose, and eagle, has its own life, its details of feeding and resting, of flight and predation, of courtship, of egg laying, and of nurturing young in the hollows and inlets, out in the open or hidden in the cracks and crevices. Rich and dense with life, the shoreline is the margin, the cutting edge of the action between earth and sea.

There are natural hazards to traffic in the sound. There is good weather and more bad—sudden squalls, fog, and high winds. One day in six is clear. The weather kept Riki Ott from flying to Valdez on March 23. It affects boats differently according to their size. During a storm, a fishing boat will pull into a protected cove and set anchor. Also on the night of the twenty-third, reports of ice floating from Columbia Glacier into the tanker channel put the Exxon *Valdez* an hour behind schedule.

The glaciers and other freshwater outlets into the sound affect the level of salinity, the water temperature, and so marine life in all its detail. The water surface of the sound measures approximately 2,500 square miles, and its dimensions otherwise include the subaquatic world. The mountains on the land merely happen to be higher than the mountains beneath the water. The sound varies in depth from next to zero at, say, Bligh Reef, to 2,850 feet off Lone Island, and there are surprises, even for experienced boat people. There are more channels under there, canyons, sand bars, and tidal flats that change shape, underwater eddies and powerful crosscurrents that interact with other forces—the wind, the tide, the predominant current.

All this, the large habitat, is the arena for the March 24 grounding, and through it, at a depth of about 480 feet, runs the channel designated for tanker traffic. But for a stretch at the Valdez Arm and running through the Valdez Narrows, there are two lanes, incoming and outgoing. Beginning with the Port of Valdez, the outward path runs southwesterly through the narrows, out the arm and alongside Freemantle Point. Here the pilot must be wary of the growlers and bergy bits that float free from Columbia Glacier, which is the largest of 20 tidewater glaciers in the sound. In 1973 the balance of the glacier was disturbed by an abrupt emptying of a glacially dammed lake. This caused the glacier's rapid retreat in recent years—an event not anticipated in the planning of the pipeline and terminal. Over the next 20 to 50 years, the glacier is expected to lose over two cubic miles of ice annually. The chunks of ice are sometimes huge, white and pale blue and streaked with black mud. Birds gather on them. Seals rest on them. The drifts move out from Columbia Bay and around Glacier Island and sometimes fill the shipping channels, causing the ships to change their route, as would the Exxon *Valdez*, and immediately before it the Arco *Juneau*.

The channel passes Bligh Reef, which is marked with a lighted buoy, and then from a point that lies midway between Glacier and Bligh islands, it swings first southerly and then southeasterly in the direction of the Hinchinbrook entrance. The openness of the water in this section provides a greater margin of safety. In good light, the Naked Island complex becomes visible off the starboard side. In the distance, Knight Island rises to view. Even in the summer the peaks of Knight Island are snowcapped. Narrow and spindly-looking, they rake the sky. The peaks seem a vertical recapitulation of the complication of the island's ragged shoreline. The lower slopes are dark blue, nearly black. Big enough to be mistaken for the mainland, Knight Island seems to float on the water. Straight ahead lies the opening between Hinchinbrook and Montague islands. Between Knight Island and the channel are smaller islands—Smith Island, Little Smith, Seal. The color of the water is a pale blue tinged with green and the milk color of glacial silt. Terns and gulls float in the water, riding the swells. Cranes might fly overhead. A pod of killer whales might pass by. If there's a tanker in the channel, fishing boats will give it wide berth, darting clear of its ponderous trajectory. The green in the water gives the appearance of depth to the blue and the milkiness gives it an opacity. This makes an extraordinary mineral-like color that I would see again and again and for which I had no name. Aquamarine does not suffice. Even in good weather, the seas darken and take on a hard chop as the ship approaches the Hinchinbrook entrance. In bad weather, it can be a treacherous place.

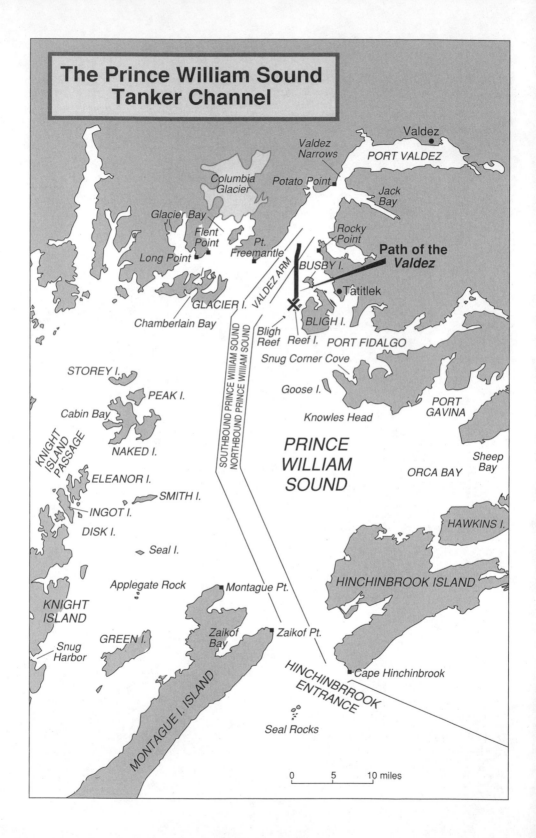

The Prince William Sound
Tanker Channel

Valdez

Valdez
Narrows

PORT VALDEZ

Columbia
Glacier

Potato Point

Jack
Bay

Glacier Bay

Rocky
Point

Flent
Point

Pt.
Freemantle

Path of the
Valdez

Long Point

BUSBY I.

VALDEZ ARM

•Tatitlek

GLACIER I.

Chamberlain Bay

Bligh
Reef

Reef I.

BLIGH I.

PORT FIDALGO

SOUTHBOUND PRINCE WIIIAM SOUND
NORTHBOUND PRINCE WIIIAM SOUND

Bligh
Reef

Snug Corner Cove

STOREY I.

Goose I.

PORT
GAVINA

PEAK I.

Knowles Head

Cabin Bay

KNIGHT
ISLAND
PASSAGE

NAKED I.

PRINCE
WILLIAM
SOUND

Sheep
Bay

ELEANOR I.

ORCA BAY

SMITH I.

INGOT I.

DISK I.

HAWKINS I.

Seal I.

Applegate Rock

Montague Pt.

HINCHINBROOK ISLAND

KNIGHT
ISLAND

GREEN I.

Zaikof
Bay

Zaikof Pt.

Snug
Harbor

HINCHINBRROOK
ENTRANCE

•Cape Hinchinbrook

MONTAGUE I. ISLAND

Seal Rocks

0   5   10 miles

Chapter 4

THE IMAGINARY JOURNEY OF CAPTAIN JOSEPH HAZELWOOD

These days, after much of the media hype and lunacy has abated, [I am] left simply with a gut feeling of frustration. Had to learn the hard way the lexicon of the 80's and discover exactly what "spin" means. The truth hasn't been allowed to come to the fore either for any number of legal reasons or it wasn't lurid enough for print or airing.

Oh well, I'll get my day(s) in court soon enough and the cause [of the oil spill] will seem pretty mundane and simple after all . . .

—Joseph Hazelwood in a letter to a friend, quoted in *Time*, July 24, 1989

And taking Jokanaan's head, all three went off towards Galilee. As it was very heavy, they each carried it in turn.

—Gustave Flaubert, "Herodias," 1977

On Wednesday, March 22, following a passage through rough seas in the Gulf of Alaska, the Exxon *Valdez* arrived in Port Valdez and docked at the Alyeska Terminal at 10:48 P.M. Chief Mate James Kunkel and Captain Hazelwood were on the bridge of the ship. The crew spent the night on board. The ship measures 166 feet at the beam and 987 feet from bow to stern—longer than three football

31

fields. The 1,286,738 barrels of crude oil she would take on was a little under her capacity of 1,484,829 barrels, or 211,000 deadweight tons.

Early the next morning, the crew began the laborious process of discharging ballast water and filling the 12 cargo tanks with crude, which included handling the delivery hoses from the terminal to the ship and at all times meticulously monitoring the flow of water out of the ballast tanks and of oil into the cargo tanks so as to maintain the proper stress levels in the ship. By 7:24 P.M. on Thursday, March 23—minutes before Riki Ott began her telecommunication to Valdez—the loading was completed, and the final checks were being made. The crew members who worked the deck during the day—including Able Bodied Seamen (A.B.) Maureen Jones and Robert Kagan, Third Mate Gregory Cousins, Second Mate Lloyd LeCain, and Chief Mate Kunkel—were tired.

Kunkel, who was in charge of all deck operations including docking and loading procedures, had stayed up from the time of arrival until 8:00 A.M. the following morning. He then took a nap, arose at noon, worked the deck again until 4:00 P.M., and went on his normal 4:00 to 8:00 watch.* If the congressionally mandated requirement that officers have six hours' off-duty time within the 12-hour period prior to departure had been adhered to, the Exxon Valdez would never have cast off that night. The required rest period, however, was rarely observed. In testimony before the National Transportation Safety Board, Exxon Ship Group Coordinator Captain William Deppe would say, "We don't have any program to give six hours of rest to any deck officer before we get under way."

It has proved difficult to determine just what was binding and what was not in the maze of federal, state, Coast Guard, and company regulations that govern the crewing and operations of tankers in Prince William Sound. As a matter of practice, general crew fatigue was common on tankers following loading and unloading. In a cost-cutting measure that had little regard for safety, Exxon had used the increasing automation of ships as a justification for reducing the size of its crews. At the same time, the company pressed for as speedy a delivery of the product as possible. The result was that it was impossible for crews to both do the work and adhere to manning regulations. Remarkably, prior to the spill, Exxon Shipping had an additional objective of reducing crew

* Bridge watches—that is, command of the ship's navigation and its piloting—were divided equally among the three mates. Each took a shift of 4 hours every 12 hours. In addition to taking his turn on watch, the chief mate has command of deck operations. The captain, who functions as a chief executive, has command of all operations. In a four-mate system the chief mate and captain would not stand regularly scheduled watches, but would stand in as required. In the three-mate system, such as that in place on the Exxon Valdez and most other tankers, the chief mate is performing double duty.

levels even further by 1990—from 20 to 16. This is a company that is part of an energy conglomerate (Exxon Corporation) that reported net revenues to its stockholders of $5.3 billion in 1988 and of $3.5 billion, after oil spill expenditures, in 1989.

Joseph Hazelwood spent part of Thursday in the town of Valdez. Between 11:00 A.M. and noon, he made several phone calls from the office of an oil agency, the Alaska Maritime Agency. From there he went to the Pizza Palace and had lunch with his chief engineer, Jerzy Glowacki, his radio electronics officer, Joel Roberson, and the man who would pilot the Exxon *Valdez* out of the harbor and Valdez Arm, William Murphy. According to Glowacki, Hazelwood drank iced tea during lunch. From the Pizza Palace, Hazelwood, Roberson, and Glowacki went to the Pipeline Club, a bar popular with tanker crews, and there, by the accounts of witnesses, Hazelwood drank either two or three vodkas "straight up." In his interview with Coast Guard investigators, Hazelwood said that he'd had two beers.

From the Pipeline Club, Hazelwood, Glowacki, and Roberson returned to downtown Valdez. Hazelwood entered a shop to order Easter flowers for his wife and daughter, then rejoined Glowacki and Roberson in the Pizza Palace, where Glowacki ordered pizza to take to the ship's engineers. There, Hazelwood drank something, but witnesses have not confirmed what it was. The three took a cab to the Pipeline Terminal, passed through the gate, where a policy on alcohol—either in the form of its possession or influence—is enforced. They climbed the gangway to the Exxon *Valdez*. It was raining and the gangway was steep, but neither Roberson nor Glowacki noticed any hesitation in Hazelwood's step.

Following the loading of the ship, Third Mate Cousins had run the standard systems check on the navigational and electronic gear. At 7:48 P.M. the test was successfully completed. At 8:20, Pilot Murphy had arrived on the bridge. Pilots are employed by Alyeska, and at that time one was required on each tanker as it passed in and out between the terminal and Rocky Point at the mouth of the Valdez Arm. After Murphy's arrival, Cousins was relieved by Chief Mate Kunkel at the bridge so that Cousins could go down to his docking station to direct the handling of the lines. It was then, at about 8:30, that Captain Hazelwood appeared, and that Murphy smelled alcohol on his breath. Murphy's observation would make the newspapers soon afterwards and be taken as evidence of Hazelwood's drunkenness, although Murphy had otherwise detected no evidence of impairment in the captain.

Hazelwood went below with a shipping agent for Alaska Maritime Agencies, Patricia Caples, in order to complete paperwork pertaining to the cargo. Later, at Hazelwood's trial, Caples would first testify that she detected a "slight sway" in his step, that his eyes were watery, and that he "seemed jolly." When cross-examined, she acknowledged that the watery eyes might have been due to the fact that he'd just come in from the cold damp weather outside, that the sway she'd observed had been extremely slight, and that his jolliness might have been her impression as it was cast in relation to the last time she'd seen him—the night before, following his arrival after a passage through rough seas.

In about ten minutes, Caples departed for shore and Hazelwood returned to the bridge. From this point, throughout the journey, and continuing past the events that followed the grounding, no one on the ship observed any deficiency in Hazelwood's demeanor or in his ability to give clear, concise orders. While damaging reports of Hazelwood's drinking had been widely circulated, there is no incontrovertible evidence that Hazelwood was drunk at the time of the spill. His crew members would assert that he was not, and indeed, the Coast Guard would find the measures he took to secure the ship after the grounding to be exemplary.

The blood alcohol test administered to him ten hours following the grounding would give a reading of 0.061 percent, or a little more than half the 0.1 percent drunk-driving limit in the state of Alaska and 50 percent higher than the 0.04 percent limit set by the Coast Guard for seamen operating a ship. A toxicologist who testified at his trial conjectured through a controversial process called retrograde extrapolation (calculating backwards) that his blood alcohol level at the time of the grounding might have been 0.22 percent, which likely would have left him dead, staggering drunk. It's more plausible that Hazelwood—and not surprisingly considering the circumstances—took a belt sometime in the period between the grounding and the blood test. Hazelwood himself had claimed to have consumed two Moussy beers—a form of very-low-alcohol beer permitted on board ship. Two of them would not have produced the 0.061 percent blood test reading. A search of Hazelwood's quarters conducted by Coast Guard investigator Mark Delozier was perfunctory at best. By Delozier's own admission, it did not include all the cupboards.

Because of the lack of Coast Guard provisions for the possibility that blood samples might have to be taken from a tanker crew, the samples themselves followed their own quixotic journey. Scott M. Conner, a Coast Guard health services technician, who happened to be in Valdez on other business, was called out to the tanker to take the samples from Hazelwood and other crew members. He temporarily placed them against his motel room window in hopes of keeping them cool, then stored them in the walk-in refrigerator in the galley of the Valdez Coast Guard station. The next day he carried them to Anchorage, put them in his own refrigerator, and finally turned them over to an Anchorage Coast Guard commander. By all early reports, the samples had arrived safely at Chem West Analytical Laboratories in Sacramento, California, but later— in July 1990, well after Hazelwood's trial in Anchorage—it was learned that the samples had been misidentified by either Conner or the lab.

In any event, the Anchorage jury rejected the prosecution's arguments regarding Hazelwood's drunkenness, but testimony at the trial creates the impression that at some point Hazelwood violated Coast Guard and Exxon rules concerning alcohol consumption and perhaps the possession of alcohol in his quarters. Although this is speculation, it seems possible that by making him tired or distracted, whatever drinking he did prior to boarding the ship was a part of the web of factors that indirectly influenced the coming catastrophe.

At the time, Hazelwood was 42 years old. In retrospect, two qualities in his record would rise to prominence: first, his problems with alcohol and, second, his rare intelligence and skill as a mariner. He began drinking at weekend parties while a student at the New York Maritime College, an elite and rigorous state-run school in the Bronx. Later, he earned a reputation as a hard drinker among some of his fellow seamen, who said that he also had a sense of when to stop so that his performance would not be seriously impaired. In 1984, while off duty, he was arrested for drunk driving in Huntington, New York. At the urging of a friend and Exxon supervisor, Captain Mark Pierce, Hazelwood entered a rehabilitation program. Through a coincidence, the Exxon brass became aware of his problems, and company records showed that according to Hazelwood's physician, he was "depressed ... demoralized," and had been "drinking excessively [and] episodically," which resulted in "familial and vocational dysfunction." In May 1985, an Exxon administrative manager, Ben C. Graves, addressed a memo to the company law department which reported that in the past Hazelwood had by his own admission returned "to vessels in port in an intoxicated state on several occasions, and that shipmates of Hazelwood's reported that he had violated company alcohol policy on at least several occasions."

Hazelwood was given a 90-day leave following his first drunk driving arrest and then returned to duty. By 1988 he had resumed heavy drinking, and according to reports his marriage of 20 years was on the verge of divorce. He was arrested once again for drunk driving. Despite Exxon's strict policy on alcohol, and despite Exxon Chairman L. G. Rawl's postgrounding letter to a Senate investigating committee, which claimed that from the time of Hazelwood's rehabilitation he had become "the most closely scrutinized individual in the company,"* Hazelwood's second arrest and his renewed drinking apparently escaped company notice.

From his boyhood on Long Island, New York, Hazelwood was drawn to the sea. Even as a teenage member of the Sea Scouts he distinguished himself for calm and courage by climbing the 50-foot mast of a schooner to haul in a mainsail that had been blown out by a violent storm. Upon graduating from New York Maritime College, he was one of a select group of his classmates hired by Esso, as Exxon was then called. His first commanding officer, Steve Brelsford, said that Hazelwood "had that sixth sense about seafaring that enables you to smell a storm on the horizon or watch the barometer and figure how to outmaneuver it." In 1985, Hazelwood's command, the Exxon Chester, ran into a freak storm. High winds knocked out the ship's radar and electronics gear, and with 30-foot waves and 50-knot winds overcoming the vessel, some of the crew prepared to abandon ship. Hazelwood calmed them, rigged a makeshift antenna, and guided the Chester out of the storm, only to be chastised by company officials for bringing the ship back to home port instead of taking it on to its destination. In 1987 and 1988, under his command, the Exxon Valdez received a prestigious company award for "safety and performance."

At 9:12 on the twenty-third, the Exxon Valdez cleared the dock and set out under the escort of the tug Stalworth. Pilot Murphy had command and in his company on the bridge were Hazelwood and Kunkel. A.B. Harry Claar was posted as a lookout on the bow, and the helmsman was A.B. Paul Radtke. The helmsman's duties at this point consisted of following the pilot's directions for steering the ship. In other words, he turned the wheel to the proper setting, which was registered before him on a rudder indicator. The wheel itself was nothing like the romantic image of a ship's wheel, the long wooden spokes tipped with brass, but a foot-and-a-half disk that communicated its position to the ship's rudder by a hydraulic system. Between 15 and 30 seconds would pass before the ship noticeably responded to a course change. The bridge itself was not the least bit rustic, but more like a highly secured stateroom, well-appointed,

* For reasons of liability, it seems to have been important to Exxon to separate Hazelwood's personal failings from company failings. State of Alaska documents, including its "Findings and Recommendations" to the National Transportation Safety Board, suggest that it has been interested in establishing, first, Hazelwood's drunkenness, and second in tying that to Exxon's responsibilities.

spacious, carpeted, loaded with technical gear—control consoles, radar screens, radio equipment, a Loran (long range navigation device by which position is determined by radio signals), a depth finder, and rudder indicators, five in all, including one in the adjacent chart room.

At about 9:35, Hazelwood went back down to his quarters to take care of more paperwork. He would not return until an hour and a half later, just before Murphy was to disembark at the pilots' station at Rocky Point. In Hazelwood's absence, the contingent left at the bridge—Murphy, Kunkel, and Claar—fell outside guidelines requiring that there be two officers on the bridge in such waters. These and other guidelines, such as the requirement that watch commanders have an endorsement for Prince William Sound (which Cousins, who would soon take the command, did not have), were murkily established and not always followed. Murphy, an old friend of Hazelwood's, would testify that it wasn't "unusual for masters to leave the bridge periodically . . . [though] it wasn't typical, probably, to be gone that long."

At 9:50, Cousins returned to the bridge from the deck to relieve Kunkel. Kunkel went to his quarters to sleep and would not awaken until a few minutes after midnight, when he heard a noise like a car running its side against a stone wall. Customarily he would have expected to come back on watch at 4:00 the next morning, but Hazelwood, knowing his chief mate's state of fatigue, had agreed to stand watch in his stead. It's important to note this, because in addition to the paperwork he was to complete, it raises the possibility that one reason for Hazelwood's spending so much time in his quarters following embarkation was that he, too, wanted to rest. Second Mate Lloyd LeCain, who was scheduled to come on watch at midnight, had also put in long hours, and Cousins himself, who had agreed to stand watch a little past midnight in order to allow LeCain more time in bed, had had no more than three and a half hours' rest in the 12 hours prior to resuming his work. This was the fashion in which the crew cobbled together its duty so as to accommodate its condition.

At 10:20, the ship passed Entrance Island near the mouth of the Port of Valdez and began her turn into the Valdez Narrows. There was fog at first. Here, traffic was restricted to one-way passage only, and as the fog lifted the land grew visible on either side of the ship as a darkness deeper than the sky. The sea was calm. The wind was light. The tide was rising, but the currents were weak. There had been reports of ice ahead in the Valdez Arm. The ship moved gently through the night, its 2,800-horsepower engine felt on the bridge as only a tremor like the rumble of a distant train. At 10:45, the marker light at Entrance Point came abeam.

Eight minutes later the channel broadened and the ship passed the light at Potato Point on her starboard side.

As the ship came out of the narrows, visibility stretched to eight miles, well enough to take sightings on the lights mounted ahead at Point Freemantle, Rocky Point, and Busby Island. The ship entered the Valdez Arm, where two lanes were established for inbound and outbound traffic. Hazelwood now returned to the bridge, and the ship's engines were reduced from half ahead to slow ahead to allow for the disembarkation of Pilot Murphy at Rocky Point—a place, some would argue afterwards, that had been selected as the staging area for pilots more for reasons of convenience than for navigational safety. Here, the tankers were still running at a relatively low speed, and in foul weather the waters would be less choppy than at Hinchinbrook Island, which had been the original staging area. Also, the distance itself back to Valdez was shorter—a cost-saving factor.*

Hazelwood directed Cousins and the lookout, Radtke, to assist in disembarking the pilot. At 11:24, Murphy was off, climbing down the side of the tanker to the pilot's boat that cruised alongside. Cousins was gone for a little over ten minutes. The state of Alaska would charge that the fact that there was only one officer on the bridge and no lookout again violated the Exxon Manual, which required a lookout and two officers on the bridge during Condition C—a measure of navigational hazard that indicated closely bounded waters or limited visibility. There would be dispute over whether or not the ship was in fact in Condition C. Even if it had been, the next question would remain: Considering the journey that lay ahead, how wise would it have been for Hazelwood to awaken one of his exhausted mates ahead of schedule?

Hazelwood called the Valdez Traffic Center (VTC) to report Murphy's departure, and then again several minutes later to request permission to change from the outbound to inbound lane. He was preparing for a maneuver to take the ship around the ice from Columbia Glacier. Gordon Taylor, who was then on duty at the VTC, testified that it was common for tankers to change lanes, and that as the ice flow increased it was not uncommon for them to deviate from the shipping channel entirely. He and his relief at the VTC Watch, Bruce Blandford, indicated that the focus of their radar was on the narrows, and that it often did not reach to Bligh Reef—a fact that many of the officers navigating tankers through

---

* Months later, speaking before the Commonwealth Club, Admiral James Watkins, secretary of the Department of Energy, would say, "It's preposterous that we took the pilot off at the harbor entrance. It's easier to do there, but that's not enough."

Prince William Sound had not been informed of. The radar system had been downgraded as a cost-saving measure during the early 1980s, even though the Coast Guard operations manual still stipulated that the Valdez Arm, which extended to Bligh Reef, be "continually monitored."

When Blandford came on duty just before midnight, Taylor told him that the radar image of the Exxon *Valdez* was "getting hard to hold onto." Blandford made no effort to see or contact the ship, and described this practice as "routine." He went downstairs to make himself a sandwich. The VTC was administered by the Coast Guard. The condition of the radar system and the general sloppiness with which the VTC monitored the Exxon *Valdez* and apparently all tankers that passed into and out of Valdez, together with the fact that blood tests administered to Taylor and Blandford afterwards showed, respectively, traces of marijuana, and alcohol use (but in Blandford's case not incontrovertibly linked to consumption prior to or during his watch), would eventually result in the investigation of the grounding of the Exxon *Valdez* being taken over from the Coast Guard by the National Transportation Safety Board (NTSB).

The ice in the shipping channel was heavy. The Exxon *Valdez* had been informed of this prior to departure, and now, though the weather had misted up, the ice was visible by sight and quite clearly on the radar screen, a little over two miles before them. It stretched in a cone shape clear across the lanes from Point Freemantle to within nine-tenths of a mile of Bligh Reef. This presented Hazelwood with two alternatives: either slow the ship down and go through the ice or go around where the ice was thinnest. By 11:24, the ship was back up close to 11 knots, the speed at which it maneuvered most effectively. A function of design and load, this is contrary to the common belief that the slower the ship goes, the better it handles.

Hazelwood informed Cousins that they would "divert around the ice" and then ordered a 180-degree course change, which would take them to a point just off Busby Island. Hazelwood ordered helmsman Claar to put the ship on autopilot, or the "iron mike," without informing Cousins. For a time, this was widely regarded as a contributing factor to the grounding, and evidence of Hazelwood's disarranged state of mind, but it had nothing to do with the grounding. It was probably a brief stopgap measure on Hazelwood's part while arrangements were being made on the bridge. Moments later, when Robert Kagan came to relieve Claar at the helm, Claar said, "I'm steering one-eight-zero and I'm on the iron mike." Cousins was standing next to Claar and he took the ship off autopilot. In any event, if the ship had been left on autopilot, this would have been discovered immediately when an attempt was made to steer manually, and disengaging it would have consisted of pushing a lighted button on the console.

Hazelwood told Cousins that he wanted to "bring it down to abeam of Busby, and then cut back to the lanes." Cousins went to the chart room and plotted the course. According to Cousins, Hazelwood went through the course change with him three times. In his testimony at Hazelwood's trial, which was slightly at variance with his previous testimony before the NTSB, Cousins said that he fully understood his orders, and that there was no doubt in his mind that the maneuver could be made. Cousins said, "He asked if I felt comfortable with what we were going to do and I said, yes. He said, do you feel good enough that I can go below and get some paperwork out of the way. And I said, I felt quite comfortable. Matter of fact I was asked that twice." It was a simple maneuver. The 180-degree change was already established. All that remained was a ten-degree rudder right at Busby Island, which would take the ship back into the channel.

Hazelwood directed that the engines be placed on "load program up." The command put the engine under the jurisdiction of a computer program which would increase the engine speed from 55 rpm to sea speed full ahead at 78.7 rpm, or to a little over 14 knots. This command, too, would become the subject of a furor—another signal of Hazelwood's disarrangement—and yet it was, according to the testimony of officers both from the Exxon *Valdez* and other vessels, a routine practice. At the time the command was given, the Exxon *Valdez* would remain within the parameters of peak maneuverability as long as it was in the area of Bligh Reef and, ponderous as the tanker was, it would not attain sea speed for 45 minutes.

At 11:52, A.B. Maureen Jones relieved Radtke on watch and A.B. Robert Kagan relieved Claar at the helm. At about the same time, Blandford was taking over for Taylor at the VTC in Valdez and going downstairs to make his sandwich. Jones was directed to stand watch from the starboard bridge wing as opposed to the bow as specified under Condition C. This was yet another of Hazelwood's commands that would be questioned, but Jones's primary duty at this point was to keep watch on the red buoy light at Bligh Reef. Being on the bow would have given her no advantage, while being on the wing kept her in close physical contact with the bridge. Hazelwood directed Cousins to call him by phone when the turn was begun, and then at 11:54, he once again went below to his quarters. Hazelwood was 15 seconds away, down a flight of stairs and a few steps along a hall—so near that Cousins would say he felt Hazelwood "still had control of the vessel."

Hazelwood's departure left Jones on watch and Cousins and Kagan on the bridge. Though employed as a third mate, Cousins was licensed as a second mate. He had made the passage through Prince William Sound between 26 and 30 times, three of them on the Exxon *Valdez*. Half of those times, he had been on the bridge. His qualifications were not questioned by anyone, and Chief Mate Kunkel characterized his abilities as "exceptional." A.B. Kagan, on the other hand, who was at the helm, was not as highly regarded. In a previous trip, he'd had some trouble keeping the ship on course. Left to his own resources, he was likely to oversteer, or to "chase the compass." Of Kagan, Kunkel would say, "I felt that Mr. Kagan needed extra supervision when assigned a task. . . . If I told him to go paint a bulkhead, normally you can send a sailor to paint. Mr. Kagan, I would have to make sure that he used the right paint, that he was applying it properly, using the right brush, et cetera. As far as his tendency to drift off, that is, in his steering ability, in my opinion he needed practice." During testimony at Hazelwood's trial, Kagan would blurt out almost endearingly, "I get so confused."

Another factor may have been that since Cousins was extending his duty over into Second Mate LeCain's watch, he was working with A.B.s not normally under his command. It was the first time Cousins had had Kagan under him at the helm. Nevertheless, the first command Kagan would be given that night—ten degrees right rudder—was the most elementary of commands, which all agreed Kagan was quite capable of executing. It consisted of revolving the wheel until the ten-degree turn was registered right in front of him on the rudder indicator, or put a bit more directly, of knowing one's right hand from one's left and of being able to read the number ten.

At 11:55, Cousins took a sighting on Busby Light, which was abeam of the ship, then moved to the chart room, apparently to double-check his orders. The lookout, Jones, reported seeing the flashing red light for Bligh Reef on the starboard side. There's a phrase that anyone with any experience at sea has had driven into them: red right returning. It means always keep red buoys and red channel markers on your right when returning to port or harbor, and keep them on your left when departing. The Exxon *Valdez* was departing. Jones had sighted the buoy light on the right side of the ship. Cousins, who had seen the same thing on the radar, was not alarmed for the moment because of the exception to the rule: At a given point, and at sufficient distance from the marker, an outgoing ship by virtue of its angle may well find the marker on its right side. There's a follow-up rule: Make sure the ship is turned well before you reach the marker. This was the right rudder Cousins was about to order.

He returned to the bridge and gave the ten-degree right rudder command to Kagan, then called Hazelwood to tell him that it looked as though they might get into the leading edge of the ice. Hazelwood asked if it looked like a problem and Cousins said no. Reassured, Hazelwood responded that he would be back up in a few minutes. During the minute-and-a-half conversation, Cousins had his back to Kagan. When he returned to the port radar and looked at the rudder indicator, he saw that it read between six and seven degrees right rudder. He immediately ordered the 10-degree right rudder again, then—in a fateful move—stepped out to take a visual sighting on the Bligh Reef light. Once again, for a moment, he was not watching Kagan. According to a computer mockup presented by Peter Shigume at the trial, if the right turn had been decisively executed at this moment, the ship could still have cleared the reef. The Exxon *Valdez* was still not far off the course of the ship that had preceded it out the channel, the Arco Juneau, which in its deviation from the ice had successfully executed a far closer and more dangerous maneuver than the one Hazelwood intended. When Cousins returned, he ordered a 20-degree right rudder because, as he put it, "We hadn't turned." Somewhere in here, too, the ship's automatic recorder indicated that an inexplicable counter-rudder might have been made—perhaps another gesture of confusion, perhaps a desperate effort to slow the ship down (for which the counter-rudder, which directs the ship against its existing trajectory, could be used), but it was now too late for anything. There was no way to either stop or turn the ship before it reached the reef.

Sensing the depth of his trouble, Cousins moved back into the chart room and "in haste" marked a chart, then returned to the bridge. It was an odd gesture—like a person falling and groping for the ripcord to the parachute he doesn't have. Maureen Jones appeared in the doorway in a state of alarm over the position of the Bligh light—red right returning. Cousins would testify, "This is the time when I'm becoming very concerned about the movement of the vessel toward the reef. . . . I gave the hard right command." This was, according to Cousins's testimony before the NTSB, at 11:56 P.M., though the automatic records kept on board the Exxon *Valdez* indicate that the turn wasn't begun until 12:01 A.M. Robert LaResche, the Alaska oil spill commissioner, compared the five-minute gap to the 18-minute gap on President Nixon's Watergate tapes. At the trial, however, Cousins suggested that his NTSB testimony might have been mistaken.

At Hazelwood's trial, Cousins went on to say, "I called the captain, told him that I thought we were getting into trouble. He said, where's the rudder? And I said it's at hard right. I turned. It hadn't moved to hard right, it was still at twenty. At that point we suffered the first shock, and within a matter of seconds we were hard aground. . . . There was a, you know, a mutual hang up of the telephones." It was now, according to Cousins, 11 or 12 minutes past midnight.

Because of its mass and the lightness of its metal hull, the tanker ploughed into the reef with extraordinary softness. The rudder was finally angled for the hard right and the ship pivoted, swinging its stern to the left. Cousins, fearing that the engine room would be hulled, and fearing for the people in it, ordered a hard left to correct the swing. When Kagan hesitated, Cousins himself grabbed the wheel and turned it. He switched on the exterior floodlights. Over the edge of the ship, oil was visible, bubbling up from deep beneath the surface. By that time Hazelwood had returned to the bridge and ordered Cousins to take a fix on their location. Hazelwood had been gone for 15 minutes. The "mundane" thing was, first, Kagan's confusion, and second, Cousins's failure to observe the rudder angle indicator after his commands. Testifying before the NTSB, Hazelwood would say, "I should have been up there."

Hazelwood ordered the engines shut down at 12:20 A.M., and sent Cousins and Jones down to wake people up, preferring that method to sounding the general alarm, which might have caused panic. He would be questioned for that, but later Kunkel would say that considered in retrospect it was the correct decision. Kunkel had been awakened by the sound of the grounding. He in turn awakened the pumpman and LeCain, announcing, "Vessel aground. We're fucked." Kunkel then went below. In the cargo control room, Kunkel saw to his alarm that a large quantity of the "product" had already escaped, that "there was movement in all the center and starboard tanks." The gauges were hard to read. He called the bridge, and Hazelwood directed him to take stability and stress tests. The radioman, Joel Roberson, saw oil shooting up 40 or 50 feet into the air from one of the tanks. Also, inside the cargo control room, LeCain saw oil spouting out of a tank. They managed to shut it off. Kunkel calculated that they'd already lost in the vicinity of 100,000 barrels of oil—in less than half an hour. The oil was exchanging with seawater.

At 12:26, from the bridge, Hazelwood called the VTC in Valdez to report the grounding, and added, rather dryly, "Evidently, we're leaking some oil." When Blandford, who had taken the call, switched on the radar, the Exxon *Valdez* came right up on it, perched on the reef. The on-duty officer assigned to the VTC was not on the premises, but at home. Blandford called the Coast Guard commander, Steve McCall, who went immediately to the VTC. Alyeska's top Valdez executive, Chuck O'Donnell, was awakened at about 12:30 by a call from the terminal and informed that a tanker was possibly aground on Bligh Reef. O'Donnell ordered a subordinate to go to the terminal, then rolled over and went back to sleep.

At the ship, the fumes grew stronger and the oil continued to bubble out. Kunkel took a computer readout up to Hazelwood and reported that as best as he could determine, the stress level on the tanker was too high, but the ship seemed stable. Hazelwood replied, "Okay, we can't go out to sea." Kunkel then asked again if the captain wanted the general alarm sounded. Hazelwood declined, but ordered the lifeboats and rescue gear readied. Kunkel would testify that Hazelwood gave him "the impression that he had command of the situation and I felt comfortable that he would be taking charge." Hazelwood sent Kunkel back down to the control room to get more information. The pumpman and engine crew were also sent down to assess damages.

At 12:40, Hazelwood commanded the engines up from stop to dead slow ahead, and then gave a succession of engine commands over a 40-minute period: "Half ahead, full ahead, full ahead, slow ahead, dead slow ahead, stop." At the same time, he gave rudder commands to Kagan, who was still at the helm. This action would produce one of the more puzzling episodes in the story. A few minutes after 1:00 A.M., Commander McCall radioed from the VTC and asked for an update of the situation. Hazelwood told him that the ship was in "pretty good shape . . . stability-wise" and that he was "trying to extract her off the shoal."

Hazelwood's account of the ship's stability was accurate enough, but if his report that he was attempting to get her off the shoal, or reef, were true, it would, first, very likely have been a dangerous maneuver. Some would argue that if the ship had been freed of the reef, it ran the risk of capsizing.* Secondly, it appeared once documents were examined that no matter what he said, Hazelwood had not in the least attempted to free the ship, but on the contrary, tried to drive it deeper onto the reef. Even some members of his crew, including Cousins and Jones, indicated in early interviews with the FBI and NTSB that they thought the captain was trying to float the ship free of the reef, but later they would pull back

---

* Others, including the man who subsequently directed the salvage operation, said that the ship would have floated if it had been freed.

from their impression. Hazelwood hadn't told them what he was doing.

In his testimony at the trial, Kunkel was especially clear in his argument that Hazelwood's efforts were directed at stabilizing the ship on the reef. One essential fact is that the engines were never ordered into reverse, which would have been necessary to extract the ship from the reef. Also, Hazelwood's commands to Kagan seemed intended to stabilize the ship and to successfully correct a list that it had developed. Finally, after Kunkel's second report—to the effect that the vessel was still intact but not fit to proceed—Hazelwood directed him below to monitor the ruptured tanks and to find a way to "ballast it [the ship] down" with seawater without opening any sea valves. He wanted Kunkel to find a way to make the ship heavier so that it would stay where it was. In Kunkel's view, Hazelwood's orders were prudent, and in fact "the only option we had." Kunkel said, "I felt safer. After the ship had listed to starboard . . . it stopped . . . and started to ease back to port, well, to zero list."

The question of what maneuver Hazelwood was attempting was critical both to his reputation for drunken wildness in the days following the grounding and in the course of his trial. Why he told McCall that he was attempting to get the ship off the reef is a mystery. He may have been confused, or still making up his mind, or expressing his disdain for Coast Guard authority. Perhaps he was unable yet to allow the outside world to come into what he knew, or maybe he still hoped for a retrieval that he knew otherwise, by his touch for the relation of a ship to sea and rock, was impossible. As it happened, the actions he did take to stabilize the ship and protect his crew—whether only hazily understood by him or perfectly understood and so offering a demonstration of his prowess at sea—were the best actions that could possibly have been taken.

A little after 3:00 A.M., the ship was approached by a party consisting of Coast Guard Lieutenant Commander Thomas Falkenstein, Chief Warrant Officer Mark Delozier, who himself had had a couple of beers at the Pipeline Club before being unexpectedly called to duty, and the redoubtable DEC representative, Dan Lawn, armed with his videocamera. Oil was boiling along the entire starboard side of the vessel. According to Delozier, it was "spreading all around. The oil was coming out of the vessel at a very intense rate . . . bubbling up into the air, sometimes up to sixteen, eighteen, twenty inches high. Against the hull, it was a foot, a foot and a half deep."

They boarded the ship and found the captain on the bridge, standing near a window and looking out. He was drinking coffee, and had been smoking. He had his hand over his mouth. Delozier took these as signals that Hazelwood was trying to cover something up. When he came near Hazelwood, Delozier smelled alcohol on the captain's breath. When Delozier asked what had caused the accident, Hazelwood said, "You are looking at it."

At his trial, which was held in Anchorage between February 5 and March 23, 1990, Hazelwood was charged on four counts under state law: criminal mischief in the second degree, driving a watercraft while intoxicated, reckless endangerment, and negligent discharge of oil. He was found innocent of the first three counts and guilty on the fourth, and given a $1,000 fine, an additional $50,000 reparations fine, and sentenced to 90 days in jail. The jail sentence was suspended in lieu of 1,000 hours' community service on projects designed to eliminate environmental damage caused by the spill. The guilty count is presently under appeal.

In a July 1990 administrative hearing before Coast Guard officials, charges of drunkenness and misconduct against Hazelwood were dismissed. Hazelwood pleaded no contest to charges of violating Coast Guard policy by drinking liquor less than four hours before taking command of a vessel and of improperly leaving the vessel's bridge while it was headed for Bligh Reef. The result was that his license as a ship's master was suspended for nine months, with consideration given for the time that he had already undergone without his license.

In August 1989, some five months after the spill, the U.S. Coast Guard undertook another study of tanker traffic in U.S. waters. To a large degree, the study was prompted by the Exxon *Valdez* grounding. The study was completed in October 1989, and though not intended for public scrutiny at that time, a copy of it was obtained by the *Seattle Times* through the Freedom of Information Act. The study is wide-ranging in its field of scrutiny and surprising for the frankness with which it presents Coast Guard deficiencies, particularly in regard to its undermanned, undertrained, underequipped, and sometimes demoralized corps of inspectors. This trend has occurred, the study notes, simultaneous with a decline in construction and maintenance standards for U.S. tankers, and with an increase in the number of 700-foot-plus vessels, which experience more wear and cracking than shorter ones. Discharges at sea through cracks are commonplace. The study observes that during recent years there has been increasing pressure upon shipping companies to compel their masters to drive ships hard in order to meet schedules, including operating vessels at maximum speed in rough seas. "The game rules now," the study says, "are for a professional investor to move freely within the marketplace spending as little as is necessary. Today's adage is to do more with less, make two tankers do the work done by three previously." This may be why the Exxon *Valdez*, and immediately before it the Arco *Juneau*, and before that scores of other tankers, diverted around the ice at full maneuvering speed rather than slowing to go through it. Doing so saved them at least a half-hour and as much as four hours in transit time.

The Coast Guard study is especially critical of reduced manning levels on tankers, the effect that it has upon crew fatigue, and the excessive reliance placed upon new technology both in and of itself and as a means for reducing crew sizes. "Coast Guard manning standards are primarily intended to ensure that the vessel is adequately manned for the safe navigation of the vessel," the study reads, and then, without naming the Exxon *Valdez*, nor Kunkel, LeCain, or Cousins, it goes on: "The standards do not adequately take into account other duties that the ship's officers and crew are required to perform when not on watch." The study questions the over-reliance on technical systems, their maintenance, the expertise of crew members to deal with problems in technical systems when they occur, and the tendency of officers on watch to experience "information overload." Again without mentioning the Exxon *Valdez* or, in this case, Cousins by name, the study observes that the bridge design—which places the chart room off to one side, where Cousins went to look at his chart, and to scratch a pencil mark on it, at the very moment his last opportunity for making the course adjustment had passed him by—should be reexamined.

Perhaps most tellingly, the study asserts that the Coast Guard itself "cooperates with the owners and operators of the tankers by allowing ships to be unprepared for inspections by using the old excuse that we are facilitating commerce. . . . inspectors are, in many instances, acting as quality control agents for the owners." The study recommends that owners again assume responsibility for maintaining quality and regular inspection schedules, and for assuring safe conditions for crews, and that the Coast Guard put the bite on the failures of the companies by refusing to certify them. At present, such refusals are virtually unheard of, or about as likely as shutdowns in the pipeline system for its violations.

The Coast Guard study articulates a basic question about the relationship between government and private enterprise. If private enterprise will not regulate itself, if government will not reasonably regulate private enterprise, or even itself, even when it comes to soiling our sustenance, and if money managers are allowed to drive the conduct of commerce, then our society becomes dangerously compromised to private power.

Not wishing to face that, not wishing to face our role as the final arbiters in the matter of oil consumption through our purchase of it in excess, it is no wonder that we hung the weight of disaster upon a single human head and, filled with self-righteousness, refused to carry our share of it, standing back to watch as it grew heavier and heavier like the head of Jokanaan, or John the Baptist, severed from his body after Salome's dance to satisfy the manipulative spite of Herodias.

Hazelwood's voyage took on an imaginary dimension for a host of reasons. The external safeguards that surrounded it were outright fabrications or so faulty that they functioned as fabrications. The Alyeska contingency plan that had promised to handle what was termed the 200,000-barrel-spill scenario was based on a plan, formulated in 1986, which projected the likelihood of such a spill occurring as once every 241 years. The Coast Guard–administered Vehicle Transport Center in Valdez, charged with monitoring tanker traffic in Prince William Sound, had downgraded its radar system. A quietly executed change in Coast Guard pilotage requirements allowed commanders without endorsements for navigating Prince William Sound to be at the bridge, and before the change the opposite regulation hadn't been enforced; even ships' officers were confused about what the regulations were and how much radar coverage the VTC had. The Exxon Shipping Company policy forbidding the use of alcohol by crews was not consistently enforced. Oil shippers had reduced manning levels on tankers. An underfunded Coast Guard failed to properly maintain tanker inspection schedules. The level of quality in tanker construction had fallen, and oil companies subordinated all aspects of oil transport to profitability. All these things and more do not absolve Hazelwood of responsibility, but they did make the continued exercise of safe operations imaginary. A catastrophic breakdown, as Riki Ott had predicted, was merely a question of time.

For Hazelwood, the journey became imaginary in the sense that once the Exxon *Valdez* struck Bligh Reef he would be propelled into a version of his life that was hardly his own—from master mariner to a drunk held on a million-dollar bond in New York, his deed compared to the bombing of Hiroshima, to a fool who tried to refloat his dangerously crippled ship, the one upon whom blame must be fixed, to an inside-out Earth First! hero who finally ruptured the oil industry's seal of secrecy, and through it all a media wonder, the butt of jokes on talk shows, his face on T-shirts, his name in headlines, and a made-up story about him drummed into the living rooms of every other house in the country for days on end. The nation could fix its sense of outrage and guilt upon him.

Through it all, Hazelwood, for legal reasons, maintained silence on what occurred on the Exxon *Valdez*. At the end of his trial, he thanked the jury for their care. The judge chastised him for failing to apologize. He had apologized when he first came to land from his wrecked ship. He was asked again and again for his apology, but, taciturn and self-contained, he declined to add the weight of servility to the wild weight already placed upon him.

Chapter 5

CITY LIFE

On April 8, two weeks after the spill, I flew to Prince William Sound. In Seattle, I asked for a window seat on the right side of the plane in hopes of having a view of the coastline, but the plane entered the clouds above the southern end of Vancouver Island and did not drop beneath them until, over the Gulf of Alaska, it began its descent for Anchorage. In a few minutes, Prince William Sound presented itself—an expanse of gray-green water rimmed by jagged, snow-covered peaks. We passed above Hinchinbrook Island, and then above the eastern portion of the sound. The mountains were the section of the Chugach Range that extends between Cordova and Valdez and beyond them north and easterly as far as the eye can see, white peak upon white peak vanishing into the white sky. In a moment, the pilot announced that we were passing over Naked Island, where the Exxon *Valdez* had been towed on April 5, and he tipped the 727 deeply to the right. It was down there, a tiny, toylike dark thing anchored in Outside Bay. It looked like a token to a gameboard. The two arms of the island made a backwards C to embrace it. A portion of the slick, a harmless-appearing shine darker than the water, surrounded the tanker and extended before it in long fingers and down, out of sight beneath the fuselage of the jet.

A hush fell over the passengers and everyone craned to see. There was the sense of unanimity to the silence as if of prayer, or as if the tiny thing down there were a terrible icon. The silence held sway for a moment after the pilot righted the plane and continued the descent, and then the conversations started up. The snatches I heard had to do with the tanker, with how much oil it had spilled, with the latest on Hazelwood, with the gasoline price spike in California. Everyone had a story. By then I'd come to understand that the better part of the passengers were headed for Prince William Sound. Among them were scientists, technicians, and fishermen heading home. The man seated next to me, Max Stone, said, "The objectives have to be clarified." It was a simple but singularly prescient remark, and he was speaking as much to himself as to me. He had a sheaf of papers on his lap and he was staring at one that was filled with numbers and small diagrams.

Max was in his midsixties, a retired chemist who had worked in the oil industry for years, mainly for Arco and Richfield, and most recently for Global Environmental Systems out of Bakersfield, California. He was a work-hardened, slightly bemused-looking man, disarmingly soft-spoken and kind. He had worked spills and seeps off Santa Barbara and was proud of his work and, I gathered, pleased to be called up out of retirement. I also gathered that he had become a chemist as much through experience as through academic training.

Before the pilot had dipped the plane for the view of the tanker, Max had been telling me that he thought his job here was to help build and operate a plant to salvage water-saturated oil and clear the water. I asked if I'd understood him right—build a plant? Unfazed, he said yes, but that he wasn't sure if it would be stationed on land or on the water. He'd said that Exxon had called his company, then given him 24 hours to get here. I suspected he'd been offered a good deal of money. I would learn that Exxon was culling the ranks of recently retired oil specialists, just as it was combing the West Coast for boats, barges, and equipment to bring to Prince William Sound. Although Exxon had taken over responsibility for the cleanup from the woefully unprepared Alyeska Company, the furor over who was truly in charge was raging full tilt at the very moment we were in the air. According to the newspapers, the state of Alaska had pleaded with President Bush to federalize the cleanup. Bush had initially declined, but then just the day before, on April 7, he had reportedly relieved Exxon of control, put the Coast Guard in charge, and promised to send troops. Actually, the question of who was in charge, of what was the proper relationship among the four institutional entities that came to the fore—Exxon, the Coast Guard, the state of Alaska, and various agencies of the federal government—would never be resolved.

By this time much of the oil had formed what was euphemistically called mousse, a water-saturated mixture, and Max had told me that in his job the whole trick was to separate the oil from the water. Once that was accomplished, the water would be returned to the sound and the oil would be salvaged. In principle, it was simple enough, like Alyeska's water ballasting system, but of course the scale of oil out there, and the extent to which it had spread, presented formidable obstacles. The water-saturated oil might be heated, Max said, and run through a series of tanks and filters to separate it. He thought it possible that they could use a centrifuge, but he doubted it. He didn't know where he was headed. All he knew was that somebody would meet him in Anchorage. He said, "If we're not trying to get perfectly clear water out of the salvage operation, then we can recover a lot of oil. We might make a macrochange that way. But if they want clear water it'll be a very long haul. That's why you have to clarify the objectives."

Although I didn't fully appreciate it at the time, Max Stone had touched upon two critical matters. His uncertainty over what exactly he was supposed to do proved typical of the confusion of efforts that went on for weeks. The question he raised about what degree of water clarity was desired would persist indefinitely. Indeed, it would make impossible what Exxon would come ardently to desire—the sense of an ending to the cleanup. When was the water clean? When were the beaches clean? What was clean? Where was the uneasy margin between pure enough and not pure enough. For some—but not Max Stone, who was a practical man—the question of purity and of its sullying would assume visionary proportions.

Back on March 24, late at night on the fateful Good Friday, Captain Hazelwood had been relieved of his command of the Exxon *Valdez* by Exxon Group Commander William Deppe. Hazelwood returned to Valdez. On Sunday, he met with members of the National Transportation Safety Board, but on the advice of his attorneys declined to cooperate with the NTSB inquiry. On Tuesday, the twenty-eighth, the news media broke the story of Hazelwood's drinking record and the national uproar began. That same day, Hazelwood again refused to cooperate with the NTSB. He shaved his beard to evade recognition and left Valdez without the knowledge of either Exxon Shipping or investigators for the state of Alaska (under the laws of which he would be charged on the four misdemeanor counts). For a week, he dropped from sight.

On March 30, the NTSB announced the results of the blood tests, which appeared to show that Hazelwood had been too drunk to legally operate a ship. On the same day, in an action it might well come to regret (since the charges of drunkenness did not stand up in court), Exxon Shipping responded by firing Hazelwood. Hazelwood resurfaced at his home on Long Island, and on April 5 he turned himself in to New York police. In court, an assistant district attorney referred to him as "the architect of an American tragedy." His bond was set at $1,000,000 and his bail at $500,000 by New York Supreme Court Judge Kenneth Roth, who himself came from a maritime background. Roth said that "these were misdemeanors of such magnitude that had never been equalled in this country." He compared Hazelwood's deed to the bombing of Hiroshima. The next day, April 6, bail was reduced to $25,000 by another New York Supreme Court justice.

The tanker remained perched on Bligh Reef until April 5, when it was floated and towed to Outside Bay on Naked Island for temporary repairs. From the outset, there had been two priorities for officials to address: contain the spilled oil and pump out the oil that remained on the ship—42 million gallons of it. Both things had to be done at once, and quickly. Pumping out (or "lightering") the Exxon *Valdez* clearly fell under the jurisdiction of Exxon Shipping, and by the time its president, Frank Iarossi, arrived in Valdez early Friday evening, arrangements were well under way. There were problems, such as locating fendering material to put between the *Valdez* and the second lightering tanker, the Exxon *Baton Rouge*, which had been diverted from taking on cargo at the Port of Valdez. Mainly, there was the problem of determining the sequence for taking oil off the *Valdez* and reballasting the ship so as to avoid its collapse or capsize. It was an extremely delicate and dangerous operation that would preoccupy not only Captain Deppe and his crew of over 20 but Exxon officials on land. After several setbacks, including pumps that didn't work, additional spillage from hoses, and weathering a storm that spun the rafted ships—two tankers and four attending tugs—12 degrees, the operation was successfully completed.

The spilled oil was another matter altogether. By Friday evening estimates had the quantity of oil on the water at 10.1 million gallons. As it happened, this was the first of three unusually calm days for the season, and the slick slid over itself and spread by force of gravity until by Friday evening it occupied an area of 18 square miles. The four entities that might take responsibility for controlling the slick—Alyeska, Exxon, the state of Alaska, and the Coast Guard—had quite different visions of who was in charge and what should be done.

Alyeska, it was understood by the state, was to provide the first line of action on spills in Prince William Sound. For spills in excess of 200,000 barrels, its contingency plan assured a response within two to five hours and that 50 percent of the oil would be ultimately retrieved. As it turned out, Alyeska didn't reach the scene for 15 hours and then with woefully insufficient gear. Equipment had been buried under piles of boom in warehouses. Some had to be dug out from under several feet of snow. A damaged equipment barge had been unloaded for repairs and left for two months. Loading it took ten hours. Other Alyeska employees in Valdez waited by their phones to be called to work. An oil container barge that Alyeska had been trying to get since 1988 still hadn't arrived. Eighteen hours into the response, no boom had been deployed around the tanker or slick, and only two small skimmers were operating. The skimmers, boats equipped with devices to draw the oil from the surface of the water, were full within a short period of time but had no barge in which to unload the oil they'd collected and, so, no further function.

For the next few days, Alyeska maintained a slightly enlarged but essentially token presence and at the same time declined to respond to calls from fishermen in Cordova and Tatitlek, who stood ready to throw dozens of boats into the recovery operation. Riki Ott, who twice flew through the haze above the spill on the morning of Friday the twenty-fourth, said, "I was stunned. There was no boom, no containment. Just a tanker on the rocks with two fishing boats coming up to it. Where was everybody?" Rick Steiner, an assistant professor with the University of Alaska's Marine Advisory Program, and stationed in Cordova as the marine equivalent of a county extension agent, flew over on Friday morning and saw the same thing. Steiner saw a group of Stellar sea lions trapped in the slick. Chuck Monnett, a marine mammal scientist stationed in Cordova, flew over once with Riki Ott, and then again with fellow marine mammal scientist Lisa Rotterman. Monnett and Rotterman were alarmed by the increasing reach of the slick and by the menace it presented to marine life, sea otters in particular. The lumps they saw in the oil were animals. They flew some 20 miles southwest to Naked Island, a prime otter habitat, and found a tongue of oil there. When they dipped for a closer look, the plane's engine faltered. The fumes from the oil were making the engine run dangerously rich. Later, when Rotterman and Monnett informed National Oceanic and Atmospheric Administration (NOAA) representatives in Valdez that there was oil at Naked Island, they were told that it wasn't so.

According to its plan, Alyeska should have recovered 100,000 barrels of oil by the end of the third day (Sunday), but it recovered only 3,000 barrels. Its projected 50 percent oil recovery rate was far beyond the standard of between 10 and 15 percent for previous big spills worldwide, and twice as much as the 25 percent experts posed as the absolute top performance under ideal conditions. As it happened, conditions for mechanical recovery were ideal for three days, but a few weeks later, Alyeska's public relations officer, Tom Brennan, would beg off Alyeska's failure by saying, "I myself flew over at 8:30 A.M. [on the first day], and yeah . . . I expected to see booms surrounding the ship, but that just wasn't what was called for. No one envisions anything like that. . . . It was obvious we weren't going to be able to contain it. . . . We knew that from the first."

Even without seeing the spill, Exxon Shipping's Frank Iarossi apparently suspected the same thing, and probably also understood that Alyeska's ability to undertake any mechanical measures was next to nil.* Before leaving Texas for Valdez, he'd begun making arrangements for spraying the slick with dispersant. There were several problems with this. Iarossi thought he had received permission to spray from the On Scene Coordinator (OSC), Coast Guard Commander McCall, but DEC Commissioner Dennis Kelso, by then the state's chief representative in Valdez, thought otherwise. There were not sufficient quantities of dispersant in Valdez, Anchorage, or anywhere in Alaska to do any good. Nor were there airplanes with which to spray it (before departing for Valdez, Iarossi had ordered shipments of dispersants and two C-130s and a DC-8). Finally, the use of dispersants was a highly complex and controversial issue and would persist as such through the summer and into the next year. It would become a critical point of dispute in litigation between Exxon and the state of Alaska.†

Applied under the correct conditions (moderate turbulence, so as to

---

* In his testimony before the NTSB, Iarossi said, "I don't think there was a power on earth that could have removed that oil from the water prior to those winds blowing that came up Sunday night, Monday morning. . . . The only technology that could have worked or had a hope to work was chemical dispersant."

† In 1988, a U.S. federal court decision concerning damages stemming from the 1978 Amoco Cadiz spill had penalized the French government for restricting the use of dispersants to waters deeper than 50 meters. The presiding judge, Frank McGarr, observed that the imposition of the 50-meter limit "seems to have been solely the result of pressure from ecology and nature groups." Exxon apparently took this as a signal that if they could show that the use of dispersants was impeded by Alaskan or U.S. officials, the company would fare much better in the damage suits that were certain to come. Consequently, as much or more of Exxon's early effort was directed at creating a paper trail to document impedance as it was at actually using the dispersants to good effect.

In October 1989, Exxon filed suit against the state of Alaska for opposing dispersant applications in the early stages of the spill. The Exxon complaint stated: "The state knew or should have known that its vigorous and active opposition to the use of dispersants would cause the Coast Guard to delay granting permission for the use of dispersants."

mix with oil), dispersants were considered the best existing quick fix for oil spills. The key components are "surface active agents" (surfactants), or high-powered versions of what are otherwise loosely known as detergents. Surfactants break up the natural cohesiveness of oil, causing it to fracture into tiny droplets that cease to float on the surface but instead sink down into the water column. The fracturing of the oil into droplets increases the total surface area of the oil and therefore hastens the process of degradation and bacterial breakdown. Dispersants make oil do what oil normally does, only much faster. They work best when applied very soon after a spill when the oil has weathered as little as possible— preferably, according to experts, within one to 18 hours (judging from his testimony, Commander McCall understood the window to be 24 hours). After that time, the effectiveness of dispersants drops off sharply, and in any case they would work on only 5 to 30 percent of the oil. Their main attraction is that when applied under favorable conditions and in open water, they reduce the amount of oil that reaches the shores. A second attraction, and a very important one from a public relations standpoint, is that they make the oil *seem* to go away. It would have made a huge difference to Exxon's image if the oil hadn't hung around to be photographed.

The problem with dispersants is that unlike washing machines, natural systems don't come equipped with drainpipes, and so the use of dispersants involves trade-offs. Dispersants themselves have "low to moderate" levels of toxicity—much lower recently than the notorious dispersants used in previous spills, such as the 1967 *Torrey Canyon* spill. Even so, by forcing the oil into the water column, dispersants cause for a brief period—six hours or so—a severe toxic hit by virtue of the rapid release of hydrocarbons from the oil itself. The hit is much greater upon the marine environment than it would be if the oil were left alone, floating on the surface. This is why it is far preferable to apply dispersants to open waters as opposed to near shorelines where life is much denser. The exception would be when there is something like a phytoplankton bloom or a heavy fish migration, which can make even deep waters extremely sensitive.

It presented a classic high-tech dilemma, like chemotherapy or insecticide applications: Do something destructive in hopes it'll make things better. And if one considers massive oil spills and chemical responses as late-twentieth-century extensions of the "horrid beauty" of our great machines that William Carlos Williams articulated in 1925, there were also elements in dispersant use of yet another notion— nearly as indiscriminate in its effects as the oil spill itself, and equally hostile to life—the presumption that the natural world would behave in the way we wanted it to.

The choice was this: oil by itself or oil with dispersant. Even practically speaking, the choice presented complexities over which there was genuine scientific disagreement and doubt—partly because there had been very few field studies of dispersant use prior to the Exxon *Valdez* spill, and partly because of the presence of a host of highly discrete variables, the combination of which take the ability to predict results well off the end of the graph. The success of dispersants depends not only upon water conditions but upon water temperature, too, and salinity level, the thickness and specific chemical makeup of the slick (crude oils vary widely in their composition) and of the dispersant itself (there are many formulations and Exxon wanted to use its own), upon the carrier, or solvent, with which the dispersant was applied (the carrier for Exxon's dispersant, Corexit 9527, is kerosene), upon the ratio of dispersant applied to the oil, and upon the method of application. In short, even given the rather limited range of their optimum effectiveness, dispersants might work and they might not work at all.

Riki Ott would emphasize the fact that dispersants introduce to the water column quantities of the toxic lightends (hydrocarbons) of oil which would otherwise have evaporated, and that once lodged in the marine food chain the toxic molecules are persistent. All, including the panel of scientists under the chairmanship of one oil spill guru, James N. Butler, who co-authored the National Research Council's *Using Oil Spill Dispersants on the Sea*, agree that dispersants should be used in combination with an effective retrieval operation, at which Alyeska had so thoroughly failed. Everything considered, and knowing in retrospect what happened once the oil got away from Bligh Reef, it probably would have been a good idea to use dispersants, had they been available. But taking the same sort of logic to its extreme, it might also have been a good idea to evacuate the nearby villages of Ellamar and Tatitlek and the Exxon *Valdez* herself, and firebomb the holy hell out of the slick. That would have abbreviated news coverage. Otter and bird bodies would have been hard to locate, and once the 42 million gallons left in the ship took to the torch, the obstruction Bligh Reef presented to marine commerce might have been eliminated forever.

The truth is that the decision on dispersants was never made. As it happened, Alaska, the federal government, and the oil industry had agreed earlier in the year, on March 1, on yet another state-of-the-art plan, the Alaska Regional Contingency Plan (ARCP). It mapped out Alaskan seaways into segments and, in the interest of facilitating speedy response, gave the OSC (in this case, McCall) permission to approve dispersant application in certain areas. Initially, the bulk of the spill was near Bligh Island, or in what the ARCP designated Zone 2—an area that required consultation with the Regional Response Team (RRT) and approval from the EPA and the state of Alaska prior to dispersant use. Additionally, McCall may at first have been unaware of a provision in the plan stipulating that the preapproved area, or Zone 1, into which a portion of the slick would begin to enter—the deep water of the tanker channel—was Zone 1* only from October 1 to February 28. During the rest of the year, because of fish migration, spawning, the phytoplankton blooms, even this Zone 1 was considered too sensitive for automatic approval of dispersant application. The eggs left by spawning fish were especially sensitive to the toxic elements in crude oil and dispersants.

The ARCP also included provisions for stockpiling equipment and supplies, and a Decision Matrix, or flow chart, intended to help the OSC take prompt action. James Butler and his National Research Council group had questioned Alaska's Decision Matrix, observing that, "The user must assemble a significant amount of information prior to making a dispersant-use decision, including a comparison of the effects of dispersed oil and untreated oil on populations at risk. . . . However, this system gives no guidance as to how to make the comparison and appears to assume a fairly high level of expertise by the user."

They were right. In addition to the Zone 1 conundrum, and the necessity for him to seek out approvals and scientific advice, McCall immediately found himself subjected to intense pressure and infighting from and among Exxon, the state, the fishermen, the environmentalists, the press. The interim solution was to conduct a series of test applications. The first was run at 6 P.M. on the twenty-fourth (18 hours after the spill) and made use of the only available aircraft equipped to spray dispersant, a helicopter with a 300-gallon bucket called over from Anchorage, and drew from existing dispersant stores (a total of 364 drums spread out between Valdez, Homer, and Anchorage).† The first test, according to McCall, showed "no positive effect," and the several tests

---

* For the remaining designation—Zone 3—dispersant application was not recommended since it was defined as the area in immediate proximity to sensitive resources (usually shorelines). Application required the same consultation and approval as Zone 2 and also that decisions be made on a specific case-by-case basis.

† Each drum contained 55 gallons of dispersant, for a total of about 20,000 gallons. Dispersant is applied at a rate of 1 to 20, so the dispersant on hand on March 24 was enough to treat 400,000 gallons of spilled crude. Had all other factors fallen in place, including the weather, the 5 to 30 percent effectiveness rate (McCall and Exxon claimed 35 percent) meant that between 20,000 and 120,000 gallons of oil would have been dispersed.

run over the next few days were repeatedly characterized as "inconclusive." McCall had by then enlisted the advice of Gordon Lindblom, a field dispersant specialist and former Exxon employee, who, according to McCall, agreed with all his decisions throughout the test period. McCall and others connected with the response team (including the EPA's Carl Loutenberger) would observe that the state of Alaska did not in any way impede dispersant application, but that the weather and the lack of supplies and equipment did. A later dispersant test run on Tuesday, March 28, included the accidental spraying from a recently arrived C-130 of a Coast Guard contingent on the deck of the Exxon *Valdez*, which raised questions about the ability of aerial personnel to hit their targets.

The net result was a standoff between the state, Exxon, and the Coast Guard, deepening a paralysis that would become one of the central features of the spill response and that would enrage the public, especially the fishermen. Alyeska in the meantime was withdrawing farther and farther into the shadows, and with it, incidentally, went the other six oil companies, which naturally wished to minimize their association with the spill, even though through co-ownership of Alyeska they were connected to the failed mechanical remedy. Exxon had taken over the response, and yet three days into the spill, well beyond the optimum application period, the original 364 drums of dispersant had increased to only 900 drums, and by that time rising winds had made aerial application hazardous. A full week after the spill, Exxon had on hand only about 2,000 of the 5,000 drums they needed. Later, Exxon Chairman L. G. Rawl would use the supposed obstruction to the use of dispersants Exxon didn't have as a means of browbeating the state, and perhaps of laying the groundwork for Exxon's coming legal position. In the May 8 issue of Fortune magazine, Rawl, flying in the face of every known fact about dispersants and the events in Prince William Sound, stated that "we could have kept up to 50 percent of the oil from ending up on the beach."

After the oil had laid there for three days in a state of relative docility, nature decided to step in. At dawn on Monday morning, a storm blew down from the Chugach Mountains. The planes were grounded. Boats were confined to the harbors. The winds blew the slick by the Naked Island complex of islands and into the southwestern portion of the sound, down to Knight Island, past Chenega Island and Green Island, and through the channels between Bainbridge, Evans, Elrington, and Latouche islands, up Resurrection Bay toward Seward, and on along the Kenai Peninsula. Twenty-five-foot waves slopped it up on the rocks. Everything was different now. The quick fix was gone, and the oil had to be dealt with on a new level of detail. To that end, the callup of equipment and personnel that had begun on the first day intensified. Max Stone was one of hundreds.

Max Stone and I parted company when the plane landed in Anchorage. I did not see or hear of him again. I boarded an ERA flight from Anchorage to Valdez. Forty-five minutes later, the Convair jet prop slipped between two ragged peaks, dropped precipitously, banked steeply, and landed in the Valdez airport. The plane was loaded to the gills with men and equipment, so loaded, in fact, that our departure from Anchorage had been delayed while several crates were taken off the plane to bring it within legal weight limits. In Valdez, the runway was lined with military helicopters, and flights passed in and out on top of one another. I would learn that what had once been a schedule of 8 to 12 flights a day had gone up as high as 600.* The small terminal was jammed with confused people. They were looking for their luggage, or waiting for the next flight, or they milled about, searching for whoever was supposed to pick them up.

There were men and women in National Guard uniforms. One man, who was headed out to Naked Island to work on the Exxon *Valdez*, wandered around with a steel diving helmet hanging from his hand. Television crewmen carried cameras over their shoulders. On the floor were mountainous stacks of luggage and gear in duffel bags and hard, protective cases. There were scientists, consultants, and electricians, plumbers, carpenters, a heavy dose of the press from all over the world, bureaucrats, politicians, insurance adjusters, the scam artists, and the scavengers. There would be high-tech medicine shows, people coming in with their schemes and inventions—super steam-cleaners and anti-crude chemical elixirs. Word had it that the whorehouse was hiring.

A merchant seaman, whom I'd met in the Seattle airport, had got here before me. He'd been called suddenly to duty. In Seattle he had told me in no uncertain terms that the grounding was the Coast Guard's fault, that Hazelwood had his drink after the grounding. He'd said, "Of course they drink on the tankers. After three days at sea, we're climbing the walls." The press, at this point, had the story otherwise. News of Hazelwood's drunken piloting was still spreading across the country. Now, the seaman was working the telephone, trying to find lodging. A line built up behind him.

Finding a place to stay was a problem. The churches had people sleep-

---

* For the 12-month period ending in June 1989, air freight cargo at the Anchorage airport increased by 60 percent, due largely to supplies connected to the cleanup.

ing on the floors, and the once dignified bed-and-breakfast industry had run out of control. Some, including myself, would pay over $100 a night to sleep in a living room, and the people, I would soon learn, wanted to be paid in hard cash. There would be two or three of us there each night. At that rate, the income came to a tidy unreported $7,000 a month. I learned that the place was 15 miles out of town, and tried to rent a car. Those prices had gone through the roof, too; moreover, all the agencies were out of cars. If I put my name on the waiting list, the people said, I might get a car in a few days. There were trucks hauling rental cars from Anchorage . . . *the road.* It was not just the airport, but the road to Anchorage, too. The road was fundamental to what Valdez was becoming. Cars loaded with tents and people looking for work were coming down it, vans and buses filled with people who had work, and semis loaded with gear, refrigerator trucks filled with food, trucks hauling equipment, supplies, computer systems, reams of paper, boom, boats, hosing, engines, compressors, Caterpillar tractors, more modular buildings, cases of rubber suits, bales of absorbent pads, digging tools, snacks and coffee machines. By then, eight skimmers had been hauled from the North Slope to Valdez.

Eventually, I caught a ride out to my place, and then another back into town. The overtaxed services, the general practice of gouging, and the scams that were being run were the down-side of the situation. One part of the up-side was that many, including Valdez residents, would give anyone a lift. After trying and failing to talk to somebody at the temporary Exxon office and otherwise cruising the downtown, I went into a restaurant called the Totem Inn. The place was as crowded as the terminal had been. As I waited for a seat, I asked the manager, a large, florid-looking lady, what she thought of the crowd. In my innocence, I expected her to betray weariness at least. She said, "It's not bad," then smiled knowingly. "But it's not near as good yet as when the pipeline came in."

Service took an hour. The telephone in the entryway also had a waiting line that stretched outside the double doors. When I got a seat, I discovered that the customary sense of boundaries between tables had completely dissolved, that the general atmosphere was somewhere between a church camp and a dog pack. There was an endless din, and shouts across the room. Two disaster reporters who hadn't seen each other since Bhopal thumped each other's arms. The waitresses had trouble keeping track of who had ordered what and could be seen wandering from table to table with lost expressions. It didn't matter. You ordered and then ate what you got. People found themselves sitting with strangers. Eavesdropping was acceptable behavior, even expected, and any conversation was open for entry. All conversations were mere channels leading to the one conversation, anyway: the tanker, Hazelwood, President Bush, the crowd, the press, the closed herring season, the otters, the death, the money, the cleanup wages ($16.69 an hour, 12-hour shifts, seven-day weeks, and time-and-a-half for overtime), and the oil, which was off Hinchinbrook Island and down along the Kenai Fjord National Park, 175 miles from Bligh Reef and covering an area over 2,500 square miles.

"We're a boomtown again," said Gari Norman, a Valdez schoolteacher who was seated across from me. Gari was concerned about the destruction in the sound, and especially concerned about the lag between that and what was going on here in town. There was a distinct fatalism to his attitude. "But the boom's built on a disaster, and it'll make us into a company town." He was referring to the fact that Exxon was leasing out warehouses, buying up buildings to house its specialists and managers, constructing camps for the workers, running the city planning office ragged, and generally spending money hand over fist. The bill was already well into the millions, and even the accountants brought in from Houston, I would learn, were getting white knuckles over the level of the flow. The evidence of the bottomless bankroll was everywhere in Valdez.

Exxon had taken out ads in newspapers and magazines across the country and apologized for the spill. L. G. Rawl had repeatedly assured the public and the U.S. Congress that "Exxon takes full responsibility and has done so from the start." The apologies, though, had a hollow sound, and many felt doubt over just what "responsibility" amounted to. Exxon was clearly capable of calling up millions of dollars' worth of equipment in reasonably short order, that is, of poising itself for action, but there was continuing confusion over just what the action would be, and taken according to what guidelines, with what devices, and for what purpose.

The fishermen of Cordova and Valdez, who had protected their hatchery sites and begun recovering oiled otters and birds essentially with their own resources, were finally invited by Dennis Kelso into the inner sanctum of the tripartite authority (now Exxon, the Coast Guard, and the state), where they were consulted on such matters as the patterns of currents in the sound, about which no one knew as much as they. They came back with more tales of confusion.

Coast Guard Admiral George Nelson had been in Valdez for several days, having come to assist the overwhelmed Commander McCall, but there remained at the heart of everything an ongoing dispute over who had final authority. At this point, the state of Alaska was still begging President Bush to federalize the cleanup and to establish clear control. Bush finally declined on the day I arrived in Valdez. Admiral Paul Yost, commandant of the U.S. Coast Guard, explained that federalization might leave an opening for Exxon officials to "close their checkbook" and force the government into assuming costs. Yost was also worried about his own thin budget. In a clear echo of the blurring of the line between economic power and regulatory authority that had created the inadequate response capability in the first place, the question of who now was in charge and who was to pay continued to clog up the bureaucratic channels.

In Valdez, it was hard to get much in the way of explanation from Exxon. Having taken repeated beatings from the press, local citizens, and fishermen, Exxon now refused to send representatives to press conferences. With justification, no doubt, Frank Iarossi would later explain that the press conferences, which were initially held twice a day, were also taking too great a toll on the stretched resources of himself and other managers. Soon, Exxon would muster a complete onsite platoon of what the company referred to as the Communications Group, but for now daily written press releases were passed out. These painfully upbeat announcements reasserted the company's intent to take "full responsibility," told of what equipment was arriving, and gave overoptimistic assessments of where the oil was, what it might do next, and how much of it had been recovered.

Exxon and the city of Valdez had invested heavily in security guards. Besides the airport, there were guards at the Exxon offices, guards at the Civic Center, and increased security at Veco, the largest of several oil service companies that would be hired out as cleanup subcontractors by Exxon. There were guards in all the public buildings. It had struck me early that considering the degree of confusion and the heat with which rumor was generated and passed, it might be a good idea to talk to a few scientists. I began what would be a long and often frustrating quest for hard information by seeking out a marine biologist a mutual friend had referred me to—Kathy Frost of the Alaska Department of Fish and Game (ADFG). Along with her husband, Lloyd Lowry, Kathy is a highly regarded specialist in marine mammals. When I went to the ADFG office, I found guards. They had constructed a barrier in a hallway made out of cardboard boxes. There was another line here, in this case a dozen or so men sprawled along a wall. They were looking to be taken on by Fish and Game. I gave my name to one of the guards, told him who I wanted to see, then moved down along the hallway to wait. In a moment, two electricians were called up to the barrier, and the other men in line cursed under their breath. There were a couple of carpenters there, and an X-ray technician who had quit his job in an Anchorage hospital and driven here in expectation of making $7,000 a month working in the ADFG morgue.

There was a guy with a grizzled, wild look. His hair sprayed out from under his dirty stocking cap and his eyes glared fiercely when he talked. He said he was sleeping in his boat down in the harbor. He hit on everyone who passed by in the hallway on the chance that he might find a lever, any kind of lever. He made a special point of the location of his boat—slip 52. He was from Anchorage and he wanted a job right now, any job. He had an aluminum-hulled boat with a six-cylinder, 175-horsepower jet-prop engine. He claimed that it was the fastest boat in the harbor. He'd hauled it here down the road from Anchorage. His frank rapacity was arresting. He was one of the few people operating with complete clarity. He knew the money was floating free, and he wanted some.

He got me to thinking about the food chain as I waited for Kathy Frost, who it turned out had left for the sound early that morning. I thought about the position of scavengers on the food chain, of the adventurers. Out there on the water, the oil slick slid along, breaching the habitats in place after place, touching its leading edge to barnacles and anemones, to the long trails of delicate, pearlescent herring eggs that stretched across the water, overcoming the birds and otters and leaving them as waste for the bears and eagles to eat. Here on the edge of land, a surfeit of human nature had gathered in a pack. The situation on either side of the shoreline was an expression of the likelihood that had been in place for years: one of the ecologically most productive and richest places in the world had spawned colossal greed and heedlessness whose predictable aftereffects now drew citizens in droves, pulled up close to the dark table, eating deeply, lost in the last dark petroleum dream that had made the American twentieth century possible. It was unsettling to consider that the guy with the boat in slip 52 was merely continuing on to the end in his own very defined way.

I went to see the Animal Rescue Centers that had been established in Valdez. Exxon had hired professionals to manage the centers, among them Randall Davis and Terrie Williams from Sea World Research Institute in San Diego and Jessica Porter of International Bird Rescue and Research Center (IBRRC). Porter and her associates, however, had the advantage of the established, field-tested organization founded by Alice Berkner. Every oil spill creates oiled birds, and by 1989 IBRRC had standardized techniques for cleaning and determining the birds' readiness for release. Porter was contacted at 6:30 A.M. the morning of the spill and was setting up shop in Valdez by Saturday morning. Randall Davis, who was put in charge of the Otter Rescue Center, did not arrive until after the oil had been blown through the sound, and had to create procedures on the spot for diagnosing and treating oiled otters. At the same time, he had to assemble his staff, build a facility, and otherwise handle the complications that developed around what he referred to as "the most political of marine mammals." The otter would become the intensely scrutinized, international symbol of the Alaskan spill.

The creation of the centers had been ordered by the Department of the Interior at the time when Exxon's attention was riveted upon lightering the Exxon *Valdez*, but in a parallel development to the federal government's approach to cleanup, the Department of Interior agency normally charged with primary responsibility for protecting wildlife, the Department of Fish and Wildlife (DFW), had refused to take an active role in the process. Troubling questions about the department's role in actually obstructing both animal rescue and scientific research were about to break surface.

In the early days the centers had been staffed largely by volunteer townspeople, whose care for the animals offered a little different take on human nature from what Valdez otherwise offered. To these as time passed were added volunteers from the lower forty-eight. Many of the volunteers would say that their work was an exercise in penance. For Exxon, it became a form of damage control. Here, too, Exxon paid all the bills. Suzanne Stolper, public relations officer for the animal centers, said that the funding was sufficient, that Exxon was not interfering in the least with operations. Although such statements invited suspicion, this one was by and large true. Stolper herself was forthright, skilled, and remarkably patient even with TV crews that had come expressly to get a few shots of death for the homefolks.

The Otter Rescue Center was located in the old Growden-Harrison Elementary School, which had been closed down after the pipeline boom. A front-end loader worked the parking lot, clearing huge piles of snow left over from winter. In the open space carpenters were constructing holding cages. As of that day, 103 otters had come in. Half of them had died. Here, the dead were hustled out the back door to avoid the press. Out in the sound, a quarter of the 10,000 or so otters were considered either dead or imperiled, and they were found floating in the water, or writhing in agony, desperately attempting to groom their fur. Thick ribbons of oil hung from their recta. As I passed the carpenters, a van pulled up and several otters were carried inside. They were inert, coated with oil. If still alive, they would be tested, warmed, and cleaned, and if they continued to survive they would be attended to with great solicitude.

Most of them arrived hypothermic because of the oil's effect on their insulating underfur, upon which they depend for warmth, unlike whales and seals, who have layers of blubber. Otters' fur has to be kept clean and arranged just so. For this reason, they groom continually. Many suffered from chemical pneumonia. R. V. Chelan, a veterinarian and toxicologist from California, explained to me that the pneumonia caused gasping, which in turn created air sacks in the lungs. After a brief exposure to the toxic fumes in the crude, many of the otters developed emphysema and it progressed rapidly to an advanced stage. If they ingested the crude, which they did as a matter of course while they groomed themselves, their livers would go. Compounds were also absorbed through the skin, producing the same effect on the lungs and liver. The benzene in the crude caused bone marrow depression, immune deficiency, and neurological breakdown. Those that died, Chelan said, would usually do so in agony.

Two blocks down at the Prince William Sound Community College, more carpenters were hard at work on the Bird Rescue Center. I spent the afternoon and next day there, learning the process. The birds came in hypothermic, too, because of the way oil breaks down their natural oils. They also suffered from various forms of toxic shock. They were warmed, tested, washed with Dawn detergent, then rinsed and put in pools to see if they floated. If they floated, they were sent to the drying room and fed a mash through a tube until they recovered to the point where they could eat fish. From there, in the case of both birds and otters, there was a question as to what to do with them—send them to the lower forty-eight, release them back into the oily sound, or what? This, too, would soon provoke a bitter controversy. By the time I'd arrived, eight birds had been released back into the sound.

"The Procter and Gamble reps have been here," my partner said as we washed an Arctic loon. I held the bird and she worked with a toothbrush and Water Pik. We had been advised that the loons and pelagic cormorants were dangerous, that the cormorants could slash the flesh with their beaks and that a loon could put a hole in your chest. I held the loon warily, keeping it low in a small plastic basin. It was a large bird. "They came to check out the Dawn," my partner said. She was cleaning, stroking each feather with the toothbrush, squirting on the Dawn, then working under the feathers with the Water Pik. The effect of Valdez upon the consciousness was such that my partner was suggesting the possible Procter and Gamble ploy: a high-toned ad, a bird, maybe, standing off to the side of the picture and a bottle of Dawn in the center. I never saw such an ad and in fact Dawn was remarkable stuff—a domestic surfactant. We rinsed the loon and cleaned it again, and then again, going through the process four times. It seemed strange, and in a way wonderful and calming to work on the wild things with such implements—Water Piks, toothbrushes, small plastic basins—and then check to see if they floated. The loon felt docile in my hands, as accepting as a baby. The melodic, mournful cry of another loon echoed through the hall from the drying room at the far end of the building. The loon I held didn't move a muscle.

A Valdez couple had rented me a car for 20 dollars. This was more of the up-side of human nature, and an expression of the Alaskan cordiality to strangers. The couple hardly knew who I was, and did not ask for identification of any sort. They had merely heard from someone else that I was stranded. At sunset, as I drove to my bed in the living room, I stopped alongside the highway to look at the Alyeska terminal across the bay. It was bathed in bright sunlight. To the right of the terminal, to the left, and behind it were the snowy mountain slopes, brilliant in the sun. The concrete holding tanks and control buildings began about three-quarters of the way down from the mountain peaks. I had already been over there, and the holding tanks were very large indeed. There was a sign every 50 feet that said, "Don't Litter. Keep Alaska Clean," and the ditch on the shore side of the access road was black with sludge.

From the highway, a distance of a couple miles, the tanks looked small, and it was then that I was struck by their Third Reich-like appearance, the extremity of function in their design. I counted the 18 of them. Beneath the tanks was the power plant, beneath that the vapor recovery facility, the metering building, and then the ballast treatment facility, the maintenance building, the control center, and the impound basins. Long pipes stretched to the water where three tankers were loading up. The traffic was gradually coming back up to capacity. The ships looked small and precisely silhouetted in the sunlight. The whole business, set off against the tremendous slopes, looked like a slightly larger toy than the version of the Exxon *Valdez* I'd seen from the 727.

The next evening, I boarded the ferry from Valdez to Cordova, a fishing town with a fast-developing reputation for outrage and activism. In the

Valdez harbor, a couple of fishing boats with oil-encrusted hulls were being steam-cleaned. Helicopters and seaplanes flew incessantly back and forth over the harbor. In the distance, two more tankers were docked at the Alyeska terminal, taking on crude.

The atmosphere on the ferry was as different as it could be from the atmosphere in Valdez. Here, too, the conversations revolved around the oil spill, but the voices were muted. It was partly the calming effect of being on the water, the sense of patience and deliberateness that comes with that, and partly a sense of grim expectation. Most of the people on board were Cordovans, heading home from often far-flung places. What they had heard was bad. What they expected to hear and see would be worse.

Among them was Tom Cumming, a fisherman who had been crabbing off Washington state and had driven 3,000 miles in 55 hours to get here. We were up on the third level of the ferry, standing outside the solarium. The water we'd been passing through and the shorelines were clear of oil. I had yet to see the oil, as a matter of fact, except on animals, boat hulls, and rubber boots worn by workers. Tom was in his thirties, blond and bearded. He wore one tiny, bright earring. He spoke softly and had the name for every island, inlet, mountain peak, and point. We passed Potato Point, a hump of land on our right as we came out of the Valdez Narrows and entered the arm. A few minutes later we passed Rocky Point, the place where Pilot Murphy had disembarked. Tom pointed out Ellamar Mountain to our left. We then saw the first sign of the bergy bits that had drifted into the channel from Columbia Glacier. Their color was extraordinary, white, and pale blue, and sometimes an intense deep blue, the result of their density. Some of them were indeed as big as houses. It was at this point that Hazelwood had informed the VTC that he was changing lanes.

"The Native village of Tatitlek is in there," Tom said. He nodded toward an opening in the shoreline, the Tatitlek Narrows. "They could be wiped out by this. The spill was in their backyard." I gazed at the inlet, into the intricate, winding darkness there of water and rock, and saw a sheen of oil, a long, thin shine. The water was that blue and green and milk color. The shine was dark gray.

In a few days, Gary Komkoff, the Tatitlek council president, would tell me that nearly everybody in Tatitlek had lived in a white town for a while. "But we chose to come back. We don't like the city life." On the first weekend of the spill, Exxon had conducted one burn test, but hadn't informed the Tatitlek people. They found out about it when they saw the flash and then smelled the fumes drifting their way. I would see

Tatitlek later, a neat row of houses with blue roofs, a Russian Orthodox church with a blue parapet, more scattered houses with red roofs, a landing strip, a community building, a dock with a few fishing boats and a float plane. One hundred five people lived there. Many fished commercially for income, but their main concern was over the damage to their subsistence resources.

"We fish, hunt, and trap," Gary would say, speaking evenly and with remarkable calm. "We eat deer, fish, clams, urchins, almost anything that tastes good. It's been our lifestyle for years. To have it suddenly jerked out from under us like this by an oil company causes a lot of hurt. This is the way we live, and now it's taken away." He would tell me that North Pacific Rim, an organization that serves Native villages in the Chugach region, would sue Exxon for damages, but then he would add sadly, "What the effects will be is unknown." I would take him to mean not only the effects of the spill itself but of engaging in the lawsuit, as well as of entering that channel.

From the ferry, Bligh Island came into view, and before it the illuminated buoy—red right returning. It was on our left. It was okay. We were going out. Now, three sea lions were resting on the base of the buoy. They lay close together, touching each other, and their heads came up to watch the ferry. Tom smiled and said, "They never let up." Then he fell silent and I could sense the anger rising in him. He repeated what Admiral Nelson had said, what many had come to say—that a child could steer a tanker through this channel, the Valdez Arm, which at this point was ten miles wide. Tom said, "Exxon's gonna get it." I'd heard that in order to avoid the ice and save time, the ferries used to take a similar shortcut that the Exxon *Valdez* had attempted. Not surprisingly, this ferry stayed within the channel.

"Most fishermen wouldn't be sorry to see the sea lions bite it," Tom admitted. They are profligate eaters of commercial fish. "But it's not so with the otters. I catch otters in my nets and throw them back overboard. They don't eat that many fish." Tom had a passion for the sea, a hunter's sense of the earth, and now a great, quietly held anger.

"I don't know what'll happen," Tom said. "The oil will drift around for a long time. It'll get the crustaceans and coat the eel grass and popweeds. The deer will eat the eel grass. The bears will eat the deer carrion. The pop weeds will get in the nets, and then we'll have a little oil coming off the net onto the fish. Is the fish contaminated, then? What is contamination?"

By the time we began the turn around Knowles Head, Bligh Island had fallen away from view. Five tankers were anchored off Knowles Head, though, awaiting their turn for the run to the terminal. These ships, too, looked oddly tiny at first. As we neared, they became huge. They flickered in and out of their bigness and smallness. A nasty silence fell over the people on the upper deck. Near the tankers was an oil slick. It had a dark shine, as if polished, almost the luster of a patent leather shoe. It came from one of them, not the Exxon *Valdez*. We had still not seen any significant portion of the main slick, and our route was now taking us farther away from it. At that time, the reports of what happened on the *Valdez* were still obscure and loaded with contradictions, and Tom shook his head and said, "I have a real hard time figuring it out. That tanker was miles off course. Way inside the buoy. From the buoy it's two miles to the reef."

At twilight, the sun sank in the west. There was a wide, white wake behind the ferry. On either side of the wake, the water was lead-colored, and further to the sides were the black crags. In the distance the tankers were alight like tiny cities. They could well have been independent cities with their own sinister codes of conduct that set them apart. Beyond were the jagged snow-covered peaks, turning a luminous pink, and above the gray clouds, the same color as the sea had now become. Tom said, "It looks just the same to me here, but all the tidal grounds out in the sound are finished." He fell silent, then gestured to the right and said, "I shot my first black bear on that hill."

Later, after the lights of Cordova had come into view, I saw Tom standing over in a front corner of the solarium. He was gazing at the lights of Cordova, watching as we came near. His body was slouched against the wall and his head touched the glass.

Chapter 6

CORDOVA

|t tore up its own face," Richard Newman, a photographer
|from California, said. He was talking about a sea otter. The
day before, Richard had been out on a float plane, and had seen the
general slaughter by air and from the shore. His first response when he
stepped to shore was to throw up, a reaction that came in part from
disgust, but in the main from the effect of fumes. It was a common
enough reaction, but striking for its occurrence two weeks after the spill.
The bulk of the most toxic aromatic hydrocarbons should have evaporated off the crude oil within the first 48 hours.

"Knight Island is thick with crude," Richard had told me. "Green
Island is gone." That was just the beginning of the gruesome litany. The
latest reports had the slick splitting out in the Gulf of Alaska, one finger
curling around the corner of the Kenai Peninsula and headed into Cook
Inlet and the other finger pointed at Kodiak. In the meantime, by the
action of tide, wind, and twirling currents, the islands in the sound had
been smeared and resmeared with oil. Knight Island, which lay directly
in the path of the oil, was among the hardest-hit places. Knight Island
was considered by many to be the heart of the sound, the wildest,
richest, most exquisite, complex, and magical of places.

"The fishermen say the area normally swarms with birds," Richard said, "but now they're simply not there. Maybe they're dead and washed under. Maybe they flew away. There are places that are completely covered with crude." Huge pools of crude sloshed up onto the beaches, he said, and made oil-filled lagoons that seeped into the crevices. He had taken his Hasselblad camera with him, but couldn't focus it. "There was nothing to focus on, no rocks, no bushes, nothing, just crude oil."

We were in Cordova, a town as different as it can be from Valdez. It had a population of about 2,600 that swelled annually to about 5,000 during the peak of fishing season, when cannery workers and Prince William Sound fishing permit holders who live elsewhere during the winter arrived. Valdez had a steadier population of about 3,500, and a city budget at least six times the size of Cordova's, thanks in no small part to the property tax levied against the Alyeska terminal. In Valdez, occupations are apportioned among education, small business, fishing, tourism, the Coast Guard, and Alyeska. A good percentage of the people put in their hours and go home to their climate-controlled houses. Valdez is a microcosm of the sharp occupational tensions one finds in most American cities. Tourism and fishing have long been at odds with oil shipping. With the oil spill, the differences became conflicts.

In Cordova, everything is directly or indirectly addressed to fishing. Before the oil spill, divisions in the community tended to take the form of close-in body punching followed by clinches, as if among relatives. Although Cordova itself, protected by the sound's prevailing westward currents and Knowles Head to the northeast and Hawkins Island just across the bay, had not been struck by the slick (nor had the nearby, prolific fishing grounds off the Copper River Delta) the town depended upon all of the sound for its sustenance. In response to the spill, the townspeople formed a solid wall of protest. On the Tuesday after, the first of several town meetings found the high-school gym packed with upwards of 2,000 hissing, hooting, contentious people, furious over the lack of action. The Exxon and Alyeska representatives arrived late and wanted to leave early. They couldn't.

Through loss, Cordovans' feeling for the beauty of their place and for the way their lives were entwined with the sound had taken on new force. Fishermen have a not always deserved reputation for being roughnecks, or cowboys of the sea, who dump their trash and pump out sewage into the water, who catch all manner of things besides fish (such as sea otters, Tom Cumming's remarks notwithstanding), and who sometimes cut loose their damaged nets and let them float to the bottom, where they became ghost nets. Made of plastic, they trap fish forever. Now, it was not uncommon to hear the crustiest among them say, "We should have been paying attention," or "The environmentalists were right." They also resented the way Exxon, especially at the beginning, had treated them as incidental. The question, finally, would be to what extent Cordova and its fishermen could form new alliances or renew old ones with other fishing interests, environmentalists, tourism interests, and independent oil shippers, such as Chuck Hamel, and what steps they could take to counter the inherent imbalance in power between themselves and the oil companies.

At the moment, Richard Newman and I, each of us outsiders, were becoming aware of what Cordova already knew. We sat in the loft of the Killer Whale, a delicatessen-style restaurant that operated in the same building as the Orca Book and Sound. Valdez had no bookstore, and this one in Cordova, though small, had a stock that ran from bestsellers to esoteric literature, philosophy, and natural history. It bespoke the community. The store was also a center of oil spill response in the town, one of many private establishments where the margin between the conduct of business and community action grew so thin as to be invisible. The owner of the deli, Jeff Bailey, and the owners of the bookstore, Susan Ogle and Kelly Weaverling, husband and wife, were involved in the response. Ogle had been the first director of Cordova's Oil Spill Disaster Response Office (COSDRO). Since the fifth day of the spill Weaverling had coordinated an effort to rescue oiled wildlife—first birds, then birds and otters. While Richard Newman and I were talking, volunteers were busy pounding together plywood bins to make what Kelly hoped would be the Cordova Otter Rescue Center just across the street, a place to treat the animals Valdez could no longer handle. Paths had been beaten by the steady stream of people between the bookstore, the prospective animal center, and the offices of CDFU and the Prince William Sound Aquaculture Corporation (PWSAC—pronounced pizzwac) a couple doors down, the City Hall down around the corner where COSDRO was located, and below that the harbor where because of the storm and the closures by then of herring, shrimp, sablefish, and crab seasons, the better part of Cordova's fishing fleet was docked against its will. The salmon season remained in doubt.

Richard had purchased the store's last navigation chart of Prince William Sound and we had it spread out between us. Richard touched the places he'd been to. I let the map emblaze itself on my mind, especially Knight Island, which had the shape of a very ornate palladin. To one side of us were windows that overlooked the harbor. Beneath us on the other side, a window faced First Street. People passed by. A clump of them had stopped and were engaged in intense conversation. One burly man in an orange coat thumped his palm with his fist as he spoke. A pickup jerked up against the curb and the driver jumped out and lurched up the sidewalk. Outside, it rained steadily, but the atmosphere on the street was electric. The rain was the tailing of the second major storm that would move the slick during the otherwise unusual period of calm for late March and early April.

Richard said that he'd seen a blacktailed deer trapped in the crude, and a sea otter that had scratched its eyes out. He made a motion with his hands, scraping down from his eyes across his cheeks, and it was then that he said, "It tore up its own face. It scratched out its eyes because of the hydrocarbons. It died with its paws folded on its chest, where they stopped from the scratching. Another otter had chewed off a paw. There was a starfish, still alive, but half-eaten through by crude."

Richard had felt sick since he'd got back, as if he had the flu or a cold. As time went by, similar symptoms among beach crews and workers in the animal rescue centers would become the subject of dispute. Some would argue that it was the effect of the fumes. Others would say that it was merely an influenza passed among people working long hours in sometimes close quarters. I was never able to learn the truth about that, but my suspicion was that the answer was not simple. Nothing about the oil, from its chemical makeup to the manner of its mobility, and nothing about the response of stressed organisms to it, whether that of humans, animals, or vegetation, was simple. As we spoke, the slick was out there roving around in all its complication. Driven by wind and current, it was an infinitely malleable, elastic blob that could vary in thickness from a couple of feet to a hundredth of an inch. It picked up sediment and grew heavy. It coated the birds and sea otters. It was death, possibly, to the microscopic lower reaches of the food chain, and to fish. It might cancel the fishing for the year. Richard's chair creaked as he leaned back. He got a hollow look in his eyes, and said, "The place was devoid of life. Ever since I've felt a weird detachment from life."

I would see him several more times in the next few days. He couldn't shake his sore throat. Each time I saw him, he looked gaunter and more hollow-eyed than before.

The corner of First Street and Council Avenue, a few steps away from Orca Book and Sound, offered a view of the town. Above, up on lower slopes of Mount Eyak, was a residential section that the earthquake had left intact. There was a dense quiltwork of walls, and of roofs set at crazy angles to each other. The houses were sometimes large and sometimes tiny, sometimes filigreed and sometimes plain. Among them were vestiges of narrow boardwalks from way back to the early part of the century. The boardwalks passed between the boundaries of adjoining lots to reach landlocked homes. In the yards and driveways were bicycles, old cars, turned-over skiffs, and heaps of fishing net. The residential tangle expressed the history of the place, recent and old. The colors were blue, white, rust, and the deep silver of weathered clapboard made luminous by the steel gray sky. Spruce trees fringed the upper edges of the neighborhood. Between the trunks lay the dark gray rock of the mountain.

Down toward the water was Railroad Way and a line of new buildings erected since the earthquake, which had damaged the waterfront: metal equipment outlets and drydocks, a new brick post office, and City Hall. Much of the traffic, the cars that careened between First Street and Railroad Way, came from the harbor. Directly beneath the corner where I stood was the Reluctant Fisherman, a popular motel and restaurant that overlooked the harbor.

First Street runs parallel to the shoreline, and strung out along it to the northwest are the canneries, the ferry terminal, and at the old New England Cannery, the offices of the Chugach Native Corporation. In the opposite direction is a road that leads out of town, past Lake Eyak to the airport, and then northerly and inland over a series of concrete bridges that span the Copper River Delta. There, the country grows harsh. The silt-laden river is white with froth, and the land around it, the sandy banks and muskeg, the bush and gaunt, windblown trees, have a scoured look.

The road is the Copper River Highway, built on an old railbed. It represented another boom. Copper, discovered in 1900, brought an influx of Guggenheim money, and a railroad completed in 1911 between the Kennecott Mine and the Port of Cordova. In those days, Cordova had been what Valdez was now, a major terminus for raw materials. The mine closed in 1938 due to the collapse of copper prices, and the town began the long process of reconstituting itself as a fishing port. The rails were pulled out for salvage during World War II.

Practically speaking, the highway stops about 60 miles out of town at the Million Dollar Bridge, a four-span steel and concrete railroad structure completed in 1910. The earthquake had dumped the end of one of the spans into the river, but the bridge had been pieced back together, the fractures in the standing spans strapped with steel plate, the collapsed span judged to be stable enough even in its wild tilt, and reconnected to the adjacent span by a big steel stairway, lashed with U-bolts, turnbuckles, and inch-and-a-half cable. Over the stairway were laid two-inch planks which made a bridge upon the bridge and rather tenuously permitted single-file vehicle traffic to the shore across the river. Beyond that point, the road gradually dwindles to nothing.

The question of upgrading and extending the road to the point where it would connect with the Richardson Highway, and thus to Valdez, Anchorage, and points beyond, had been controversial in Cordova for years. The absence of a road made the town an island of sorts, accessible only by sea and air, and eliminated the incursion of certain classes of traffic—the casual traffic of tourists and the insistent traffic of truckers. Road advocates bemoaned the fact that Cordova could not be a cleanup staging base, which reduced the amount of Exxon money that came into town. Others were grateful that Cordova could not become another Valdez. Too much Exxon money was coming in as it was, they said. As much as anything else, the absence of the road contributed to the town's integrity. It defined motion, reduced interruption, increased continuity, and encouraged reflection. It made relationships different, because it was not easy to just go away. One could drive only so far, then one had to turn around and come back.

When I moved away from the corner and headed back along First Street, past Orca Book and Sound and toward the CDFU and PSWAC offices, Tom Cumming appeared. He moved quickly across the street, stopping for a moment to talk to a group of men out in front of the grocery store, then ducked into the alley that led to the Club Restaurant. I'd had breakfast there. The place had been filled with fishermen who would have been happier to be out fishing for herring. Instead they'd been stopped in their tracks, which in itself was frustrating enough, never mind that they also didn't know whether they would fish at all that year, for anything, or how, in many cases, they would survive the loss of livelihood. Fishing was a precarious business, anyway, dependent upon the whims of nature and the stringent regulations applied by the Alaska Department of Fish and Game (ADFG), whose job was to control the pressure of fishing upon a run. Fish now, Fish and Game would say, and then order a stop five days later, or two days, or 12 hours. Exxon had announced that all losses suffered by closures would be compensated, but given the circumstances that seemed a chancier thing than fishing itself, and in all respects far less desirable. The fishermen were unsure how or when or to what degree that compensation would appear. In the restaurant, the word Exxon rose repeatedly and cut through the rest of the low, swirling talk like a curse.

One man said, "Exxon's already made eighty million off the spill by raising the prices at the pumps. It's a damn tax."*

I reached the doorway leading to the PWSAC and CDFU offices and stood there for a moment, reading the notices that had been taped to the windows. The burly man in the dirty orange coat and Greek fisherman's cap that I'd seen through the window of the bookstore stood next to me. His name was George Velikanje. I asked what he thought of what was going on. He turned it straight back, asking what I thought. It was not in the least necessary for us to name what we were talking about. I said I guessed the people were pretty angry.

"Angry!" George said, turning to me. His broad, bearded face had hardened and his eyes turned steely. He lurched toward me and stopped about four inches away, close enough for me to take on a little spit. "Angry!" he said. "Do you know what rage is?"

---

* The figure is probably mythical. In April, L. C. Kumins of the Environment and Natural Resources Policy Division of the Congressional Research Service observed that between the beginning of March and the first week of April 1989, there had been a little over a 10-cent average increase in per gallon gasoline prices at the pump. In certain West Coast locations, the jump went as high as 20 cents. This was due partly to gradual price increases prior to the oil spill caused by then newly installed EPA regulations governing the volatility specifications of gasoline, and by a slowly developing shortage of crude supplies relative to demand for refined products following the raising of prices by OPEC at the end of 1988. As of March 1989, pump prices had not yet caught up to the rising price of crude. To all of this was added the brief shutdown at the Alyeska terminal, and then the 11-day slowdown, which resulted in approximately a 16 million-barrel delivery shortfall, two-thirds of which was to be refined on the West Coast. Since the Alyeska terminal operates all the time at capacity, the shortfall could not be made up. The shortfall and accompanying doubt over when full-capacity operations would be restored precipitated allocation assignments by refiners and then a rash of speculative spot-buying by wholesalers. The 16-million-barrel shortfall from Alyeska constitutes about one-sixtieth of the daily 975-million-barrel crude oil working inventory needed to keep the nation's fuel supply system in operation. The effect of the Alaskan shortfall upon the market was analogous to what an ecologist would call a perturbation.

The lesson to be learned from this applies not so much to a specific instance of profit taking (profit-taking as a general practice is another question) as it does to the heavy demand on a very sensitive market, and consequently to the potential effectiveness of the lever which the Alyeska consortium *could* apply to the fuel supply system. At the time of the spill, public scrutiny upon the oil industry was quite sharp. In fact, many West Coast Exxon dealers held their prices below par in order to placate their customers. In another scenario, the consortium might reduce the flow in the pipeline for profit-taking or for political reasons. Over a year later, in July of 1990, in a walkdown with the EPA and DEC, the consortium threatened to shut down the pipeline and did reduce the flow for one day as a protest against being held liable for violating state and federal air pollution laws. A federal judge intervened with the result that the matter once again was thrown onto the negotiating table. The cost of a shutdown or protracted slowdown would be felt by the federal government and Alaska state government in the form of lost tax revenues, and then by the public in the form of increased prices at the pump. By the summer of 1990 Alyeska was well back on the offensive again, and the public demand for cheap gas, especially when it lacks an oil spill to serve as a reminder of the tradeoffs that are at stake, is finally the consortium's most valuable bargaining chip. To this attenuated set of circumstances was added the 1990 late-summer Iraqi invasion of Kuwait.

He pulled back and lightened up a bit. "Some of the people here are shy, but if you went into the living rooms at night, you'd see that this thing's tearing them up. Pretty soon the rage will spill over.

"There are a lot of Vietnam vets among the fishermen, and they damn sure don't want to get wasted all over again," he said. "They've been through that." He said the vets had brought weapons home with them and that some of them were talking about loading up the Cordova fleet with guns and explosives and blockading the Port of Valdez. He paused, waiting to see the effect of his words, and smiled. "The right wing and the left wing have met in this town, the oldtimers, the vets, the ex-hippies. Look," he said. "This is a small town. We know who you are. Let the lower forty-eight know, because when that happens it's time to watch out."

His notion was fairly compelling—the new union, a project for revolution—but just exactly how seriously George meant it was a bit hard to read. I'd seen him working the street with admirable energy, buttonholing one person after another. He was an operative, a catalyst. Loquacious, articulate, and theatrical, he'd been called to that, as others in Cordova had been called to do other things. Later on, David Grimes, who at this time was in Valdez serving on the ad hoc citizens' advisory committee, would explain to me that one of the striking things about the oil spill was the way it called people beyond themselves, and made them rise to find their own necessary roles.

That process had begun two weeks before on the morning of the spill. When Riki Ott and acting CDFU president Jack Lamb reached the CDFU office at 7:30, Marilyn Leland, CDFU executive director, was on the phone, making and receiving call after call. Shortly thereafter, Riki made her flyover with the marine biologist, Chuck Monnett. They saw the slick, the Exxon *Valdez*, the Exxon *Baton Rouge* pumping its ballast into the sea, and no cleanup activity. They then flew on to Valdez in search of information. There, Monnett was cornered in a restroom by a reporter who'd heard he was a biologist. Monnett sent the reporter to talk to Riki Ott, and Ott, who would tell me that she'd "left professional science because of the numbers of scientists who wouldn't come out from behind closed doors to speak to the public," found herself cast into the role of the conscience of science. During the first Exxon press conference, she stood up from the audience and offered a lone, dissenting voice to the account Exxon's chief environmental scientist, Al Maki, was giving of the way oil dispersants would make the oil "disappear." Ott's effect upon the attention the press would give to that and other issues was immediately decisive. Later, Iarossi would say that one of the reasons he stopped giving press conferences was because Ott took up half the time.

Chuck Monnett was then in the sixth year of an otter population study project run under a contract with the federal Department of Fish and Wildlife. Knowing that he and his colleague Lisa Rotterman were more informed than anyone else on the otters in the sound, fearing for their study, and for the animals themselves, who represented the most diverse genetic stock of sea otters anywhere in the world,* Monnett wanted to do a count, to firm up a baseline on the population against which damage to it could be measured, and to track individual otters. Since no one knew at that time where the oil would flow or how much more would be released from the ship, it was also not known how imperiled the entire otter population was. Monnett and Rotterman were seeking a way to protect a portion of the population. On Friday, Monnett secured "unlimited funding" from the Minerals Management Service (MMS). Three days later, the Department of Fish and Wildlife threatened to cancel Monnett and Rotterman's long-term project and quarantine all their equipment. Then they were allowed to continue with their surveys. Two weeks after the spill, Monnett and Rotterman were shut down, and then again later yet they were put back into operation again. For the duration of the summer, they were run through a gauntlet of bureaucratic machinations in which they found themselves at odds with their own agency, at odds with the Otter Rescue Centers, which they helped establish, and their work and careers jeopardized. Monnett would tell me, "Early on, we felt like Fish and Wildlife was trying to control damage, that it was ANWR. Two weeks later the ANWR bill was dead and the agencies turned around and started taking samples of otters, but it was too late."†

Back in Cordova on the morning of the spill, Rick Steiner, the Marine Advisory agent in Cordova, was awakened at 7:00 by a telephone call. He went to his office at the harbor where he worked the phone, seeking information. He also tried to get two Fish and Wildlife agents stationed

---

* As the oil spill wore on, the damage to the genetic stock of several sometimes highly localized species was, from a scientific point of view, a far more serious matter than the death of individual animals.

† The bill was wounded, at least. Legislation that would have approved limited oil drilling in the Arctic National Wildlife Refuge had passed through the Senate's Natural Resources Committee and was expected to receive congressional approval during the 1989 summer session. Although President Bush continued to advocate the bill, the consequence that oil companies feared most, that the oil spill would change the thinking of senators previously supporting the legislation, had happened. By early April the bill was moved to the back burner—for a time.

in Cordova to go out and assess the spill, but they wouldn't move. Steiner then walked up the hill to the CDFU office, where he found Jack Lamb, David Grimes, Jeff Guard, and Marilyn Leland, who was still on the phone, taking calls and otherwise trying to get word on what was going to be done. She called Exxon, Alyeska, the Coast Guard, the DEC, EPA, and DFW. At 9:00 A.M., she informed Exxon that she had 30 volunteer boats ready to assist with containing the spill. At noon, she informed Alyeska that she had 75 boats, including 15 from Tatitlek. What she eventually heard from Alyeska and Exxon on Saturday was that they were "reluctant to use the boats because of the liability connected to using amateurs."

As Steiner, Grimes, Guard, and Lamb talked in the CDFU office, they were joined by other fishermen. The place was loaded with confused, worried people. Lamb pulled out the Alyeska contingency plan. It said that any spill within 50 miles of the terminal could be contained in 12 hours. The group knew a few things from the reports they were receiving: first, that the spill was much less than 50 miles from the terminal; second, that so far, eight or nine hours after the spill, nothing at all had happened; and third, that no one had any idea what was going to happen except that the spill would spread. They talked of the threat to the imminent million-dollar herring fishery, and the likely effect of a storm upon the slick. Steiner decided to take a flight out to see for himself what was going on, and he saw the same thing that Ott and Monnett had seen: the spill, the Exxon *Valdez* listing on the reef, the *Baton Rouge* deballasting, and no boom, no barges, no skimmers, and nothing coming, and lumps in the oil that were sea otters, and sea lions swimming in it.

Steiner returned to Cordova and spent most of the night talking to fishermen about what they could do. Many of the fishermen had already geared up their boats to fight the spill. Steiner is a tall man, blonde, bearded, lean, pleasant, and smart. He has a way of listening closely that inspires trust, and—as his role would develop over the next year and a half—a way of maintaining effectiveness and hopefulness even in the densest tangles of power politics and litigation. He held the fishermen's respect not only for his knowledge of the sound as a biologist but also for the fact that he ran his own seiner boat. His knowledge had been trued by reality.

The next day, Steiner flew over the spill again and found that it had expanded toward Naked Island. He went on to Valdez in hopes of getting information there to pass back to Cordova. Like Riki Ott, he found chaos, the national press installed, federal scientists who had come more to monitor than to take action, the DEC completely lacking in the equipment to do anything, Exxon keeping people out of its makeshift head-quarters in the Westmark Hotel, and Alyeska not answering its telephones. Steiner called his friend, David Grimes, and told him to get over to Valdez. Grimes, himself a fisherman, an accomplished musician and poet, a natural historian, and a man possessed of an uncanny ability to bring diverse people together, would become the oil spill's metaphysician.

The Cordova contingent in Valdez came to consist of Steiner, Ott, Grimes, Lamb, and Guard. Their forces were augmented by, among others, Doris Lopez, a Valdez fisherman, Ray Cesarini, a Valdez cannery operator, who provided temporary living quarters, Jim and Nancy Lethcoe, Valdez tour boat operators, historians, and activists, and Theo Matthews of Soldatna, the president of United Fishermen of Alaska. By the third day of the spill, Sunday, the twenty-sixth, the population of Valdez had almost doubled, and at a press conference that afternoon, the group heard Frank Iarossi announce that the oil spill had progressed beyond the point where it could be contained mechanically, and that plans were being formulated to use dispersants and laser-ignited burns. To the group, the news was chilling.

They stayed all Sunday night, as the first gale blew the oil slick around, and put together what Grimes referred to as the "educational press conference" in which several of them presented various subjects—fisheries, ecology, oil pollution, dispersants, local history. The press conference was held the next day. It built on the ground Riki Ott had first taken in the Exxon press conferences and resulted in wide national coverage and yet more pressure placed upon Exxon. The interests of those concerned with wildlife and fisheries had been permanently lodged as a factor in the battle. Afterwards, the DEC second-in-command, Larry Dietrich, who had been ordered by Governor Cowper to "do something," arranged with his boss, Dennis Kelso, for members of the group—Steiner, Grimes, Ott, and Lamb—to join the brass at a meeting of the oil spill triumvirate that night. Jack Lamb was the only one among the group with a family. He was by nature more conservative than the others, more patient, more given to working within regulations, and a bit uncomfortable at being cast in the role of a rabblerouser. He was the best at talking to the brass. Unassuming, clean-cut and square-jawed, Lamb looks like a high-school football coach. David Grimes would tell me later that Lamb "was brilliant, a pillar. Though he took some heat for it later back in Cordova, he became the de facto spokesman for fishermen."

At the meeting, the group found that the brass knew very little about the currents and tidal patterns of the sound. The result, thanks largely to

Kelso's insistence and Iarossi's willingness to listen, was that they were heeded and, then, to their amazement, given the power to order equipment and formulate plans. Considering that the oil spill was completely out of control, they decided to focus their attention on protecting selected spawning streams, herring catchments at Knight Island's Herring Bay, and the hatchery system. David Grimes said, "When it looks like everything's lost, you're freed from limitations. You can go for it."

Back in Cordova, many of the fishermen were vascillating between blockading the tanker channel and continuing to marshall volunteer forces to fight the spill, first more or less independently of the group in Valdez, and then in tandem with it. Some, such as Tom Copeland, preferred independent action. He outfitted his boat with a pump and five-gallon buckets, then went out looking for oil. Near Knight Island, the first day they pulled out 1,500 gallons, and on their best day they drew 2,500 gallons, while Exxon's best skimmer collected just 1,200 gallons a day, which raised fairly compelling questions about what might have happened if the authorities had turned the "amateurs" loose to begin with.

What came to be known as the mosquito fleet, a small armada of seiners, bowpickers, long-liners, and skiffs and the ferry *Bartlett*, commandeered by the DEC from the Alaska State Ferry System, eventually made their way to the Koernig Hatchery at Sawmill Bay on Evans Island. Despite Iarossi's initial receptivity, battles with the Exxon system continued. There were unending complications, shortfalls of equipment, and lapses in communication. Steiner would say, "The disaster was unfolding minute by minute. None of us had gone through anything like this before, so we were winging it. . . . The fishermen needed stronger boom, more skimmers, and better logistical support. . . . Exxon's people were trying, but the company was still our biggest hassle. . . . We'd say we needed something and they'd say, 'Yes, we've ordered it. Yes, it's on the way.' Then it took days. At first we believed them. Then we realized they were just trying to get us off their backs. There were so many people in the chain of command that if one link goofed, nothing got done." Finally, the hatcheries were saved from the main onslaught of oil, but questions of lingering damage to the salmon fry and to the hatchery grounds awaited returns from the 1989 release, which would not begin until 1990.

George Velikanje moved off and I went inside the doorway that led to the CDFU and PWSAC offices. I met Heather McCarty, the PWSAC news officer. In previous years, Heather had been the editor of *Cordova Times*. She fishes commercially with her husband, Max. An Englishwoman, both she and her husband had graduated from Whitman College, an elite liberal arts school in Washington. She'd majored in English. Max had majored in theatre, and they'd come to Cordova on a shoestring in the early seventies. They, too, were typical of a new breed of fishermen. Max, a rebellious man with a sharp wit, had described the first planeload of lawyers that flew into Cordova as the landing at Normandy. Heather gave an impression of intensity and solidity, and because of her position and the changed reality in Cordova, she had emerged as something more than the PWSAC news officer.

"Our seiners get the prime catch," she told me. "Our boats get the first, highest-quality catch of the run. Each boat takes in about a hundred fifty thousand fish a day." I stared at her for a moment. It was strange to imagine that many fish—a pile of them, silvery, mountainous. Heather pressed on, explaining that 20 percent of PWSAC's annual budget comes from a 2 percent tax the state of Alaska collects off the top of each fisherman's gross. Eighty percent comes from the contract seiners that are stationed at PWSAC's hatcheries at the beginning of the run. Once PWSAC makes its budget, she said, the run is opened to commercial fishermen, for whom $20 million is generated annually from the aqua-culture's Armin F. Koernig and Esther Island hatcheries.

Roughly speaking, the hatchery system works this way: Salmon return-ing from the ocean to spawn are captured. Females are slit open, their eggs removed, and placed in buckets. Male salmon are held over the buckets and squeezed, so that their semen squirts over the eggs. The fertilized eggs are then washed, placed in incubators at the hatchery sites, and kept until they hatch. Up to this point, the process is a form of interdiction and enhancement intended to increase the numbers of young salmon, or "fry," that will be released into open waters. The young fry are kept in net pens in the bays at the hatchery sites until they are ready for release. By this time, their olfactory sense, or "chemical memory," has been "imprinted" with their place of origin, and those that survive would return after an ocean journey of between 2,000 and 10,000 miles and a lifespan of two, three, four, five, or seven years. The length and duration of the journey varies according to species. The en-hancement process with eggs and fry simply improves the odds on substantial returns.

The remarkable and not fully understood ability of the fish to return to their home ground to spawn and to die, the precision of their timing, and their food value have made salmon a staple resource of fishing cultures (and a staple of myth) for centuries. The predictability of their runs makes them especially vulnerable to being overfished, as they have been, but also capable of being managed toward recovery. There are definite hazards in the management process, too, such as the overstocking of a habitat with one species, and the huge numbers of identically imprinted salmon returning to one site as opposed to diversely imprinted wild salmon returning to various estuaries and streambeds.

What PWSAC and other hatchery systems in Alaska were about was restoring and sustaining the salmon runs, especially of pink salmon, the primary commercial species. Most of the pink salmon catch was canned. At the time, PWSAC operated three hatcheries, one of which, Esther Island (later renamed the Wally Noerenberg Hatchery), was devoted to producing a variety of species in addition to pinks, including chum, chinook, and coho salmon, all of which are at sea for longer periods than the pinks, were less abundant to begin with, more sensitive, and as sport and table fish more valuable per pound. Because of their locations off the main path of the oil slick, however, neither the Esther Island Hatchery nor a third, Cannery Creek, was under immediate threat.

Pink salmon spend three to five months in the estuaries, inner bays, and channels, then begin a 2,000-mile migration in the Pacific. In the spring and summer of their second year of life, they move back toward their home streams. PWSAC's Koernig Hatchery, located on Evans Island, was under a threefold threat: first, to the pink salmon fry that were soon to be released; second, to the year's returning salmon; and third, the possibility of lingering toxic effects on future releases and returns. Potentially, the damage could be exponential. The result of the second of the threats—that to the annual run, and so to the 80 percent of PWSAC's budget Heather was speaking of, and to this year's income for fishermen—would not be known for two to three months, when the return runs began. As noted above, the results of the third threat—lingering effects—would not be fully known for years.

The first threat was immediate. As Heather and I spoke, 8 million pink salmon fry were in the net pens at the AFK hatchery and 600,000 more were emerging each day, their movement toward maturation at least as ineluctable as the oil that hovered in the bay. Heather explained to me what PWSAC, the canneries, the fishermen, and the town stood to lose. The hatchery system, though granted seed money by the state and the canneries, had been established and literally built by the volunteer labor of the fishermen themselves. The first and fairly modest returns from the system came in 1974, but it was hoped that during 1989 and the succeeding few years the success and viability of the system would be firmly established. It became easier to understand the character of the fishermen's rage.

To the effort expended in developing the salmon run and the possible financial fishing losses this year were added the $300,000 that a permit to fish with a seine net currently cost, or the $50,000 to $70,000 that a gillnet* permit cost. The permits—regarded as real property, not unlike leases on Bureau of Land Management pastureland for cattle ranchers in the West—are bought, sold, and passed down through inheritance. "It's not unusual for a seine fisherman to be carrying three-quarters of a million in permit and equipment investments," Heather said. "On top of that come the annual fees and operating costs—fuel, labor, nets." The permit fishermen here had bought the farm, so to speak.

At the time, Heather thought there would be no fishing at all in the sound this year.[†] PWSAC's prime concern was to protect the fry in the net pens. They had received a million dollars from Exxon toward funding the effort to protect the hatcheries—in the form of a signed personal business card that Frank Iarossi had handed to PWSAC president Bruce Suzumoto.

There were two areas of concern in Cordova. One was money: the spilled oil's threat to the fisheries and hatcheries, and then the threat of Exxon money to community solidarity. The other area was that of place, home, the environment. Normally, the two concerns overlapped to varying degrees, but by this time they had collapsed quite completely into one another. It was the merging of the left and right wings that George Velikanje had talked about.

Kelly Weaverling, who runs the bookstore with his wife, Susan Ogle, discovered his part as a preservationist carried to an extreme he himself would never have expected. A tall man with aquiline features, long black hair, and a beard, incisive, opinionated, and given to wearing sandals, baggy pants, and dark sleeveless sweaters—yet another one in whom the combination of articulateness and offbeat appearance would give the brass pause—Weaverling had been a submarine navigator during the Vietnam War. With Ogle, he had toured the sound every spring by kayak. Quite possibly no one knew the sound better than they.

* Seine nets are a mile or more long and cast in a circle around a school of fish, then drawn shut, capturing the fish within. The vessels that deploy them are called purse seiners. The much shorter gillnets are cast in a line and allowed to drift with the current. The vessels, gillnetters, are smaller than purse seiners and take smaller catches. The costs of permits reflect the relative efficiency of the two methods.

† As it turned out, the salmon fisheries were partially opened. Certain areas remained closed because of the oil. The total catch in Prince William Sound was slightly above the ten-year average of 20 million fish but well below the preseason projections of over 48 million. The lower than projected return was due in part to closures, but mainly to much poorer returns than were expected. The 1990 returns, which would still not prove or disprove oil damage in 1989, did reach record levels.

Over in Valdez, the bird rescue people, Jessica Porter, Alice Berkner, and Jay Holcomb, had encountered a surprise as they set up their center. No arrangements had been made to retrieve the birds, which were usually out there in remote, hazardous locations. They had expected that the Department of Fish and Wildlife would at least administer the retrieval operation. Traditionally, responding to wildlife damage fell under the federal department's purview, although since the eighties Fish and Wildlife had been backing away from oil spill cases because in its view the limited number of animals rescued did not justify the expense. And in this case, since the spill had not been federalized, Fish and Wildlife would point out, the agency had no obligation to involve itself with bird rescue. It was a bind of the sort that was becoming familiar: the Department of Interior had ordered Exxon to rescue animals; the Department of Wildlife refused to cooperate. The bird center was desperate to find someone who would take charge of a rescue fleet. Jay Holcomb of IBRRC had heard about Weaverling and contacted him. This was on Wednesday, the sixth day of the spill. Weaverling agreed to manage the operation, which would be funded by Exxon, and immediately set out with Holcomb to Knight Island to learn the techniques.

The next day Weaverling went to work, beginning with five boats. They brought oiled and injured birds back to Valdez. However, since they were encountering otters at the same time—lying in the water next to the birds—they began collecting them, too. It was an understandable response, driven by compassion, the urge to redress pain. Soon, there were 21 boats bringing in animals, and then 45 boats, mainly from the Cordova fleet. The Bird Rescue Center had trouble keeping abreast, and in the Otter Center animals were stacked up in cages in the hallways. The retrieval operation had become too efficient.

Randall Davis, who was in charge of the Otter Center, concluded that even the newly completed Valdez Otter Rescue Center, which I'd just seen there, would be filled to capacity in a day at the rate the otters were appearing. Davis encouraged Weaverling to open an otter center in Cordova, and Weaverling received approval to do so from an Exxon spokesman, Don Cornett. This was the center in which the carpenters were pounding pens together across the street from the bookstore. They had assured Weaverling that the center would be ready in five days.

At the time, there were several particular causes of outrage in Cordova. The fate of Weaverling's rescue project and the otter center would soon be added to them. Another had to do with 70,000 feet of boom that had been ordered from Florida to protect the Koernig Hatcheries. Exxon, it was thought by Cordova people, had intercepted the order for other purposes, and it would take two weeks for a replacement to arrive.* Exxon had representatives in town offering short-term financial relief for those immediately affected by the disaster, but only two persons had as yet signed on. The Cordovans remained wary, offended, and deeply divided over the capitalization of what had begun as a volunteer effort. Exxon now was offering $3,500 and more a day for leases on boats from Cordova's fleet, but the contract came equipped with a gag clause. Fishermen were not to express their opinions to the press. Most of the fishermen absolutely refused to have anything to do with such a contract.

A community information meeting was held each day. Sometimes the meetings doubled as a press conference, but their purpose was to disseminate information about the spill and spill response to citizens and local organizations. Some of the meetings were conducted relatively quietly. Others were volatile, especially when Exxon representatives were present. Monte Taylor, the chief Exxon liaison to the communities of the sound, came to one on April 10. Retired now, Taylor had been Exxon's Alaska manager. He is white-haired, a bit heavy around the jowls, and he looked tired. During the meeting, Ken Adams, CDFU second vice president, said that he had flown the sound the day before and had seen no active oil skimming. Taylor didn't seem to understand the point. He said, "There is a skimmer in Valdez, not Cordova." In fact, there were about ten skimmers stationed at various points out in the sound, awaiting instructions. Adams asked Taylor for a list of what materials, what boats were in the sound, where they were located, and what their instructions were. Taylor said, "We're organizing a list."

He was asked by a town councilmember about the supersucker *Vaydaghubsky*, a huge skimmer that Exxon had contracted with Russia to bring into Prince William Sound. He said, "It left yesterday and should arrive within ten days." He was not certain where it was headed. He asked the group for suggestions. When they gave them, he took no notes. When he was asked in turn what he did with such suggestions, he said, "I call around." When he was asked what was to be done with the sludge once it was skimmed off, he said, "It's not timely to know that." I thought about Max Stone and wondered if he had figured out yet what was to be done with that sludge. Taylor was asked what plans there were to test water quality near Cordova. There were oyster farms there, and the proprietors were worried. They feared that if oil were to come their way it

---

* When I later asked Fred Davis of the Exxon Communications Group in Valdez about the mislaid boom, he referred me to Les Rogers in Houston. Rogers said that he could answer the question if I produced a copy of the purchase order.

would poison the oyster beds. Taylor said, "Water quality should be a high priority."

It was hard not to feel a little sorry for Taylor. The Cordova people, though at this juncture polite enough, were not swallowing runarounds. Heather McCarty sat at the table behind Taylor with a searching, intense expression on her face. Taylor clung desperately to the obscure language of the bureaucrat. He spoke in a monotone, taking care not to give anything away by a show of emotion. He used all the half-answers and distracting asides at his command to hold his position and yet appear friendly, but finally it was apparent that there would be nothing forthcoming, only the blockage to communication and the same lack of precision and decisiveness that was encountered repeatedly with Exxon representatives.

Immediately following Taylor's appearance, Kelly Weaverling came into the room. There was a blackboard up against a wall on which a flowchart of the animal recovery operation had been drawn. Weaverling had intended to discuss that, I gathered, and perhaps to report on the progress of the new otter center. Instead, he told the group that he'd just come back from the water, that the bird people said this was the most difficult terrain they'd ever worked with. He said his group had begun collecting otters, too, and that there was trouble. He looked bad. His face was drawn, and he spoke in bursts, and paused and looked down at the floor, then spoke in another burst.

Fish and Wildlife officials had just told Weaverling that there would be no otter center in Cordova. There would be one in Seward, instead, the advice of Randall Davis notwithstanding. Moreover, they informed Weaverling that he had to cease and desist from capturing otters because his fleet was unauthorized, untrained, and had been operating without inspections. Since the otter was a federally protected species, Fish and Wildlife had stepped in. There was an uncomfortable silence in the room. The irony was not lost on anyone: the federal government would shut down a citizens' response group, but not a faulty oil delivery system. Later, Weaverling told me that at that moment he felt "so low they could have driven a snake over me."

Fish and Wildlife officials had feared—perhaps with justification—that otters that might survive on their own were being unnecessarily stressed. Nevertheless, Fish and Wildlife officials, who would decline to be identified, later said that they regretted that the rescue operation had been shut down. In an indication, perhaps, of the kind of basis upon which many choices were being made, they said the decision caused them a lot of bad press.

A few days after the Fish and Wildlife shutdown, Exxon, which still had charge of the bird rescue operation, ordered Weaverling to stop rescuing birds, but he continued anyway. "I was never personally paid by Exxon or Veco," he said, "so they had no control over me." In early July he was fired, though reports circulated that he had resigned in protest. He told me, "I did not resign. What happened was I worked on a verbal agreement and a handshake with IBRRC. You'd think the chain of command would be Exxon, Bird Rescue Center, me, my fleet. But at that point Exxon didn't want any of this stuff done, because they wanted the bird problem to go away . . . because if the birds weren't being brought in, then the birds out there must be okay. They started directing the vessels themselves and letting me and the Bird Rescue Center know later. I became a supernumerary. I did not resign."

Weaverling went on to organize an observation project at Perry Island, which had been heavily oiled. His objective was to create a record of the impact of oil and of humans engaged in cleanup. The project was staffed by volunteers, or what Weaverling called "vertical citizenry," and funded by donations channeled through the Alaska Conservation Foundation. "I'm unaffiliated," Kelly said. "I'm an independent voter. I came here to get away from society."

"Most fishermen are fair," said Belen Cook, a slight, dark-haired woman. Belen and her husband are gillnetters who fish for herring and salmon off Cordova in the Copper River Flats. "If they see that Exxon is fair, they may be satisfied, but Exxon has proven that not everything they say is true." Belen believed that Exxon should pay punitive damages, in addition to paying for the losses. "The unknown is frightening," she said. She said she had cried, and that she would never have dreamed of seeing the men cry that she had.

We were in the CDFU headquarters. Ken Adams came quietly out of the office at my back and sat down, took off his hat and ran his fingers slowly through his white hair. He was probably in his early forties, intense and handsome, and had emerged as yet another of the forceful CDFU spokespersons. We faced each other on the long side of a particleboard table, which was up against the wall that separated CDFU from PWSAC. Beside us was an open area and in it were more tables loaded with heaps of photocopied material—fishing closure announcements, press releases, newspaper articles. People passed in and out. Adams told me that he'd awakened in the middle of the night and had three visions. The first was of David and Goliath. "Should the people of Cordova offer Exxon terms? Did David give Goliath a chance?

"Bush should be impeached," he said. "He's pimping big oil. Are we still a free people?" This was his second vision—the wimp transformed into a pimp. Adams had a message for the boardmembers of big corporations: "I know you are good Americans, and so I personally invite you to come out on my fishing boat. I'll supply the gloves, boots, and chow. You supply the toothbrushes. Do you know what work is?"

His third vision was of covering the Exxon boardmembers with oil and letting them suffer the fate of the sea otters. "Then they would know." He glanced at my notebook as if to make sure I had that right, then added that most of what he was saying was personal, not necessarily a CDFU position. By this time, I understood a little more about what was at stake with the fishermen. I understood that Ken Adams, like many here, was caught in a terrific, mortal bind: his life, his livelihood, his home, his values, his family and friends, everything pitched against the oil slick. He was not a radical. Like Jack Lamb, he was well accustomed to working within the system.

Adams had an explanation for why it had taken so long for Alyeska and Exxon to begin cleaning up the spill: "They didn't want to clean it up. Who's accountable? Does accountability simply mean pay on the books? Exxon didn't understand responsibility. For Exxon appropriate measures mean confusion, manipulation, and deception. It's incomprehensible that they couldn't clean it up if they wanted to. We had phenomenally good weather until yesterday—day seventeen of the spill. Exxon can't say the weather made it impossible to clean it up. They were counting on bad weather to use as an excuse and they didn't get it."

It made sense. It was the same principle as running tankers until they broke down, of using a faulty delivery system. It was cheaper to keep things that way and sidetrack the regulators. Similarly, it was cheaper to figure that the spill wouldn't happen, and if it did, then to wait for the wind to come up, to hang tight and try to control the imagery. When I asked Exxon representatives about this later, they denied it, even exhibited outrage at such a suggestion, but an examination of the events as they occurred—the lack of preparation, the indecision, the confusion, the footdragging, the impediments, the refusal to consult the knowledgeable until pushed into it—lent credence to Adams's accusation.

The next day, I met George Velikanje again down at the docks. He invited me into the cabin of his tender, the *Salmo Point*. The boat had a pleasant, slightly sweet smell, the odor of long use in the wet. Outside, it was raining steadily, and it was warm and snug in the cabin. George sat up behind the wheel and I sat on top of a storage trunk. The boat was 60 years old, one of the older boats in the fleet. George himself was 45, a fourth-generation Alaskan. "I'm free and clear," he said, which I took to mean that his boat and permits were paid for.

It was George who introduced me to the channel metaphor. "The only people in this town in favor of working through the channels are the people in the channels," he said. "But they don't know anything, or they forgot." George spent a few years down in the lower forty-eight when he was young but didn't like it. "I came home and told my father that they've got it all fenced down there." Once, he set out with a friend on a 200-mile hike here in Alaska. They almost starved to death. Near the end, as they were climbing a slope, his friend stopped and called out for help. He thought he'd ruptured something. George, who was in the lead, told his friend that he would wait, but he sure as hell wasn't coming back down to get him. They both made it up and at dark found an abandoned Native fishing camp. They saw the silhouettes of salmon hanging from a line, and tore down the fish, gorging themselves on it. When they awoke in the morning, they saw that the fish were infested with maggots. George said that he and his friend looked at each other, and laughed, and ate some more.

George rocked back in his chair and said, "That's what we know. We know about death. I've been that close to death and I know how to laugh in its face. Those Exxon fuckers don't know anything about that." He pulled off his boots and tucked his feet underneath his legs. "You know," he said. "The pipeline can't be turned off. If it's stopped up in winter it'll freeze. It'd take one hell of a snake to ream it out." Again, he smiled. "The monkey wrench."

Outside the cabin, a raven landed on top of a piling and cocked its head at us. They are smarter than dogs, some say. They are "opportunistic" feeders. They have powerful spirits. This one surveyed us closely, checking us out. George said, "This is a chance for us to force a little responsibility on the kings of capital, the robber barons of our society. They say, be realistic. I say, what the hell do you think is real?"

Exxon and the government, in George's view, were concerned only with controlling the damage to themselves. "It's fucking image manipulation, that's all," he said. He repeated the sentiment I'd heard from many: "The fishermen have a track record of seeing things correctly. Exxon has a track record of screwing us over. Now they've proven it to everyone. How come they're getting to make the decisions? How can I love my fucking country when it isn't real?"

Chapter 7

SHOWTIME

I referred to Prince William Sound as one of the two most beautiful places on earth. I leave it to each of you individually to decide what the other one is. We all have a special Shangri-La in our hearts and minds. Think of yours when you contemplate what has happened to ours.

—Don Moore, Cordova city manager,
in an appeal to the nation, 1989

KIMO, an Anchorage ABC affiliate, staged a televised town meeting in Valdez on April 11. It was held in the Civic Center, a capacious place made of bricks and nestled among rock outcroppings not far above the ferry terminal. At the entryways, security guards searched bags. They were checking for tape recorders, they said, but they were probably looking for weapons, too. Reportedly, some of the Exxon people had received death threats. The guard I got, a wiry man with bright eyes, bowed his head and murmured apologetically as his hand moved among my notebooks and socks. Inside, the plush auditorium was packed and swirling with talk. I found a seat near the front.

John Valentine, one of two KIMO moderators, informed the crowd that Exxon had initially agreed to send a representative to the panel but then reneged. A murmur rippled across the hall. Valentine, the size of a tight-end, is handsome and shiny-looking, a universal jack who could have been plugged into any news show in the country. He prowled the stage, which was still in the process of being set up, and spoke into a handheld mike. He said he had spent three hours negotiating with Exxon officials, a statement that left a perplexing aftertaste since its main import seemed to be that Valentine had been allowed access to the inner chamber where so few had ventured. When Valentine said that Exxon's condition was that there be no audience participation, a snicker broke from one of the back rows and the murmur in the hall increased in intensity. Valentine said he had declined to meet that condition. There was spotty applause.

This was to be a "Donahue" or "Oprah Winfrey" style show, and Valentine, no doubt, understood that a fair amount of serious network weight was in town. This was akin to combat duty for a man in his position. A high-stepper could move up fast. The front row of the hall was a bank of cameras. The feel of the audience reasserted the difference between Valdez and Cordova. These people were more diverse, an internally fractious group that ran the gamut from out-of-town environmentalists to oil industry employees, from onlookers to bureaucrats and irate fishermen. Valdez was in a state of sensory overload, and the televised town meeting had promised to draw the chaos within the boundaries of readymade theatre, maybe even to tap a little of the truth from the inner sanctum. The man seated in front of me, who turned out to be the city manager of Valdez, tipped his head toward the woman next to him and said, "I'm going to keep real quiet through this thing."

Valentine announced that Bill Allen of Veco International, Inc., had come in Exxon's stead. The contingency at the back of the hall hooted. Allen was over on the extreme right end of the group of men seated on the stage. He looked like a bear-wrestler, long-limbed and heavy. His legs were stretched out beneath the table, and he lounged against the back of his chair and communicated a sense of his apartness from the others. He was a classic Alaskan type: roughcut and sly, fathomless in his ambition, adept at damming up and diverting the streams of money that flowed through the state. The public version of his life took the shape of an exemplary fable: poor as a child and raised in the small town of Ione in north-central Oregon, he dropped out of high school when his mother moved with her children to New Mexico. Allen went to work in the oil fields of the Southwest to help support his family, and by the time he was in his early twenties he was supervising projects for corporations such as Bechtel and Fluor in southern California. He appeared in Alaska as an oil rig welder in 1968. Following a series of adversities and liaisons with big oil, he ended up the owner of Veco, an oil service company, that is, a subcontracting company that managed equipment, supplies, and construction and maintenance crews for the oil principals. Alaska had long been a good place for subcontractors, for those who built the pillars that held up the expressway. It became an even better place when construction began on the Trans-Alaska pipeline.

Allen had said, "We bet everything on the North Slope." Veco prospered during the pipeline days, mainly through its association with Arco and British Petroleum. A union construction subsidiary, Norcon, was formed to meet pipeline requirements. After the pipeline days, Veco continued to diversify, and one investment into a Houston shipyard sent the company into bankruptcy court in 1982, but Allen surfaced and with the help of Arco, it was said, reassembled his company. A couple of years later, Veco was found guilty of illegally inducing its employees to make pro-oil political contributions, which increased Allen's notoriety as a front man for oil interests. By the late eighties, Veco International had essentially recovered from bankruptcy proceedings. It remained principally devoted to oil field service and construction, but entered the oil spill cleanup business in 1988 through a contract with the Cook Inlet Response Organization. In the same year—as if in an act of prescience, as if to secure in advance a Veco marker in the environmental response business—Allen's company became involved with supplying equipment and personnel to the widely reported rescue of three gray whales trapped in ice in the Arctic Ocean off Barrow. By the time the cleanup from the Exxon *Valdez* spill was over in the fall of 1989, a new Veco subsidiary, Veco Environmental and Professional Services, had been formed, and Allen had institutionalized his role as a major player in the Alaskan information game by buying out the more conservative of the two Anchorage newspapers, the *Anchorage Times*.

With him on the stage were Rear Admiral Edward Nelson, Jr., commander of the Coast Guard's Alaska District, DEC Commissioner Kelso, John Devens, the mayor of Valdez, and Don Moore, the Cordova city manager. The man who was missing, and in whose stead Bill Allen had appeared, was Frank Iarossi. Iarossi, Kelso, and Nelson (later to be replaced by Vice Admiral Clyde Robbins) made up the private, state, and federal triumvirate charged with directing the response to the spill. Although Iarossi, according to reports, had asked Nelson to take command so that there would be a clearer framework for action, Nelson had declined because the spill had not been federalized.

At this point, the hope that the newly installed administration of George Bush would step in and take control was rapidly dissipating. Bush had dragged his feet on Governor Cowper's request for a declaration of a national disaster and subsequently decided against it, and so against federalization, but agreed to send troops to Prince William Sound.

Now, that order had just been rescinded. As it happened, the Coast Guard Commandant Admiral Paul Yost arrived in Valdez in two days, on the morning of Thursday, March 13. One of his first actions was to give Exxon three days to produce its plan for cleanup operations, then a week late. Yost came, as he put it, "to take names and kick butts." He came to be widely admired for both his humanity—his willingness to be affected by the damage and the pain of the people—and his leadership capabilities. For as long as he was around, things improved considerably, particularly in the upper echelons of decision making. Execution of decisions by private and public subordinates on the shorelines and in the communities or with, say, the otter and bird rescue operation was another matter.

The Bush administration's argument was that the oiling of the sound had been caused by private enterprise and that private enterprise should therefore be held accountable for corrective measures immediately, not sometime in the future. Legally, politically, and economically, this was an eminently defensible position. Also, there was absolutely no evidence from declared national disasters to suggest that federalization would have improved the effectiveness of the response. The fact that the spill had occurred in U.S. waters, however, did make it possible to bring in the Coast Guard, and hence Admiral Yost. Eventually, Exxon managed and paid for the cleanup and supplied equipment while the Coast Guard made final decisions and approved and monitored the plans. In order to mollify Exxon's fears over government lawsuits, the Coast Guard stream-lined the process of gaining approvals and permits under the labyrinth of regulations and laws administered by state and federal agencies. Belatedly found, it was not a bad solution, at least in theory.

The KIMO show was called "The Spill." John Valentine announced the commercial breaks by saying, " 'The Spill' will continue," which provoked raucous, bitter laughter from the audience. Valentine roamed the aisles with his handheld mike. Questions concerning the lack of response to the spill were raised, and Admiral Nelson and Dennis Kelso were unable to agree on even the most fundamental matter. Admiral Nelson said that the first priority was to get the oil off the water, a proposition that by this time had come to seem fanciful at best since each passing day brought news of the oil slick's invasion of new territories, and somebody like Tom Copeland with his boat and five-gallon buckets could pick up more oil than a skimmer. At this stage 800 miles of beaches had been fouled and observers were still trying to track where else the last storm had driven the oil. Kelso more reasonably echoed the conclusion that the CDFU people had arrived at, that the first priority was to maintain the boom defense, particularly at the hatcheries, and that getting oil off the water came second.

The primary cause for delay in shoreline cleanup was the lack of supplies and manpower. A second cause had to do with the question of standards, a complex and, politically speaking, heavily freighted matter that involved several issues. It raised again the question that would never go away, the question of purity: When was a beach clean? What was clean? How was clean measured? The state and Exxon would fight over this well into the next year. It also raised the question of what cleanup methods to use, chemical or mechanical, or both, and of the further damage to shorelines that might be caused by an invasion of workers and equipment. Admiral Nelson stated that cleanup standards had not been set yet because the islands in the sound were still in the process of being analyzed for their ecology, their sensitivity, for the presence of archeological material. Kelso stated that the standards for beach cleanup had already been set. Bill Allen, who had to be prodded to respond, said that there was a communications problem and that he was in the dark so far as standards were concerned.

Mayor Devens of Valdez, who among the men on the stage probably felt most acutely the need for direction since his town was under siege, derided the Bush administration and Alaska's congressmen for not declaring the sound a national disaster area. At the same time, he credited himself for talking the Bush administration into not sending troops. He was understandably very worried about the impact of the still-developing cleanup mobilization upon Valdez, but precisely what his vision was of the federal presence remained unclear. He was also worried about underwater oil, claiming that it was distributed at some depth under the surface—15 to 20 fathoms. He was wrong about that, or basically wrong, although at the time there was talk everywhere of oil sliding beneath the surface and then reappearing as if from nowhere, of fishermen hauling up oil-coated anchors.

Jack Lamb was in the audience. He rose to his feet and asked that Exxon and Alyeska be required to hold a public conference to answer questions concerning their lack of response to the spill. As one of the group of fishermen ushered into the inner chamber, Lamb knew better than most what Exxon and Alyeska's answers would be and what they would not answer at all. He said that both Alyeska and Exxon were stonewalling, that they were offering no response to the public. He asked the panel to tell him when movement would be made on the cleanup. He wanted to be told who was running the cleanup operation. He was asking for what the audience wanted to hear. They had come in the vain hope that in a forum such as this a meaningful answer or two might emerge.

Admiral Nelson said that the Coast Guard command structure was running the operation, though effectively this was not true. Admiral Yost hadn't arrived yet. Nelson, knowing very well who Jack Lamb was and perhaps recollecting what the people in the inner chamber had decided to do, now said that the salmon hatcheries were the first priority. Otherwise, he did not respond to Lamb's questions, which were really a form of serving notice on Alaskan television in the face of an appalling misuse and concealment of information: Where were the skimmers? Where was the boom? Where were the barges? Where had Alyeska been? Where was Exxon? What about the beaches? What about reparations? What about the animals? What was next?

Bill Allen of Veco was unable even to hear the questions. They had to be repeated for him, and more than once his catchall response was that there was a "communications problem." His company had been taken on as the primary contractor for cleanup services, and his deal with Exxon was on a "cost-plus" basis, which meant that he was guaranteed a profit on every dollar spent, but Allen was able to say only that he was "in the dark." The effect of his approach, whether intentionally or accidentally guileful, was precisely the same as the approach Monte Taylor used in Cordova—plead ignorance, blur the distinctions, misinterpret the questions, talk about something else.

Quite possibly Allen, the Exxon surrogate, was truly in the dark, and if so, his failure lay in agreeing to come here when he had nothing to say or, having come, in his refusal to explain the darkness. By not articulating the source of their confusion, both Allen and Exxon hung the public out to dry. Exxon kept repeating in its ads and press releases that it "accepted responsibility" for the spill, but it sounded more and more as though the purpose of the apology was to absolve the apologist of responsibility, like President Reagan with the Iran-contra affair.

The grizzled guy I'd met outside the offices of the Department of Fish and Game a few days before reappeared here. He latched onto Valentine's mike and gave his pitch. His boat was still waiting in slip 52. His bottom line was that having exhausted his other possibilities, he wanted Bill Allen to tell him when Veco would hire him on. Allen didn't understand the question. The guy pushed the limits of decorum and Valentine, sensing the nearness of theatre, maybe, turned him loose. The guy's voice rang in the hall as he repeated his pitch, the whole garbled, frenzied thing: what kind of boat he had, what kind of engine, how fast it was, where it could go, where it was, and where he was from, which was Anchorage, and how he looked the way he did because he'd been sleeping in his boat for the last 14 days, long enough, he said, to make him an official resident of Valdez.

Bill Allen drew his legs up, leaned forward to listen, and smiled. The guy had Bill Allen's attention, and suddenly it became a moment when all the confusion, indignation, subterfuge, evasion, and even outrage were stripped away and the true meaning of the cleanup came out, burned clean to its nub. The guy wanted to make some money, that was all. Allen understood that. The audience fell silent. It was a moment in which the floor and walls of the hall seemed to atomize and drop away. Everything was suspended and into the weird, glassy, rapt space two sharks came and swam free.

After a time, Allen said that he didn't know when the guy would be hired, or for what, or how, or by whom, but that it sure sounded as though he would be hired to do something.

The next morning in the Totem Inn, I fell into a conversation with a correspondent for the Canadian Broadcasting Corporation. He told about stumbling upon a refrigerated semi-trailer down by the docks that was stacked to the ceiling with otter bodies. It was the morgue to which the dead otters slipped out the back door at the rescue center were taken. The bodies were numbered and kept for the pathologists to dissect and test.

The Totem Inn was packed again. There was a line at the telephone. A clump of people stood waiting for empty seats, and all around us was the noise of intense conversations. Everyone had news and rumor ran rampant. Two men seated next to the CBC correspondent and me joined our conversation. They were Charles Jurasz, who operated a whale observation station in Oregon and a consulting and educational operation in Juneau, and David Lonsdale, the assistant director of the John G. Shedd Aquarium in Chicago. Lonsdale had several reasons for being here, among them to encourage the establishment of an aquarium in Alaska for the rescued otters, and possibly to procure otters for his aquarium. There were disputes over everything, of course, and that included the disposition of otters once they were ready for release from the rescue centers. Public aquariums had joined the orbit around Valdez. The Shedd Aquarium would eventually send three staff members to help with the otter rescue project and take in four otter pups that for reasons unknown had been abandoned by their mothers and then cared for in the Seward Otter Center.

Charles Jurasz, whom I would come to know as the months passed, was a passionate, tendentious man. He said that the humpback whales were due to migrate into the sound any day now. "They're surface feeders," he said. To demonstrate, he craned his neck downwards, dropped his jaw, and cruised low over the surface of the table. He straightened up, eyed the rest of us fiercely, and said, "Oil floats. Can you imagine?" The best hope, he said, was that the whales would avoid the slick.

He and Lonsdale had just seen an otter die at the rescue center. Charles did the trick with compressed breath that I remembered from childhood playgrounds. He leaned back in his chair and sucked in air, then sucked in more, and more. His face deepened in color as he squeezed the air in his lungs, then suddenly he let it out in an explosion of air. The puff was as visible as breath exhaled in the cold. "It was like that," Charles said, "when the otter died. That was the pain it felt, and the constriction of its muscles. Its last breath came out like that."

At the rescue center in Valdez, the recovering animals were out in the sun. They were given ice in their cages. One of them, number 81, was dying. She had almost died an hour or so before, but had perked up after being given ice. Now, she was fading again. Two volunteer helpers, Jake Metulka and Dave Berrey, crouched by the cage. Dave said, "Alaska's been raped, but the question is, is it by consent or force?" He looked over at me to see if I was writing that down. I wrote it, though I could sense the shine of frequent use on the words. There was a troubling impulse among many here to assure that they were being memorialized along with the event. The press seemed to carry the power to do that. I'd been inside the building where otters were held in plywood stalls, and I had watched, aghast, as an NBC crewman shoved his way up to a stall, shined his lights on a startled otter, and began rolling the film. He was a big man with a taut, blunt face, and he had to be chased off.

Dave went off to find some towels to try to warm number 81. She lay on her back, moving her legs indiscriminately. She scraped at her face, bit at her paws, rolled over, and cut her lips by biting at the wire cage. The otters were readily anthropomorphized in the imagination: they were articulate with their paws. Their eyes expressed intelligence. The pain of number 81 seemed familiar and close. Her mortality was my own. She writhed in a slow, ceaseless frenzy, as if striving to locate the source of her trouble.

I headed down to the Bird Rescue Center to help with the evening feeding. Surgical tubes were inserted through the beaks of the birds down into their stomachs, and a sugar mash was forced in from a large syringe to rehydrate them after the diarrhea caused by the oil. I held them—a white-winged scoter, a common loon, a red-footed pigeon guillemot, a gray, white, and orange harlequin duck that looked dazzling in my hands. The head of a Barrow's goldeneye, seen close, had a rich purple sheen emerging from beneath the black. I was holding the birds gently, feeling the dryness of their feathers, and at the same time my mind was filled with the image of number 81, with white mountains, with Bill Allen awakening from his reverie and leaning forward to listen to the guy with the waiting boat in slip 52, with the Totem Inn, packed with people, with the raven that had so narrowly scrutinized George Velikanje and me, with the slick, the elastic thing that engulfed the beaches. I thought about Kelly Weaverling and wondered if the bird I held was one he had rescued.

A gray-haired woman in the Bird Center had had the side of her nose ripped open by a pelagic cormorant. She continued working, dabbing at her nose with a Kleenex, her blood dripping on her yellow slicker. My partner and I approached a cage of cormorants. Angular and quick, they have athletic necks and long, menacing beaks. They attack in a pack any outstretched hand. One had to move fast to catch one safely. I held its head with one hand and pressed its body against me with the other. It calmed down. My partner inserted the tubing through its beak, slid it down, and slowly compressed the big plastic syringe. The cormorant's belly swelled intimately against my palm, then it crapped on my boot. My partner laughed softly. When we finished, I set the cormorant gently in its cage. It whirled suddenly in a rush of slate-colored feathers. Its neck whipped around and its beak tore at my fingers.

The next morning, I climbed into a four-man red-and-white Cessna 180 at the Valdez airport. We flew over the Alyeska terminal where they were still skimming up a 168-gallon spill from an April 10 tanker-loading mishap. At another time, that would have caused a stir. Each of the three gray tankers moored at the terminal was encircled by a silvery boom in compliance with regulations. We headed out above the Valdez Narrows and along the Valdez Arm toward Naked Island. To the right, pale blue icebergs from Columbia Glacier floated in the dark water at the mouth of the arm. At Knowles Head, another tanker awaited permission to enter.

The sky was clear in this part of the sound and we flew at about 1,000 feet above the water until we reached Storey and Peak islands just north of Naked Island. Black oil bled from their rocky shorelines. The oil in the water had a milky tinge. We circled Naked Island twice, and the pilot banked the Cessna for a view of the Exxon *Valdez*, anchored in the bay. A repair barge was tied up to the tanker's side. The tanker was still leaking and the barge was engulfed in thick, black crude. The bay was filled with oil. All of Naked Island's shoreline was lost to the blackness.

In the five-mile stretch between Naked and Eleanor islands was a large, oval oil slick. It had the rainbow appearance oil took on in the sun—gray, white, faint blue, brown, red. The brown or red color that indicates thickness is called chocolate mousse. When the oil is thin and light gray, it is called cloud. The euphemisms seemed outrageous. The longer the oil sat out in the water the more it would harden, making it more difficult to skim.

The natural color of the bottom in the shallows near the shoreline was emerald green, which came from the fucus beds. A few patches of the color flashed by as we passed over Eleanor and Ingot islands and started down the edge of Montague Strait along the eastern side of Knight Island. Then the color disappeared. A large portion of the slick was trapped in Montague Strait between Montague and Knight islands. The rocks along Knight Island were covered with oil. Pools of crude were locked in all the coves. I spotted several brown, rectangular shapes floating in an inlet and reached for the binoculars. The pilot dropped the plane to the level of the cliffs. The shapes were motionless in the murk. They were otters, eight or nine dead ones, washed into the inlet.

The coastlines are intricate. There are coves upon coves, inlets upon inlets, twisting jagged peninsulas and complex watery arms. All the shores on the eastern side of Knight Island were coated with oil. We were near low tide and the beaches, cliffs, and shrubs were black 20 feet above the waterline. Offshore, the oil floated in elongated ribbons and congealed around the rocks. From the southern tip of Knight Island, we cut west to Sawmill Bay, the site of the Koernig hatchery. The oil had crept within a half-mile of the hatchery and I counted 20 boats down there, frantically skimming, running booms, sopping up crude with the two-foot-square sponges that could hold a gallon of oil. The efforts to save the hatchery seemed frail and desperate.

The Cessna swung out and passed up along the western side of Knight Island. The normal colors of gray rock, the ocher of dried eel grass, and the green of the shallows were utterly gone. Everywhere, the water was rainbow-black from crude. At the northwest edge of Knight Island, Herring Bay, a deep, labyrinthine inlet, was clotted with black. Because of their intricacy, all the islands and shorelines looked like computer-generated fractals, fine, complex, and infinitely specific in their structures. The complexity of the ecology along the shorelines and in the estuaries, where the exquisite chaos of commerce between microscopic organisms, fish, plant, and land animals became most intense, appeared dead. By this time, two hours out, I had long stopped fooling with my binoculars, camera, and notebook, and instead held my head still against the window and stared down at the horror.

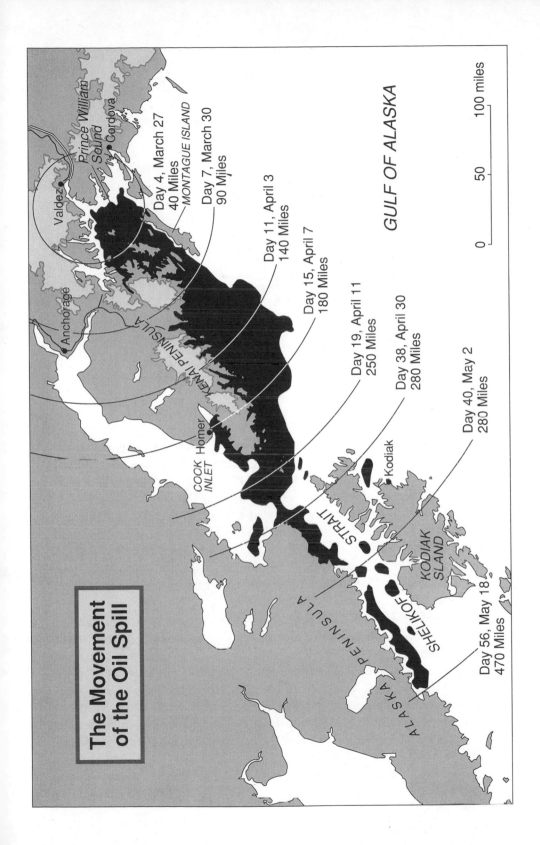

The Movement
of the Oil Spill

Valdez

Anchorage

Prince William Sound

Cordova

Day 4, March 27
40 Miles
MONTAGUE ISLAND

Day 7, March 30
90 Miles

Day 11, April 3
140 Miles

Day 15, April 7
180 Miles

Day 19, April 11
250 Miles

Day 38, April 30
280 Miles

Day 40, May 2
280 Miles

Day 56, May 18
470 Miles

KENAI PENINSULA

COOK
INLET

Homer

Kodiak

STRAIT

SHELIKOF

KODIAK
ISLAND

ALASKA PENINSULA

GULF OF ALASKA

0   50   100 miles

Chapter 8

THE TEARS
OF SCIENCE

On June twelfth, two and a half months after the Exxon *Valdez* foundered on Bligh Reef and midway through Exxon's cleanup exercise, I stood on a rocky bank beside the mouth of a stream that emptied into Resurrection Bay. The bay is a narrow, 25-mile-long indentation into the eastern side of Alaska's Kenai Peninsula. Its mouth is about 50 miles west of the edge of Prince William Sound. This bay is ice-free, protected from winds, and also for a time was the principal point of connection between the Pacific and the Alaskan interior. The town of Seward lay a half-mile to my left in the shadows of the mountains.

Between the town and the bank where I stood, the *Alpha Helix*, a 133-foot steel-hulled vessel operated by the National Science Foundation, rocked gently in the water alongside its dock. The ship's hull was bright blue. Its abovedecks and communications antennae were white. Beside it, the dock, damp from a recent rain, was a glistening gray. I could see the figures of the science crew as they hustled up and down the gangplank and passed down duffel bags and crates loaded with diving and laboratory gear to the ship's crew on the main deck. Their voices sounded thin in the distance.

Shortly, we would embark for Prince William Sound. I would spend ten days in the company of a team of natural scientists under the leadership of John Oliver. Their specialties were in benthics (sea bottom) and intertidal regions. My hope was that I could come to understand, accurately and in detail, just how far-reaching the poisoning had been. There was the pitch of emotion in Valdez, Cordova, Seward, Homer, Seldovia, and Port Graham, the ever-rising din of claims, denials, and false information, the shrill and sometimes woefully misinformed response on the part of environmentalists in the lower forty-eight. And by this time science had become partitioned into adversarial camps (again, the state, the federal agencies, and Exxon), and into camps within camps. The otter centers competed for victims. Some specialists jockeyed to get the inside track on future research papers. There had been a shift in command, too. For the Coast Guard, Admiral Yost had stayed until the end of April, then to be replaced by Vice Admiral Clyde Robbins. Frank Iarossi, who some said had come to care too deeply, was relieved by Exxon's Otto Harrison, whose mission at times seemed to be to question every recommendation and protect Exxon against every possible legal twist, which had the effect out on all the edges of the battle of undoing Admiral Yost's work. The spill now covered over 6,000 square miles. Finding the truth in detail about it was like searching in the dark for a narrow ledge to hang onto.

Of the panelists on the KIMO show in Valdez, the one who stood most apart from the others was Don Moore, Cordova's city manager. A spare, balding, and thoughtful-looking man, Moore had given notice of his resignation in Cordova for personal reasons and had agreed to accept another position elsewhere before the spill occurred. The result was that he would soon leave the town. During the KIMO show, he spoke much less than his fellow panelists, but among them he alone had raised the question of the impact of the oil spill upon Native subsistence villages, particularly Tatitlek and Chenega, the latter of which had had its resources obliterated. When the sense of the paralyzing effect of infighting among interest groups had become especially strong on the panel, Moore said, "We should seize this moment to rise above ourselves. There should be a major research effort."

That was the first time I had thought seriously of the spill as a research opportunity. It had been clear from the start that science was to be an integral part of the cleanup and recovery—to take custody of the oiled otters and birds, to try and to fail to take custody of the oil slick itself, to observe and to monitor. What I hadn't appreciated was that extraordinary energy would also be devoted to research that ran the gamut from "applied" in the strictest sense (findings might inform the response to future spills and so be closely allied with technologies; dispersants; bioremediation) to "pure" or "almost pure" (the response of organisms to toxicity might lead to inquiries that would bear upon, say, genetics). Calamity had come to be a staple resource for science-oriented government agencies and cottage industries across the nation, and the research process and its presumed results—that is, "knowledge"—would come to be heavily leveraged by the parties of interest.

At the beginning, I had visited several of the science meetings in Valdez, which were then gatherings of state and federal agency, Exxon, and free-lance scientists. In some cases, they were scouting out contracts. At first, the meetings functioned as open distribution centers for information. Later, they became fractured, even useless some would say, as the state and federal agency scientists and Exxon scientists came to be pitched against one another in complicated ways, thus reflecting the fractious relationship of their employers. They would fight, for example, for proprietorship of the bodies of the dead that were to be examined and used as evidence in litigation.

I went to one early meeting in the company of Charles Jurasz and David Lonsdale. Previously, the Shedd Aquarium had been granted permits by the Department of Fish and Wildlife to capture several otters from Prince William Sound. Then the permits had been withdrawn because of the quite understandable uncertainty over the status of the otter population. Lonsdale's mission was to barter the lost permits and expert help for the four otters the Shedd Aquarium eventually received from the Seward Otter Center. It is not my intent to question Lonsdale's or the Shedd's motives (Lonsdale is a kind, compassionate man), but Lonsdale's presence was an example of how the margins of the scientific community were being worked. Another, much more problematic skirmish involved bald eagles. The National Foundation to Protect America's Eagles wished to transport threatened eagle fledglings to Tennessee, but the Department of Fish and Wildlife impeded that effort and early attempts to care for stricken eagles in Alaska.

At the beginning, the conduct of the scientists seemed, by and large, exemplary. At the meetings, which were held in a large, well-appointed conference room of the same Valdez Community Center, reports were given by members of what was called the Oil Spill Assessment Team on the current location of the oil slick, on beach surveys and the numbers of birds found dead or captured and carried to the Bird Rescue Centers, on otters dead and captured, on the progress of the then newly opening rescue centers at other locations, on the condition—insofar as it was known—of the hatcheries, the fisheries, water quality, on the status of the expected migrations of birds and marine mammals. Arranged on a table at the back of the room were neat stacks of photocopied handouts available for the taking—maps of the latest NOAA overflights, summaries of reports, lists of contact persons, and animal counts.

The undercurrent of emergency could be heard in the voices of the scientists, in contrast to the coolness of manner with which they presented their data. Their faces sometimes looked stunned. They were fatigued. Due to the hours spent each day gathering and reviewing data, these meetings did not begin until ten at night. Nevertheless, statements were succinct and clear. The meeting itself was well organized. People awaited their turn to speak. Details were offered freely, questions were answered, and in accordance with the scientific practice of accuracy and skepticism the holes in findings were readily acknowledged—the problems with counts of the dead and the living, the question of whether or not humpback whales would see and avoid the slick, whether sea lions could survive swimming in it. The willing acknowledgment of such holes made them exactly what they should be to science—portals through which more light might eventually be shed upon mystery. This was a question of a quality of mind, of not rushing to fill all the gaps with enthusiasm, blame, and cant. There were no guards at the doors of the conference room.

Aside from the dispersant fiasco and other initial misapprehensions about winds and currents, the early impression given by scientists was that they could be counted on to be calm, accurate, and forthcoming— that is, scientific. So far as the efforts of many of the individuals were concerned, the impression would hold. Many would remain scientific in the face of physical, intellectual, and professional peril. So far as the group of them was concerned, however, the spin on the impression would reverse direction and science would come to seem a refuge from the true damage and many of its practitioners the quarrelsome high priests of disaster. This came later.

The scientists at the early meetings were invariably under 50 years old and usually much younger than that. Their clothing was neat. They were handsome or pretty, trim, fit, well washed. There was not a black face among them. A third of the Assessment Team were women. It was an upwardly mobile group of young professionals, adept at weighing hazard against advancement, and good with words and apparati. They were well paid. They had the security of their expense accounts, most of them, and they, or their superiors, saw the opportunity to get bigger ones. They had all the advantages of class and position. In contrast to the sense of immediate peril and the will to action that the villagers and fishermen displayed, they were watchers, and many would refuse to cross the line that separated their watching from action.

As time passed, as conflicts among the agency and private scientists deepened, the enlarging chaos out in the field ate at all the edges of their method. Kathy Frost was a member of the Assessment Team and told me in early May that oiled river otters and harbor seals had begun to turn up. Several premature harbor seal pups had been found dead, and the oiled adults seemed to be displaying aberrant behavior. Normally, they dive into the water when approached while sunning themselves on the rocks, but now they sat still, even when helicopters flew as close as 600 feet. She worried that the oil had caused some kind of systemic shock. Secondary and tertiary effects upon the food chain were unknown. She said, "Mussels and bivalves may get oil in their sediment, which would affect growth and recolonization, which in turn would affect the otters. The otter pups may not make it because of the food problem. We could get a double-whammy on the otters." By that time, as many as 2,500 otters were thought to have died. Eagles, sick from having eaten oiled carrion, were appearing. A squid had washed up on an apparently clean Tatitlek beach, dead of unknown causes.

There was concern over the coming arrival of migrating humpback and killer whales, over the impending spring migration of sea and shore birds. It was said that in terms of the diversity of species and sheer numbers, Prince William Sound was the single largest stopping place for waterfowl in the world. Between April and June, gulls and petrels would arrive, three species of puffins, birds in flocks coming one after another and numbering in the thousands and tens of thousands, kittiwakes, murres, auklets, murrelets, oystercatchers, snipe, dowitchers, sanderlings, surfbirds, plovers, phalaropes, whimbrels, ducks, and geese to join the resident flocks, surf scoters, sandpipers, and shearwaters in flocks as large as 100,000. Because of the forbidding nature of the adjacent country—to the south the Saint Elias region and the Kenai to the west—Prince William Sound with its tidal flats, snow-free estuaries, its islands and bays and its milder spring climate served as a feeding and resting habitat for the birds as they came north from their wintering grounds. As many as 20 million birds pass through Prince William Sound during the spring and summer months. They feed upon near shore life, invertebrate life of all kinds, clams, mussels, squid, lugworms, copepods, amphipods, schooling fish, flatfish, polluck, sand lance, capelin, and carcasses and marine mammal placenta. In April and May the outlook remained grim.

There was concern not only over the effect of oil upon birds that happened to land in it but over its effects upon the food supply, how such effects would be measured, and by whom, and for whom, and to what use the findings would be put.

A scientist in tears was one of the insistent images of the early days of the spill. Charles Jurasz told me he had wept. As Belen Cook had seen hardened fishermen weep, Jurasz said he'd seen the most stoic of scientists weep openly. The grief was a response to the removal of a presence from 1,000 miles of beach and thousands of miles of near-shore waters. The loss was felt most keenly by those whose daily life had been woven into the fabric previously, such as the fishermen, the villagers, and the scientists like Kathy Frost whose work had already put them on intimate terms with Prince William Sound. Lisa Rotterman, the otter specialist from Cordova, would say that something momentous happened "when Kathy Frost came back from Green Island and said, 'As a scientist I'm not supposed to feel anything, but it's overwhelming.' " That scientists could weep, especially the natural scientists whose business often enough was pathology just as killing, finally, was the business of fishermen, seemed to validate the loss. That the image of a scientist weeping passed so quickly among the growing numbers of people gathering around the event served as a kind of awakening to the fact that this thing had actually happened and that its substance consisted of something rather more than could be calibrated, weighed, or counted.

Between the dock and the town of Seward and around the curve of the shoreline was the Seward Otter Rescue Center. It was made out of conjoined mobile homes and garrisoned by a chain link fence. I had tried to get in earlier with Bruce Stewart, education director at the Monterey Aquarium and a member of the science crew on the *Alpha Helix*, but we were turned away by a portly, affable guard. No amount of expert talk and no display of credentials would convince him to change his mind. "There was no entrance without permission from Exxon," he said, but he was willing enough to serve as an informant himself. He said that up to that time 150 otters had passed through the Seward center and that there was now a 90 to 95 percent success rate—meaning that 90 to 95 percent of the otters brought in lived.

Considering what I'd heard otherwise and what I'd seen a couple of months before in Valdez, the figure seemed outrageous. I thought it was another lie. Bruce and I went on our way to dinner and as we walked I asked him if he thought it was possible. He shrugged. When I told him about the otters I'd seen in Valdez, he gave me a dark look, then said that if the guard here had his numbers right, the best explanation would be that the otters were arriving in a lot better shape.

It was a simple enough answer and, as it turned out, a perfectly reasonable one. By this time—June—a majority of the toxic aromatics were gone from the oil. The bulk of the otters that were hit hardest by the oil had been hit immediately, and those that remained out in the waters might have been situated in relatively clear areas to begin with. They might have learned to avoid the oil. Their main vulnerability by this point might have been to the secondary and tertiary effects Kathy Frost had spoken of.

I would eventually learn that by the summer months the success rate at all the otter centers was indeed in the 90 percent range. In October, Lisa Rotterman would tell me that as time went on, many of the otters brought in survived for just the reason Bruce had suggested, that indeed some were captured from spottily oiled areas, that whatever problems they had upon arrival in the rescue centers came mainly from the stress of being chased and captured. Some of the boat people, she said, were confused, or driven by excessive enthusiasm, or by greed. There was big money in "otter rescue," thousands of dollars a day. One reason Fish and Wildlife had proposed closing down Kelly Weaverling's rescue operation back in April—the stress upon healthy animals—had turned completely around. Otter rescue contracts had continued to be let. Randall Davis told me that there was disagreement among the veterinarians over how to judge whether or not an otter should be brought in. Some felt that any slightly oiled otter should be captured. Others felt that even moderately oiled otters should be left alone. From a boat, there was no way to tell a moderately or lightly oiled otter except by chasing it. It also became a technical question. There was no objective method for detecting oil in fur. In August, Fish and Wildlife issued a permit to capture 16 otters to test a spectrophotometric method for measuring oil. One of the 16 had detectable oil in its fur.

The lights of Seward glimmered faintly just beyond the otter center. It was 8:45 in the evening, almost time to go. There were nine days to solstice, and the pale, slowly deepening twilight had just begun. Across the bay, the mountains were dark blue, almost black. Directly before me, the pale blue water of the bay was tinged with green and the milk color of glacial silt. The green gave an appearance of depth to the blue and the milkiness gave it opacity. It was the extraordinary and changeable mineral-like color again for which I had no name. Down along the bay, the dark humps of small islands were visible. At the edge of the bank and along the mouth of the stream, eight men were fishing for pink salmon in the rising tide. Soon, the water would churn with spawning fish, and they would appear in the estuary, exhausted, dark, hook-jawed, and breaking surface with the humps of their backs. At the moment, the water was quiet. The men matter-of-factly cast and reeled in their lines, or fooled with their gear.

Seward had some 2,000 residents, although its population would temporarily rise by close to 1,000 before the oil spill summer of 1989 was over. The tsunami that followed the 1964 earthquake had destroyed its port installations. Through the succeeding years the town had broadened and stabilized its economy. Fishing and associated industries remained the chief source of revenue. There was a strong government presence, a maximum security prison, a vocational school, and a nursing home financed by oil-rich state coffers. In the last five years, 3 million tons of coal were delivered by rail, then shipped out of Seward's port to Korea. In the complicated and disturbing irony of the modern Alaskan economy, the Chugach Native Corporation was developing a timber industry, and a state-of-the-art mill would soon open. Industry practices, which were controversial both within and without the Native community, included keying long-term production to the Asian market, old growth harvesting and clear-cutting* right down to the waterlines and along watersheds. Before the oil spill, fishermen here and in Prince William Sound had considered the timber industry their most immediate threat.

Like Valdez, Seward had a highway to connect it to Anchorage. It was hardnosed about its survival, and quick to assess a changed situation and to capitalize on it. Each of Veco International's cleanup subsidiaries, Veco Inc., and Norcan, would use Seward as a base of operations. Bill Noll, then a member of the Seward City Council and one of the leaders of the oil spill response during the summer, and later to be elected mayor, would tell me in November that "Seward did not get involved with trying to pick sides. The reporters go back to New York. Sure, the spill was a national tragedy, but mooning and crying don't get it fixed. If Exxon's to blame, then pay up, Exxon. A lot of people in Seward feel like that."

---

* Old growth stands include centuries-old trees and sustain long-established and complex ecosystems. Also, because of the tightness and clarity of its grain, the wood in old growth trees is generally superior to new growth. Clear-cutting is a heavily mechanized form of logging by which, for the sake of efficiency, all timber growth is removed from a large tract of land.

Some distance out in the water from where I stood was a "sheen," a remnant from the oil that had filled Resurrection Bay and kissed the Seward shoreline on April 17, 24 days after the spill. I was surprised that so little was evident. I bent to catch the sunlight slanting against the skim and saw that there was maybe a quarter-acre or so of the stuff. On the water, the oily swirls were visible by their shine and changeable coloration—red, gray, blue, and white. On a larger scale it was the same as what one sees on an asphalt parking lot after a rain. The fish the men were jigging for would skirt the sheen.

The tide had begun to rise and suddenly the salmon were running in earnest. The surface of the water churned from their density. They could be heard, chopping through the water and slapping in the shallows of the stream. The activity of the men at the water's edge intensified. They cast repeatedly into the roil. A Native man in jeans, plaid shirt, and high rubber boots hooked one, reeled it in, netted it, and walked up the bank and dumped it out not far from where I stood. He picked up a stone and hit it over the head, then returned to the water's edge to recast his line.

I eyed the fish, looking for some sign of oil, but saw none. A five-year-old boy, the man's son, clambered down the bank and stood over the fish. He picked up a stick and hit it, circled it and hit it again. A younger brother came down. The brother found another stick and hit the fish in the head. The two of them circled the fish and struck it repeatedly. It was a two-foot salmon, a good one, silvery and scarcely mottled with decay: Oncorhynchus gorbuscha, known variously as pink, humpbacked, or humpy. The pinks were not the most favored for eating, but they were the staple of the salmon crop, like brown-skinned potatoes or field corn, the most abundant of the species and the primary product of the commercial canneries. The canned salmon for sale in the grocery stores is almost invariably pink salmon. These men were catching them to take home to be smoked, dried, or canned and stored for winter.

Soon, the fish lay still where the boys' father had lodged it between two black rocks. Down at the edge of the bank, the other men were catching fish, one after another, and helping each other land them. The stormcloud had come near to us and the light turned to a radiant gray. The white seiner cruised slowly toward the docks across the bay. The blue, green, and milk-colored water took on the gray of the cloud. The oil sheen became almost invisible. The bending figures of the fishermen were dark against the darker rock and the bright fish flashed one after another as they were pulled from the water.

I understood what the boys were doing, hitting that fish—mainly because I had been a boy, once, and had three children of my own. It was a form of play or ritual that had to do with making capture and death familiar. It was akin to setting fire to an ant hill, but touched with exquisite and complete directness upon these boys' knowledge of the world, for to them death and the taking of quarry was a daily thing. They stood above the fish and looked at it, seeing its silver against the black rock, the incipient hump behind its head, the darker curve of gill, the hook of the open jaw. They prodded the fish and found it tensile, still filled with the tautness of life. They were engaged in an inquiry, asking—*What is this?* And maybe having been told that the fish had left this stream and returned a year or more later, knowing that it would be eaten, their inquiry might become layered with spiritual and moral dimensions and so extend into their own risky time. They might also ask for rightness of mind and thought. In their looking, they asked all the questions. It was pure science.

I returned to the *Alpha Helix*. As we set out, a group of us stood on the foredeck to watch. I looked at the white seiner I'd seen previously through a pair of binoculars. Two men dressed in yellow slickers were on the deck, hoisting plastic garbage sacks to a third man on the dock. The sacks looked heavy. Their contents shifted around, making them unwieldy. The man on the dock loaded them into a pickup. They were oiled birds, I suspected, brought in for the count. After that, they would be stored in freezer trucks to be kept as evidence. The boat and three men passed from view as the *Alpha Helix* headed slowly down the long bay.

The rattle of the anchor chain playing out against the hull of the *Alpha Helix* was usually the last call for action. By the time the anchor hit bottom, one of the three inflatable Zodiacs or the wooden whaler had been lowered by the crane from the rear deck to the water alongside the ship. John Oliver, a compact bundle of energy, would be there, urging on the lowering of the next Zodiac and directing traffic . . . that gear bag into that Zodiac, that set of tanks there, those weights there, and these people together in the red Zodiac, you four in the gray one, you in the whaler . . .

His graduate students, of whom there were five among the 13-person science crew, would spin around, apportion the gear, drag the oxygen tanks across the steel deck, quickly secure the zippers and gauges on each other's diving suits, and then, once he was sure everybody was pitched in the right direction, John would be gone, the first one out with his team, down the ladder and behind the controls of the Zodiac with the biggest engine, the red one. He would cry out, "It's a good place to die," jerk back the throttle and slam through the swells at top speed toward his diving site.

A highly regarded benthic marine biologist, John Oliver is about five feet nine. He has light red hair and a complexion inclined toward pinkness. His students refer to him as "science in motion." He had been described to me by a mutual friend before I met him as "the bandit scientist." I was finally unable to resist raising the matter with John. When I did, he grinned and said, "Oh no, we're way beyond that, now." Just what he meant, whether he'd gone so deeply into banditry that he'd come out the other side burned clean, or if he'd adjusted his course, was not clear to me until much later.

On the night of the twelfth, as the *Alpha Helix* made its way from Seward to Prince William Sound, several of us sat in the galley, the principal gathering place on the ship. It was kept clean and snug. It had white walls, fixed chairs and tables. The tables had ledges and little corrals at their heads to hold things—a precaution against the roll of the ship. It was a place of comfort, inviting aromas, and conversation, a refuge against the rawness of the outside. Back in a corner, a pot of coffee was always on. Between the dining area and the kitchen stood a serving bar and beneath it a set of stainless steel coolers that were kept stocked with drink and food, most notably ice cream, which seemed to be a staple in the diet. The ship's cook, Trish Kaminsky, who knew the habits of John and his crews from previous voyages, and probably a few things about sugar and high-velocity activity, as well, had already announced that she'd loaded her freezers with extra quantities of the stuff.

We were eating strawberry ice cream on the night of the twelfth, big bowls of it, and talking desultorily about the ship, the weather, the sound, the oil. John said that what was required to chart the effects of oil were scientists who were familiar with the area and able to follow a project over a period of time. Also, he said, they should be "the sharpest possible scientists, who are also generalists, people capable of seeing things at the edges of vision."

There were others on more intimate terms with Prince William Sound than John, but he was experienced with oil spills and his own ability to use the edges of vision was excellent. Although ecological or "whole earth" thought has made an energetic entry into the biological sciences in recent years, the use of closely defined parameters to create a controlled research environment is still, and quite understandably so, the primary method of research. The universe is vast. Human capabilities are small. The trick, it would seem, is to scrupulously exercise the tools of controlled research and at the same time to retain the ability to look up, or away. There might be something in the air or out in the peripheries of the water column that is affecting the grids. There is really nothing new about this necessity of science and existence—to see what is before one, to see what is not before one. It's a function of intelligence, but not necessarily of education. The failure to see what lies beyond the edges of primary scrutiny—including, perhaps, the reason for tears—may be caused by a preexisting structure, either a real one that is exerting leverage, such as a government agency, or one in the imagination, a mind set.

As it happened, this voyage had been in the planning stages prior to the oil spill. It was originally intended as a part of a research project directed toward the feeding habitats of sea otters. John Oliver and Rikk Kvitek, of the department of zoology at the University of Washington, were seeking otter feeding sites and samples to use as a basis for comparison with other sites in Glacier Bay and along the coast of Washington, Oregon, and California. The buildup in recent years of the otter population in Prince William Sound (due to federal protection), and the resulting pressure upon otter food (clams, urchins, mussels, crabs, and fish) made the region interesting to them.

The oil spill had several effects upon their work. It came to be a part of their proposal to the National Science Foundation and therefore guaranteed their funding. It increased the pressure upon the crew, since there was now something additional to look at. There were two major planes of observation—otter predation, oil—and each was to be approached through a form of survey. This suited John Oliver. To pretend that any occurrence, natural or otherwise, was discrete would have been contrary to his nature, and this, I would ultimately conclude, was where his banditry had come to lodge—in the freedom of his spirit, the steadfastness of his trust in inquiry, and his resistance under at times difficult circumstances to being driven by a predetermined system.

The ship did have a basic itinerary, or a floating plan, which John arrived at and amended through consultation with the captain of the ship, Tom Callahan, and other principal parties. Principal seemed to mean whoever had the most specific requirements at a given time or place, and usually included Rikk Kvitek and, in the initial stages of the trip, Gordon Robilliard, whose San Diego–based environmental consulting company was doing shoreline survey work for Exxon by virtue of a contract let by Dames and Moore. Gordon had been added to the crew in the later stages of planning.

The basic itinerary, however, did not preordain what exact sites were to be examined from one anchorage to the next, nor did it necessarily seem to mean that anyone—even at times John Oliver, or Rikk Kvitek, or the captain of the ship—knew exactly what the plan was. In response to my sometimes befuddled attempts to grasp what was going on, John would several times say that we would look at "whatever was interesting." It was not unusual to see him in the red Zodiac heading off full tilt in one direction, then slowing, rising from the saddle behind the wheel and peering off in a direction tangential to his course, and settling back down, throttling and swinging the Zodiac around in a wide arc toward a previously unanticipated objective . . . a rock or small island, maybe, a shoreline with an inviting-looking escarpment.

That was the method. No electronic monitors here, and not much in the way of chunks of habitat cordoned off for extended observation, but mainly just people looking and counting, making records, scratching the bottom, digging up shell debris left by otters and prying urchins loose from rocks. By the time we were done, the diving teams would have examined and taken samples from between 40 and 50 sites. More than 20 shorelines would have been inspected. The trip was a very aggressive survey undertaken by a posse of marine range riders. John communicated the sense of everything out there in the world being ephemeral, forever on the verge of slipping away. One had to be quick to get on it. There was a definite predatory quality to all of this, the electric buzz of preparation, the demands on the students, the dives themselves probing the deep, the booty brought to the lab, and the ice cream afterwards used to jack everybody back up. But at the outset, especially, John's joy in the pursuit of ephemerality, even of joining it, was contagious. In the beginning, when he appeared on the deck before a diving sorty in his red-and-black diving suit, replete with hookups and gadgets, he looked like an impish road warrior, ready to engage in battle with the eternal Proteus.

The path of the *Alpha Helix* would be approximately backwards along the direction the oil had followed. We would enter the sound at the southwestern edge, move toward the center, then swing clockwise. In the early afternoon of June 13, the ship set anchor just north of Point Elrington at the extreme edge of the sound. Once the diving teams were off, the last group of five of us made the first shore party. We donned our blaze orange float jackets and set out in the wooden whaler for North Twin Bay. Besides myself, the group included Bruce Stewart, Gordon Robilliard, Peter Slattery, and Kathy Conlan.

The bay was deeply indented into the island. On a map it looked like a mouth agape, turned away ever so slightly from the gulf. As we entered into its protection, the chop of the sea against the whaler fell away. To our left, or on the northern side of the bay, a sea lion slid off a rock and vanished into the water. Up above, tufted puffins flew in and out of their rookery in the cliffs. There was a passage in the air filled with them. They were stout, betasseled birds that had a determined look like small, antiquated bombs. They fed by diving, or "flying underwater," and so had been thought to be especially vulnerable to the oil. The birds were passing back and forth between a feeding ground out at sea and the young in their burrows. The sky was gray. They disappeared out there. They were soundless, as is the way with puffins, who make only a guttural noise in the vicinity of their nests.

The water around the whaler was clear. We landed and the five of us spread out. The beach was composed of cobbled rock. There was no immediate sign of oil. I followed Gordon Robilliard along the northern arc of the bay toward the cliffs. A harbor seal poked its head up about 40 feet from shore and looked at us. In the curve of its skull and in the way its head lay low just above the water, it was unmistakably seal, the fur brown, the snout and eyes dark. In the equipoise of its position and its bodily address to us there seemed to be intelligence, an inquiry into our presence: *What is this?* It disappeared. Overhead, the puffins flew back and forth, as intent as small fullbacks.

Gordon found a chest-high patch of oil on a rock, and it became easy, then, to locate more oil at the same level along the outer rim of the beach. The oil had been carried in by a high tide and had left its traces like a bathtub ring. Gordon marked it down in his book. We turned and walked toward the southern half of the beach where Peter and Kathy had gone. The footing abruptly grew uncertain. I looked down. The stones had taken on a sheen. The farther we went, the darker the sheen became until it was the amber color of engine oil. The rocks grew steadily larger as we moved around from the center of the beach, and the footing became precarious. Kathy Conlan, wearing green hip boots, had waded into the shallows to search the oiled rocks. She stood in the midst of an oil sheen and called out her findings to Peter Slattery, a stout man with a red beard, who was at the edge of the shore, crouched over Kathy's Zip-Loc specimen bags, helping to organize them.

The bags contained amphipods, mainly, the tiny shrimplike creatures that Kathy planned to take home to Ottawa. The amphipods were alive. She'd found barnacles and periwinkles alive on the rocks, living in oil. Kathy returned to shore and showed us a gum boot chiton she'd found. The gum boot was a good eight inches along and flatly built. Its eight cream-colored plates were coated with oil like the rock it had been found on. Chitons fed by grazing rocks for algae and detritus. Kathy turned this one over. Its long, peach-colored foot was smeared with oil. Now, two harbor seals poked their heads up to look at the four of us from just beyond the edge of the oil sheen. They were watchful, and seemed calm. They ducked out of sight, then reappeared to look from a different vantage point. The sea lion had not reappeared. Over on the other side of the beach, a column of puffins still flew out. Another column flew back.

We all moved back to the center of the beach and then up and across a quarter-mile of densely overgrown landbridge. There were birds here, sparrows and thrushes that scuttered ahead of us and rattled sideways into the brush. It was then, because of the whip of their wings and their alarmed chirps, that the silence of the beach we'd just come from struck me. We broke out into the open at the top of another beach on the opposite side of the island, facing Elrington Passage. The scientists scattered. No one said anything. This place smelled of oil. Kathy immediately carried her net and bucket into the water and began searching a group of large rocks just offshore. Bruce and Peter poked at the algae. Gordon moved along the beach, then sat down on a log and began writing in his book. In terms of impact, he would say, this beach was maybe a four or five on a scale of ten.

The upper wrack of algae was lightly coated with oil. Below it a fresh set of deer tracks approached a line of eel grass, then stopped and broke back toward a clump of alders. It had been startled away by our approach. Fifteen feet or so down, the lower algae wrack was so heavily oiled that when stepped on, it gurgled and emitted a sharp stench. Below that, oil covered the rocks and lay in pools in the crevices and depressions. Out in the water, dense ribbons of it slipped around the protruding rocks and undulated slowly with the motion of the ebbing tide. As Kathy moved, it swirled around her boots.

A fishing boat, no doubt leased out as a cleanup vessel, was nestled some distance away against a small island. Behind it was another shoreline. It made a vista—dark rocks, green spruce trees deepening almost to black on the slopes, and gray, luminous sky. My feet were in oil. Before me the water was black with oil, then further out it took on the dreamlike color of blue, green, and milk. Overhead, first one bald eagle, then a second appeared. They flashed in and out of sight as they circled in overlapping arcs. They were looking for food to carry to the young they had nested in a snag on the landbridge between the two beaches.

On either side of the landbridge was a microcosm of the entire chaos: on the other side a half-clean, half-oiled beach, and on this side a heavily oiled beach, over there harbor seals that would become oiled if they hauled out on the wrong rock, a somewhat less imperiled sea lion, and puffins that seemed to have so far avoided the risk of diving into oiled waters, and over here one line of algae that might survive, another line that would not, a deer that might ingest oiled eel grass and die, and eagles that might tear into that fouled carrion, and no doubt a bear in the woods that might also feed on the carrion or lick the oil off its paws after walking across the beach, and in the intertidal region wildly varying levels of damage for the clams, mussels, shrimp, starfish, urchins, kelp, and chitons. Kathy found surviving barnacles, mussels, and amphipods around those rocks on this side, but the far greater hazard lay here, no doubt because this bay faced one of the channels down which the oil had flowed. The beach on the other side had more wind, more exposure, and perhaps was in its presently bisected state because of an eddying effect as the currents drove the oil around the tip of the island. The oil had less opportunity to settle over there. Some of it had already been scoured off by the wave action.

Along with Bainbridge, Evans, Latouche, and Montague, and to the north Knight Island, Elrington is one of the group of islands that form a broken barrier to the south and west of Prince William Sound. At the approximate geographical center of Prince William Sound is Naked Island, to which the Exxon *Valdez* was towed on the twelfth day after the spill. The predominant currents move counterclockwise, although this basic directional tendency is complicated not only by the irregularity of land masses on the surface but by the like irregularity beneath the surface. There are crosscurrents. The water moves in contrary directions and shears against itself. Due to the extreme differences of depth, stream flow from the land, and glacial outlets, the temperature of the water varies. Again, because of outflow from land, the density of the water changes. There are differences in the levels of salinity or sediment load.

The Japan Current, or Kuroshio, swings clockwise by the gulf. The Alaska Current, a big, powerful eddy of Kuroshio, flows counterclockwise just off the continental shelf. Within the sound, there are underwater eddies, highly variable tidal patterns, and unpredictable winds. Some of these irregularities are minor. Others, such as prevailing currents (also counterclockwise in the sound) and the wind, are significant. Taken together, they create a mosaic of forces which are in a constant state of interplay and flux. Since oil is lighter than water, it is somewhat less affected by its own inertia than water. In a wind it may shear from the surface of the water and skim. In calm water, it spreads laterally. In the presence of surface currents, it will move at their speed, and it is otherwise affected by waves.

Over time, the oil changes its nature, seeking stability. The bulk of the lighter-weight aromatic hydrocarbons—benzenes, xylenes, etc.—evaporate into the air within 48 hours after a spill. These are also the most toxic elements, and through inhalation and absorption were the primary cause of the first, devastating slaughter of animals. The heavier aromatics, which are chronically toxic, may enter into temporary solution in the water, and may be dispersed through metabolism by bacteria and other organisms over a relatively long period of time. These metabolic processes introduce toxic elements into the food chain.

If the oil has a concentration of waxes and asphaltics, as does Prudhoe crude, it may mix with water and form mousse, at which point weathering of the entirety is drastically slowed because of the sealing effect of water. Cleanup also becomes much more difficult. Most skimming machinery is designed to pick up oil, not heavy concentrations of water. As time passes, the oil becomes heavier. It may collect sediment and sink, or adhere to beaches. Eventually, Prudhoe crude becomes asphaltic. The oil has its own complex set of internal forces. It simultaneously follows its own dynamic and interplays with whatever it touches, deepening the complication of the mosaic. As of now there are no computerized models that come close to replicating the complexity of the movement and gradual decay of oil in a place like Prince William Sound, Cook Inlet, or the Gulf of Alaska.

This is one reason why the oil industry is so actively interested in a remedy, such as dispersants, which would have the real advantage of drastically increasing the rate of weathering of some of the oil, and the public relations advantage of making oil seem to disappear. It is also why it was hoped that the oil would exit to the Gulf of Alaska and keep going out to the open sea where it would disperse on its own—that is, gradually break up into increasingly smaller and less visible packages, ultimately transferring its discrete droplets into the water column. It may also be why Exxon repeatedly exaggerated both the likelihood and the facts of dispersal. A month after the spill, it still clung to the vestiges of its hope and told a *New York Times* reporter that 66 percent of the spill had been eliminated: 13 percent by cleaning, 35 percent by evaporation, 8 percent by burning, 5 percent by biological breakdown, and 5 percent by disintegration. Every one of the figures was unbelievable. The figure for evaporation represented a physical impossibility since no more than 22 percent of Prudhoe Bay crude can evaporate, and the figures for biological breakdown and disintegration were both exaggerated and blurred. When I quoted the figures to Kathy Frost of the ADFG, she laughed and said, "What's the difference between biological breakdown and disintegration? And how did they measure it?"*

By March 28, the oil had moved by both the eastern and western sides of Naked, Eleanor, Ingot, and all of Knight Island. By the thirtieth, it had ricocheted off the inside shores of Montague Island and hit Latouche Island. By the thirty-first, it had entered Elrington and Latouche passages on either side of Elrington Island. During the first few days of April it had touched all the channels in the group of strainer islands and parked itself off the coast of the Kenai Peninsula. Parts of it would wash back toward the sound, and then wash out again, and back. Other parts would go up Resurrection Bay, Cook Inlet, and by mid-May reach out to Kodiak Island and slip behind Kodiak to the Alaska Peninsula.

Those central and southwestern islands were the same ones I had seen on my overflight in early April. The channels between them vary from narrow to wide, deep to shallow, but the overall pattern as the current and the oil moved nearer the edge of the sound is one of increasing constriction, as of a funnel. The visible edges of the islands are infinitely complex, and so they provided a variable and gradually tightening obstruction to the oil that flowed by them before it was released from the sound. The effect of tidal movement works in sympathy with the irregularities of land. For these reasons, what we saw at North Twin Bay on Elrington Island and the bay across the isthmus was a primer for the diversity of damage that was in store for us. While the basic course the oil would follow might have been known, the detail of its impact could never have been predicted.

During the evening of the twelfth, the *Alpha Helix* edged toward Knight Island. It has the most intricate shorelines of any island in the sound and after the boundary islands, Montague and Hinchinbrook, the largest land mass. Its bays are so long that at several points they cut almost completely across it. We anchored for the night in Snug Harbor, a large bay near the southeastern end of the island that would be used as a site for research on dispersants and bioremediation.

Diving teams had been out to the island. They had grim tales of oil on the shorelines. Knight Island had taken the brunt of the hit. Their reports of conditions beneath the water, however, were much more hopeful.

* In one of many contrasts with Exxon's April figures, Steve Provant of the DEC would estimate in mid-September that somewhat over 6 million gallons, or a little over half of the original spill, remained, much of it on shorelines.

Rikk Kvitek was normally dour, but even he seemed buoyed by what he'd seen. In the galley, he said, "Things are carrying on as normal. It's business as usual. The barnacles are alive. The algae is still working. The polychaetes are alive." I went to the deck after dinner and gazed out at the island. It was about nine o'clock and we were still well within the long, luminous twilight. The *Alpha Helix* was parked in an oil slick. The stuff lapped and stuck to the hull. Three fishing boats were anchored near to shore. The edges of Snug Harbor glistened with oil. Beyond the beach was bush, then trees, then the snow-capped mountains. It was utterly quiet.

The next morning, the *Alpha Helix* cut back south. A party of us went to shore at Sleepy Bay on Latouche Island. Sleepy Bay is at the northern tip of Latouche, a big cavity, an opening like a waiting embrace. There was oil at least a foot down. When I tried to walk, I slid around on the rocks. When I stepped on an algae wrack, my boots sank deeply into the slime. Each step broke the seal of oil and the stink came out—oil, carrion, and decay like shit. At times, I had to reach down and grab the top of a boot to extract it. Pools of oil hung on in the depressions and crevices in the rock. It swirled thickly in the water and clung to both sides of a line of boom. Gordon Robilliard said that this beach was about a six on a scale of ten, which left hanging the question of what a ten would be like. There was no sign of life here, not a single bird. Kathy Conlan waded out into the murk, then came back and searched the algae wrack for amphipods. Here, she found nothing.

Chapter 9

THE RAPTURE OF
MACHINES

Alaska Falsejingle
Alaska Volute
Amphipod
Ancient Murrelet
Arctic Fox
Arctic Loon
Arctic Surfclam
Bald Eagle
Barrow's Goldeneye
Beaver
Black-legged Kittiwake
Black Rockfish
Black Scoter
Black-tailed Deer
Black Turnstone
Bonaparte's Gull
Broad Snow Crab
Brown Bear
Bufflehead
California Armina
Canada Goose
Canary Rockfish
Chinook Salmon
Chum Salmon
Clay Pipe Sponge
Coho Salmon
Common Eider
Common Goldeneye

Common Merganser
Common Murre
Coonstrip Shrimp
Coyote
Crisscrossed Yoldia
Dall's Porpoise
Double-crested
   Cormorant
Dungeness Crab
Eel Grass
European Starling
Feathery Shipworm
Fuzzy Crab
Glaucous Gull
Golden Eagle
Great Horned Owl
Gray Whale
Gray Wolf
Hairy Cockle
Harbor Porpoise
Harbor Seal
Harlequin Duck
Hermit Sponge
Herring Gull
Horned Grebe
Horned Puffin
Horsehair Crab
Humpback Whale

Humpy Shrimp
Kelp
King Crab
Kittlitz's Murrelet
Knobbyhand
Hermit Crab
Ladder Whelk
Limpet
Longhorned
   Decorator Crab
Magistrate
   Armhook Squid
Mallard
Man
Marbled Murrelet
Milky Venus
Mink
Northern Crow
Northern Goshawk
Northern Horsemussel
Northern Pintail
Oldsquaw
Orange Bat Star
Orange-pink Sea
   Urchin
Orca
Pacific Halibut
Pacific Herring

Pacific Sea Lemon	Red Squirrel	Spot Shrimp
Parakeet Auklet	Red-throated Loon	Stellar Sea Lion
Parma Sand Dollar	Rhinoceros Auklet	Stellar's Eider
Pea Crab	Ridged Crangon	Surfbird
Pelagic Cormorant	River Otter	Surf Scoter
Phalarope	Robust Clubhook	Tanner Crab
Pigeon Guillemot	Squid	Trenched Nutclam
Pine Grosbeak	Rusty Moonsnail	Tufted Puffin
Pink Salmon	Sablefish	Vole
Porcupine	Sea-clown Triopha	Warped Whelk
Red-breasted	Sea Otter	Weathervane
Merganser	Sea Raspberry	Scallop
Red-faced	Sei Whale	White-winged Scoter
Cormorant	Shrew	Wolverine
Red Fox	Slender Seawhip	Yellow-billed Loon
Red-necked Grebe	Sockeye Salmon	Yelloweye Rockfish
Red Sea Urchin	Sparrow	Yule Grass

—Partial list of species affected or killed by the Exxon *Valdez* spill, compiled by Jody Morgan, *Equinox*, July/August 1989

For two days the *Alpha Helix* remained in the vicinity of northwestern Knight Island and the group of islands just off its northernmost tip—Disk, Ingot, Sphinx, Block, and Eleanor. Besides Knight, two of the islands—Ingot and Eleanor—are sizable bodies of land. The others are small. On a map, the group of them look like morsels broken away from the big chunk. At close range, they seem separated from Knight Island only by the merest happenstance of water level. A shore party I accompanied would find two of them, Eleanor and Block, joined at low tide by a landbridge.

Night was a squint of darkness that closed briefly and then reopened. We retired at midnight and rose at four or five in the morning. Throughout the night, the befuddling light seeped through the portholes to the cabins. During the day, the skin absorbed the light. The body took the light into its darkness and felt oddly large and soft. The mind seemed to compose itself within in a pool of radiant white. The diving teams, driven by light, worked from six in the morning to nine or ten in the evening.

We had passed across the verge into the heart of the oil's blackness, and were close to the source of the original slick. Great fields of oil had passed here. "Knight Island is the soul of Prince William Sound," David Grimes would say to me several months later. By then his words would strike a chord in me. There is something decidedly mysterious about Knight Island, a primitive power that has to do with its size, irregularity, and the line of its peaks, two, three, and four thousand feet high, that make a jagged spine visible from great distances. "It's the lodestone. It's appropriate that it was the hardest hit," David would say, and then, veering toward animism, he added, "It opened its arms to the oil. The oil was surprised to be taken out of the earth and released from pressure. It sought stability and went to Knight Island."

The *Alpha Helix* was less than ten miles from the bay on the western side of Naked Island where the Exxon *Valdez* had been anchored for over two months for repairs, and where, despite the company's repeated claims to the contrary, it continued to leak oil. The ship was still there, since the authorities in Portland, Oregon, had strongly discouraged the company from sending it to their harbor for repairs. Given the political cast of Oregon, to have sent it there would have been to court a local display of outrage. The Coast Guard took it a step further and indulged itself in a romance of law and order when it raised the possibility of sabotage by what Captain James Calhoun called "radical elements." Exxon backed off. Calhoun's phrase provoked the public question as to just what was meant by "radical elements."

Although those of us on the *Alpha Helix* weren't aware of it, since we had been out of touch with the news, a two-million-dollar plan had just been announced to tow the *Valdez* to San Diego, where it would be repaired by the company that had built it, the National Steel and Shipbuilding Company. In another of the relentless and mind-boggling expressions of optimism by Exxon officials, it was announced by Exxon Shipping that the entire ship had been cleaned of crude oil and would not leak. When the ship was towed out of Prince William Sound on June 24, it trailed a mile-long oil sheen.

The cleanup activity was presently centered in the area of Knight Island, and what had been previously a nearly private witnessing by the crew of the *Alpha Helix* would now add machine and man to the picture. Early in the morning of the fourteenth, I heard the thudding sound of a helicopter. I moved out from the *Alpha Helix*'s galley to the deck to look. In the pale light a large gray shape loomed up, a navy vessel that Exxon had leased out. The *Alpha Helix* as it swung around the northern edge of Eleanor Island came nearer to the navy ship. Secured to the ship's starboard side were two barges that made a dock for three fishing boats. The barges also had shelters erected on them to form a cover for supplies. Overhead on the ship's deck stood a crane, used for loading. One helicopter rested on a landing pad at the foredeck. The other helicopter approached across the pale blue sky, then circled and hovered above the pad. In the distance beyond the ship was the dark outline of Naked Island. The helicopter descended to the pad. Its rotors slowed to a stop and four men in dress slacks clambered out. They were observers, presumably executives, politicians, or reporters.

An hour later, Kathy Conlan, Kim Kiest, a graduate student from Moss Landing, and myself put ashore on Eleanor Island near what is called Upper Passage, a channel between Eleanor and Ingot islands. We were not far from Block Island. The bay we came into was shallow and nearly ringed by land. There were traces of oil in the water, bands of it that encircled the protruding rocks. We cut our engine and tipped it up to protect the propeller blades from the bottom, coasted to land, then waded ashore. The beach was composed of a coarse sand and it had at first glance an inexplicable pale beige color, a whiteness.

Before me was the small bay, and at the intersection of water and earth a line of greenish, gummy matter—diatoms. To my right, the beach gave way to a line of rock faces. Kim moved that way. At my back, Kathy worked her way up a small stream, upending rocks and digging into the clumps of growth. She had her tools with her—the net, the bucket, the plastic Zip-Loc bags. To my left and separated by a line of rocks was a tidepool. Its water was dark and its far bank drenched with oil. Above it was a long, narrow landform, dense with growth. I moved that way. From the distance, the high noise of a two-cycle engine slipped in and out of audibility. Scattered all across the beach were bits of broken shell. The wrack of brown algae appeared to be alive, if discolored, but when kicked even lightly it broke free. I crouched and picked up a handful of sand. When I dropped it, a thin, clear sheen was left on my palm. What was wrong here had just begun to dawn on me when Kathy said, "It's been cleaned."

I looked up. Kathy was on her knees at the edge of the stream. "It's barren," she said. "It's like a desert." It was true. The sand was the color of the Mojave. It lacked the deepening hue of the plethora of tiny things that normally flourish on its surface. This color was wrong. The beach, we would learn, had been cleaned by the "hot water wash" method a few days before. "It looks like a sewage-polluted beach that's been taken under protection," Kathy said. "It's only the really hardy stuff that's survived."

The "hardy stuff" she referred to consisted in this case of two species of amphipods that she found in the stream. She speculated that they might have survived because of the presence of freshwater runoff. Amphipods had come to intrigue me because of their strong capacity for survival, and because they were near the bottom of the food chain. They are commonly known as beach hoppers or sand fleas, the tiny creatures found on beaches that sometimes bite and that have the ability to suddenly straighten their backs and leap. Some species are microscopic. Others grow quite large and are a food source for salmon and—the gammarid—for gray whales. The ones Kathy found were usually about a third of an inch long. Nearly flat on their two sides, they lay on the tip of a finger and wriggled.

Reproduction is triggered by "carrying," a process by which the male attaches itself to the female, sometimes for long periods, and Kathy was concerned about the lack of reproductive activity among the specimens she found but finally reached no conclusion on the matter. Amphipods are primarily but not exclusively marine animals, and many tolerate radical changes in salinity. They are usually but not always bottom feeders. Many are strong swimmers. They may be herbivorous, carnivorous, or both. They are voracious and opportunistic. True marauders, they eat what presents itself to them. In a way, they are the coyotes of the intertidal zone because of their capacity to live almost anywhere, to eat almost anything, to thrive in the face of any menace. Fishermen sometimes find their lines stripped of bait by amphipods. Several nights before, Kathy had shown me one under the microscope in the lab of the *Alpha Helix*. It lay on its side and wriggled its many appendages—legs, antennae, and a set of powerful graspers clustered near its mandible. Kathy explained that museums use amphipods to clean specimens for skeletal displays. A pit is dug, then filled with water, the specimen—a seal, say, or a whale—is dropped into the pit along with a good dose of amphipods. Before long, the skeleton is clean. On the dish beneath the microscope, the amphipod looked like a shrimp. Its body was nearly transparent, luminous as a chip of moonlight. It was possible to look right through the creature to its other side.

Peter Slattery had told me, "They're not that important, probably," by which he meant that they would probably recolonize. In his opinion, their power of survival was so strong that they would come back even if they were wiped out of a certain site. In the great debate over what happened to fouled shorelines, the power of certain creatures to survive or return was critical. Peter and Kathy had found amphipods living on oiled rocks. Generally, they found two species of amphipods on oiled beaches, and three species on the unoiled. The first beach we'd visited—North Twin Bay on Elrington Island—overlapped with an amphipod survey a colleague of Kathy's, Dr. Ed Bousfield, had conducted in 1961. She found two species there where he had found one. This was hopeful, if the flimsiest shred of a comparative finding.

In my effort to understand, it had become important to find survivors capable of containing hydrocarbon doses lethal to others, of surviving drastic changes in the chemistry that surrounded them. What if the species lost on oiled beaches were genetically discrete? If so, the amphipod gene pool would be interrupted. What if the species that survived suffered sublethal toxic effects from the heavy aromatics that might affect its reproductive capabilities or be passed on to its predators?

On Eleanor Island, I stepped into the stream to cross to Kathy's side. A dark cloud rose from the bottom and swirled around my boot. I stepped again and raised another cloud. I dipped my hand into the stream. Water and oil droplets separated from each other in my palm. The oil must have percolated to the stream bottom from the subsurface elsewhere. I turned back and dug through the sand with a stick, creating a small hole about four inches deep. Quickly, the bottom of the hole filled with oil. I dug another hole in the beach, and another, and a small trench four inches wide and six inches deep. Each time, the black oil seeped into the bottom and rose to its level a couple of inches beneath the surface. Except for the amphipods and oil-fouled diatoms at the edge of water and sand—which, Kathy and Kim would surmise, had washed in with the tide after the cleaning—the beach was dead, and for the time being deader than any beach that had been merely oiled. Aside from the amphipods and diatoms, there was absolutely nothing alive on it, and it had the oil still in its substrate.

The hot water wash, like many of the cleaning methods, had been questioned from the start for precisely the reasons we were witnessing—its destructiveness and its inefficacy. The method consists of heating seawater, putting it under pressure, then blasting the beaches with it. It is one of several related approaches that include spraying water at various temperatures and pressures by fire hoses, hand-held wands, and sprayers with eight high-pressure nozzles mounted on cranes (omnibooms). Here, the force had been sufficient to shatter clamshells into bits and to penetrate a couple of inches into the coarse sand. The heat increases the liquidity of the oil and thereby causes it to run down the beach and into the water, at which point it might be skimmed. However, it presented the plant and animal life with temperatures well beyond the range of their experience. Brown algae wilted on contact; hence its pale color and the fragility of its hold. The argument used to promote the method is that on heavily oiled beaches it impedes the formation of tar mats (asphalt), which, through their sealing effect and persistent toxicity, retard successful recolonization by plant and animal life.

A test beach in Knight Island's Herring Bay, not far from where Kim, Kathy, and I were, would be hot washed in mid-July. The test was conducted by Exxon scientists and scientists from various federal and state agencies. The lead agency, NOAA, struck an agreement with Exxon to keep the data secret. Months later, in February 1990, following an application by the *Anchorage Daily News* under the Freedom of Information Act to NOAA, the data would be released and reported in an article by Charles Wohlforth. The results showed that on the upper part of the beach 86 percent of the plant life hit directly by hot water was killed, and that some species of plant and animal life, for example, snails, sea lettuce, and brown algae, were completely wiped out. In all, 13 species of plants and animals were lost completely from the site. In the water where the hot water and oil flowed, dead starfish, crabs, and small fish were found. The magnitude of this secondary effect, according to Jacqui Michel of NOAA, was unexpected.*

The machine used in the test discharged 500 gallons a minute of 130-degree water. It was estimated that 1,300 gallons of oil lay on the beach before treatment and that half of that remained afterwards. Some 300 gallons of oil were picked up by the waiting skimmer. What happened to the remaining 350 gallons, no one knew for certain, although roughly speaking, the answer was obvious. It was dispersed in the water, or it washed back onto the beach, or onto another beach, or it mixed with sediment and settled to the bottom. The 300 gallons the skimmer picked up was probably offloaded into a bladder or into a storage barge, then transferred to a central site, probably run through a water separator, perhaps shipped by barge to Tacoma, and trucked to the toxic waste dump in Arlington, Oregon, where it would be stored or recycled as asphalt. Cleaning spilled oil was like trying to whitewash a red barn. No matter how many coats are applied, the red still seems to show through.

It should be noted that there was (and is) a general scientific consensus that there have been very few rigorously conducted field tests of cleanup methods for any oil spill. In the case of the hot wash test beach here, Jacqui Michel would assert that cleaning heavily oiled beaches by whatever method was preferable to simply leaving the oil and allowing it to harden into mats. This was an activist position, a triage, and it was supported with even greater vigor by Exxon's senior environmental ad-

---

* My requests to both Exxon and NOAA for white sheets that would include specific data on the test sites were ignored.

visor, Al Maki. In a March 2, 1990, letter to the *Anchorage Daily News* following Wohlforth's article, Maki wrote:

> The extent of the impact of hot-water washing was weighed against the alternative, which was, to leave the heavy oil concentrations on the beaches, posing a greater threat to shoreline species. Data clearly indicated that while hot-water washing caused some incremental localized impact on these species, the removal of heavy hydrocarbon concentrations stabilized the shoreline and will likely speed overall recovery of biota.
>
> The finalized report on the test results show a considerable variety of organisms still present on shorelines treated by the hot-water cleanup method. Although the numbers of several species were reduced significantly, enough remain to strongly suggest the ability to reproduce and the return of a viable shoreline ecology. This trend has been observed in several studies of other spills worldwide, showing that shoreline biota recovered in impacted areas within two or three years after the event.

With both Michel and Maki, it was a judgment call, though Maki's assessment seems overoptimistic. By "shoreline" biota, he presumably meant intertidal life—crustaceans, bivalves, diatoms, plant life, etc.— indigenous to that shoreline, and not, say, the migratory birds whose numbers might be depleted first by the oil spill itself, and secondarily by the lack of food during the two- to three-year period. The possibility of exponential effects through the reduction in food sources for predators, such as birds, is glossed over. The decision to clean any beach by the hot water wash was a selection from an array of forbidding choices, which included the various means of flushing, the various means of mechanical and manual removal (from excavating beaches with backhoes to wiping rocks with absorbent pads), using dispersants, vacuum pumping, skimming, burning, and sandblasting. The conundrum with which decision makers were presented was absolutely resistant to solution. At best, the hot wash method, when compared with other methods of interdiction, merely reduced the amount of time required to achieve what Maki calls "viable shoreline ecology" (what is meant by "viable" is open to interpretation) by a factor which is beyond accurate prediction, and which, everything considered, remained a great deal more than two or three years. Some experts put the recovery period for beaches with oil left in the substrate at 30 years, or as long or longer than if the oil were left alone.

Kathy, Kim, and I walked across the isthmus to Block Island, situated nearly in the center of Upper Passage, between Ingot and Eleanor islands. Like the other interior landbridges, this one is verdant with growth. The green and yellow plant life and the dark tree trunks and the dark, humus-heavy earth come at one in a startling rush. As we began our descent toward the water, our vantage point brought to our eye birds flying in and out of a rookery. They were black-legged kittiwakes, the most common gull of the Arctic, named after their cry. They were to our left, coming away from a cliff and flying into the trees and then around, out of sight. Their pattern of flight had an intentness to it, quite unlike the whirl and hover one customarily sees when gulls range the water for food. No doubt, they were headed out to locate food for the fledglings situated on the ledges of the rock. It was the first sign of bird life we had seen for some time, and for these birds in this place the search for food was not a happy prospect.

We swung rightwards along a narrow trail, and down, moving toward the smell and the noise, the shoplike stink, the sound of engines. We clambered down the face of a rock and into what by then had become a recurrent vision: a beach or, in this case, a line of several shallow beaches separated by jutting rock formations like knots in a rope. All that we saw was inundated with oil. The detail still held its morbid fascination, this rock six feet above the water level and yet drenched with oil, and this twisting, glossy line of algae, and this fish body cast upon the edge of the beach, and these fissures and crevices and little bowls and indentations filled with oil the consistency of mayonnaise, and this small cove aswirl with chemical colors—gray, white, brown, and rust—and that rock out there in the water, a tiny island, to which Kathy Conlan, following her ritual of inspection, waded. Her fascination was fixed once again on the durability of certain creatures, for here among the oil she found sculpins, a common fish of intertidal regions, amphipods, mussels, and what she referred to as "scads of hermit crabs."

With the fascination, however, came a certain inescapable blunting to what grew into a repetitious horror, a customary deathliness. Our fascination, or the high and low points of a day, came to reside in the detail of abuse and the detail of survival. The acceptance of the pervasive reality of abuse caused despair. As our despair deepened, we all found it increasingly difficult to speak of its source. It was there, everywhere. Oil was the landscape and so it was drawn within us. Science, when removed from the scene, referred to such assault as "aesthetics." I found myself sinking into the world of symbology in hopes of finding a way to grasp what I saw. . . . It was like the *Inferno* where the very substance of Dante's landscape, of exterior form and of the interior acceptance of that form by the condemned, was made out of evil. The three of us did not speak, but looked, and turned away to look at something else, and then at this, at this bulb on a popweed streaked with an eerie red, at that steel-colored streak in the water.

The water in the cove directly before us was closed upon itself by a stretch of blue plastic boom. The boom's purpose was to hold in what oil was here until a cleanup crew arrived. It failed in its purpose, for even then in slack tide ribbons of oil passed from one side of the boom and under it to the other side. To our left, a second length of boom lay draped across the rocks, and 30 yards and a couple of coves farther down, a group of college-age people—two young men, two women— were building a pair of shelters out of two-by-fours, plywood, and fabric. A skiff ferried back and forth from a boat out in the channel to the young people, who were there to conduct a kittiwake census under the auspices of the Department of Fish and Wildlife. There were other crews scattered throughout the sound, doing bird censuses, one of the young women told me when I walked down there. Her broad face was filled with intentness and purpose, like the kittiwakes flying out to look for food. She said there was also a DFW cruise ship roving the sound to do counts. She and her comrades had their building supplies ashore and one man had the first shelter almost constructed. At the edge of their beach was a growing stash of fuel cans, food, and equipment. A lime-green portable latrine stood at the edge of the woods.

From there, I could see that beyond the DFW supply boat was a large, bright blue and white cruise ship, a fancy vessel with big, recreational decks. It was owned by a religious organization with a reputation for swinging, and had been leased out as a work crew hotel boat. Off its bow, three large, black bladders floated in the water. They looked like dead, finless whales. They were used either as repositories for recovered oil or as storage for fuel to run the machines. The water in the channel was still and dark. The sky was clear. Downwards and across the channel was the dark, the darkness of Ingot Island across the way, and the darkness of the water and the shine on it that glinted in the sun. Beyond the cruise ship were a barge and several more fishing boats, and beyond them, small in the distance, a shore crew ran high-pressure hoses on Ingot Island. A small skimming vessel waited just offshore. The crew's yellow hardhats looked like buttons. The milk-colored ricochet of spray from their high-pressure hoses arched against the dark slope of the island.

I worked my way back toward Kim and Kathy, past them, and then out onto a point of land. Another bay came into view, an anchorage. In the bay were over 25 fishing boats, also leased out for work. Occasionally one of them, answering a radio call, would start up and ease out into the channel. There was the noise, the noise of this boat or that, the distant hum of the engine running the hoses across the channel, the noise of the DFW skiff coming and going, the racket of the hammer the young man used to put together the shelters, and yet what we saw here and heard was nothing compared to what the diving teams were seeing in Herring Bay that day, or to what I would see there later. We caught a glimpse of it that evening as the *Alpha Helix* passed down along Knight Island, retrieving the diving teams: big ships floating in the open water, smaller ships and barges crammed into all the inlets, and makeshift constructions along the shoreline, shelters, latrines, and bulldozers, backhoes, cranes, generators, compressors, a barge loaded with an omniboom. The omniboom had six oil-fired burners that heated 100 gallons of 40-degree water to 160 degrees in a minute and then shot the water out at the rocks and beaches under 80 pounds per square inch pressure. Later, a floating incinerator would be brought in to Herring Bay because the landbased incinerators couldn't handle the waste being generated at the rate of 250,000 to 500,000 pounds a day.

In some places, everything was thrown into the incinerators—oily logs, rock, gravel, sludge, broken shovels, spoiled containment booms, absorbent pads, rain suits, boots, shit from the latrines. When the DEC began strictly applying air pollution regulations, a way had to be found to ship out the oily debris. At its peak, the cleanup effort would involve 14,000 vessels, 80 aircraft, better than 500,000 feet of boom, boom dragged out of every corner of the world. There would be 11,000 workers who consumed 330 tons of food and had 10 million gallons of water delivered to them, who wore 31,000 hardhats, 600,000 pairs of gloves, 73,000 pairs of rubber boots, 53,000 lifejackets, and 167,000 rain suits. They were ferried from one place to another, herded onto the hotel boats and then back on shore into temporary camps. To fulfill their needs, maritime and cleanup equipment pulled off the shelves of supply houses all up and down the western United States, and huge quantities of food were shipped in. In order to monitor the cleanup, the Coast Guard itself had deployed seven major ships, 20 aircraft, and more than 1,000 personnel. The lists go on and on.

Vessels became unavailable on the West Coast. The price of gasoline out on one Aleutian island rose to six dollars a gallon because there were no transport barges left to deliver it. It had to be flown in by light plane. The lists were late twentieth century, computerized versions of the now seemingly quaint lists one might find in the journals of explorers, Colnett,

Cook, Vancouver, Fidalgo, Lewis and Clark, lists that served as ironic
mirrors of the lists of damaged species. A supplies list, excluding food,
for one small response vessel, for example, looked something like this:

750 ft. Expandi 4300 Containment Boom
1 each GT-185 Skimmer
1 each Pharos Marine Hydraulic Power Pack W/Spares
1 Each 1000 Gallon Oil Water Separation Tank
2 Each 16' Rigged Hull Inflatable W/50 HP Outboard Motor
1 Each Spare 50 HP Outboard Motor W/Spares Kit
2 Each Fish Totes
20 Each Bundles Sorbent Boom (800')
20 Each Bundles Sorbent Pads
10 Each Bags Viscous Sweep (1000')
1 Each Roll Nylon Reinforced Visqueen (20' X 100')
1 Each Steam Cleaner
1 Each 4KW Generator
1 Each 2" Pump (Diesel Driven)
100 Ft. 2" Suction Hose
100 Ft. 2" Discharge Hose
2 Each Response Boxes (Storage Containers)
12 Each Boom Lights W/Batteries
12 Each Anchor Buoys
12 Each Mustange Float Suits (to be sized)
12 Each Sets Carhart or Refrigewear
2 Cases Rain Gear (1 Lg, 1 X-Lg)
12 Pair Rubber Knee Boots
12 Pair Insulated Arctic Pack Boots
24 Pair Felt Boot Liners
12 Pair Safety Glasses
12 Pair Ear Protection (Peltor)
2 Dozen Rubber Gloves
4 Dozen Glove Liners
4 Dozen Cloth/Canvas Gloves
5 Cases Plastic Bags
1 Case Ear Plugs
1 Set Hand Tools (Rakes, Hoes, Shovels)
2 Sets Mechanic's Tools
2 Tool Boxes
4 Coils ½" Poly Line
4 Coils ¾" Poly Line
2 Coils ½" Nylon Line
2 Coils ⅜" Nylon Line
12 ¾" Shackles
24 ½" Shackles
1 55 Gallon Hydraulic Oil

2 Cases Outboard Motor Oil
5 5 Gallon Gas Cans
1 Set Spare 2″ Camlock Fittings
1 Fully Equipt First Aid Kit
1 Drum Motor Oil (30 Wt)

When he arrived in early April, Admiral Yost had said, "This spill is a war. I intend to fight it as a war." It became an event on the order of a military call-up, marshaling platoons of people and incorporating immense quantities of big things and tiny things—the navy frigate, the ¾-inch shackle, a box of Ritz crackers. By the time the cleanup was in full swing, on-scene Coast Guard commandant Vice Admiral Clyde Robbins would say, "As far as my actual authority over the cleanup, I have none, unless I take over the spill. My only hope is to get Exxon to do what I want to get done through jawboning and coercion."

Exxon was called upon to do what it did best: organize and transport equipment, position that equipment, call up the specialists and the work force, make arrangements with a host of subcontractors, and keep track of the money. It tended to use three basic approaches—beach washing, chemical applications, and bioremediation. Bioremediation, which used fertilizer to enhance the oil-eating capabilities of resident microbes, proved promising, but generally the predisposition was for massive, systemic remedies applied by armies of workers and hundreds of machines. To a degree this was an inescapable condition of the situation, and it was not entirely Exxon's fault. The state of Alaska and the public generally were applying intense pressure to remove all possible unsightliness, even beyond reason.

In another time, 50 years ago, or maybe only 30, Americans would have eulogized the display of machine and muscle, but that time is gone, even for Alaska. Instead, what we had was the awful detritus, oil on the beaches, and then the whitened, steam-cleaned beaches, pale as the whiteness of Melville's "transcendent horror," and beneath the surface of those beaches the oil still there, thick in the substrate, and the intrusion of the workers, the graffiti carved on the rocks, the trash, the beaten-down growth, the dance pounded out to the beat of internal combustion engines both small and large, running day and night, upon "pristine"*

---

* Just what constitutes "pristine"? The waters of Prince William Sound were already heavily affected by fishing and, historically, by the fur trade. The landforms are somewhat less heavily affected than the waterways, although there is mining, the growing timber industry, and the tourist industry, which includes activities such as glacier climbing and aerial hunting, and in general the new rage for adventure as hobby. Practically speaking, Prince William Sound is (or was) relatively pristine. On the other hand, the Alaskan historian, Morgan Sherwood, argues in his essay, "The Wilderness and Alaska," that any area acces-

environments. The culture was locked inside a loop, an infantile solipsism on a massive scale.

The culture that perfected the mechanized way of being, then spilled the oil, stayed true to itself. It proposed to redeem itself by using the very mental set that had caused the spill in the first place. In the process, incidentally, it consumed yet more of the raw material that it used to drive itself, and its way of being, than it had spilled. Eighteen million gallons of refined fuel (gasoline, diesel), or in volume about 160 percent of the 11 million gallons originally spilled, were used to operate the cleanup machinery, and this says nothing of the fuel that was used to manufacture and ship the equipment, or to bring the workers here. There's a large leak in the system, which would be a great deal less troubling if the oil spill and cleanup were a discrete event. It was not. The parallel systemic leak occurs across the land. Despite improvements in the efficiency of motor vehicles, American consumption of petroleum has continued to rise in the last 15 years. In the meantime, the culture lives within its own mythology of machines and world proprietorship. Exxon is the second largest corporation in the United States and the world's third largest energy supplier,[†] but to ask it to stand apart from the delusion of the dominant world culture is to ask a great deal.

In Prince William Sound, the alternative—once the oil had been spilled, once the initial retrieval and dispersant strategies had failed—was to come in softly, discreetly pick up what oil could be picked up, employ what beneficent means were available, such as bioremediation, and leave the rest to winter. Once the oil was there, the die was cast. To accept this meant to acknowledge one's own lack of purity. This line of thought is not intended to undercut individual and early grassroots responses such as those undertaken by Tom Copeland, or Kelly Weaverling's animal

---

sible to modern transportation, which all of Alaska, indeed all of the world, now is, no longer constitutes a wilderness. It logically follows, therefore, that there is no longer any such thing as wilderness. The Exxon call-up, for the potential it displayed, and the pressure from the Alaskan government to advance that potential, would seem to validate Sherwood's point quite completely.

Exxon and the state of Alaska waged a war of semantics over when a shoreline was environmentally stable—and this became a pivot in the ensuing litigation. Exxon proposed that environmentally stable meant capable of supporting viable life; the state, actually supporting that life—two different views of damage.

[†] In 1989, according to rankings by *Business Week*, only IBM was larger than Exxon among U.S. corporations. In 1980 Exxon was the world's largest oil company, but by 1988 it had fallen behind the state-owned Saudi Aramco and Royal Dutch/Shell. The rise of OPEC and increased nationalization of oil sites and concessions during the 1970s and 1980s heightened the competition among members of the old oil trust, including Exxon. This, together with the American demand for low fuel prices and shareholders' demand for high revenues, is a factor in the cost-saving measures applied to petroleum production and shipping.

rescue fleet, or the ad hoc citizens' advisory committee in Valdez. Quite the contrary. Their work was heartfelt, genuinely effective, and conducted outside the bureaucratic channel that was dug once Exxon and the government entities took control. They were among the first to appreciate their own failings, but if one of my children were drowning, I would want to have Tom Copeland, Kelly Weaverling, or Riki Ott there.

As the *Alpha Helix* passed it that evening, I stood on the deck and looked into Herring Bay. It had a broad opening and I knew that it penetrated deeply into the island. Its mouth was conveniently cocked in the direction the oil had come from. Its ragged shores were a series of coves and inlets. It had its own small islands and peninsulas. It was like a Prince William Sound in miniature, and a favored haven for seals, otters, sea lions, and migrating birds.

We were in the heart of the long twilight. I could see the pale rigging lights of small boats, the outlines of large boats and barges, the sometimes resplendently illuminated hotel boats. Distant laughter came faintly across the water from the bunches of vessels crammed together like small towns.

It was impossible not to think of the animals. The beaches were now ghettoes. The power of despoilment came from somewhere else, made its visitation, then passed on, leaving its waste of noise and junk. It was an assault by oil supplanted by a like assault of machinery and chemistry. These places had never heard such engines, or felt such focused high-pressure spray or such heat, or been stripped, as they sometimes were, of gravel and rock. They had never been walked upon by so many feet, had never been left this way, black with death, white with death.

Chapter 10

THE RAPTURE
OF SCIENCE

The *Alpha Helix* drew away from Knight Island, then passed Ingot and Eleanor islands. I stood outside on the rear deck and gazed down along our wake through the legs of the crane mounted on the stern. The clusters of lights faded slowly from view. We passed the same navy ship we'd seen early that morning. It was a gray outline resting on the dark water. In the distance were the ragged peaks of Knight Island and over to the west the mainland. Bruce Martin, the ship's Able Bodied Seaman, came out and began checking through the whaler and Zodiacs, the engines, lines, tanks.

He moved fast. He was a Yup'ik Eskimo from Nome up on the Seward Peninsula. A small man, hardly over five feet tall, he had at times an explosive personality. Quick to anger when his deckhands screwed up, or when he felt pushed by the science crew, but just as quick to laugh, he was trusted implicitly by the captain, Tom Callahan. He called me over to the rail of the deck and pointed eastward. "Tanker," he said. We had now come into the open water between Eleanor Island and the Naked Island complex and had a good view across the tanker channel. A tanker had come into sight from behind Naked Island as it steamed toward the Hinchinbrook Entrance. I stared at it, impressed by its tininess in the distance.

A few days earlier, I'd asked Bruce how he felt about the spill, and he'd spat out his response, "It's another bullet!" According to Bruce, it all began with the forced relocation of Eskimos by the Russians for the sake of the fur trade in the eighteenth and early nineteenth centuries. When the Russians sold Alaska to the United States in 1867, the Russians asked the United States if it wanted the Eskimos as part of the deal or if it wanted Russia to move them out. "That tells you everything," Bruce had said.

Prior to the passage of the Alaska Native Claims Settlement Act in 1971, the controversial resolution in law to the question of Native land claims, Bruce said he'd traveled around to the villages to tell them not to vote for acceptance. The primary impetus for the legislation was the push to open oil production on the North Slope, to which the Native land claims were a legal impediment. By turning the land over to Native corporations as private land (as opposed to the "trust" or reservation system), Congress presented the Native people with a host of legal and economic problems that they were not initially prepared to deal with and that would change their lives forever. Bruce said he'd told his people to send their children to school to become lawyers so they could defend themselves and not pay out all the money to corporation lawyers. He'd said, "At first a village would think it could hire one lawyer, then they were told they had to hire a firm, so the villages ended up paying ten lawyers. The village elders who were put in charge of negotiations were picked by the government, not by their own people. So the elders were put in a very bad position. How could they decide all these things? The settlement act was just a way for the outside corporations to get their hands on the land."

Bruce said he'd got disgusted and had gone down to Seattle to live, that he'd joined the Seattle Native Corporation. "But then finally I had to come back," he said. I had the definite impression that he'd had a hard time in Seattle, that he'd nearly lost his life there, that he'd passed directly out of the crisis of his people and into a personal one.

Now, in the few minutes we'd stood side by side at the rail, looking out, the tanker had grown abruptly larger. They had that capacity to appear small, to appear to be barely moving, and then suddenly to seem huge and fast. Fishermen told of seeing a tanker in the distance and of starting to cross the channel, but then discovering before they were in the clear that they were barely going to make it. The Alpha Helix altered its course northward. In a few moments, the tanker grew smaller again. Members of the science crew began to drift out to the deck, then work their way up the gangways toward the foredeck. We were going to pass

the Exxon *Valdez*, one person said. At times, the science crew transformed itself into tourists.

Out of the blue, Bruce said, "It's all lost now. Only a handful of the
Eskimos still believe in the old way." Then he fell silent. I leaned out,
looked toward the bow, and caught a glimpse of the *Valdez*, its long,
slender shape on the water. Bruce and I stayed where we were, our
bodies rocking gently to and fro with the motion of the ship on the
water.

"The Eskimos believed in dimensions," Bruce said. "This life is lived
on one dimension. If you do well, you will pass on to the next dimension, but you'll still be here. If you do bad, if you commit suicide, then
you have to do this dimension over again."

The *Alpha Helix* made an arc and now we had a good view of the *Valdez*.
There were smaller boats scattered around it, and a large work barge
pulled up to its side. In the water, strips of boom and patches of oil
sheen caught the fading light. By then, I felt as though I'd seen the ship
a thousand times. Bruce said, "Everything considered, it's a positive way
of looking at things."

Many times after that, I would think of what he'd said, of the idea of
dimensions as opposed to the remote afterlife I'd been raised to believe
in, and of the fluidity of the relation between ethical behavior and the
several levels of life as opposed to the rigid dualism of heaven and hell,
and most of all of the idea of the other dimensions being here as opposed to somewhere else. It seemed to me that to have the other worlds
of one's life bound up inextricably with where one happened to be now
was at its very foundation a less fractured and more adult way of seeing.

Later, a group of us gathered in the galley. John Oliver came and
dawdled over a bowl of ice cream, then disappeared. There was a re-
flective air among us, probably because we had pulled away from Knight
Island. The most demanding and the worst was over. Some of us were
still finishing dinner. What had begun on the first day out as a set schedule for meals had by now dissolved into shifts that stretched into the
evening. Trish Kaminsky accommodated the crew by working irregular
hours herself. I gathered that she liked this group, as opposed to some
of the other officious science crews she'd cooked for.

Trish was in the kitchen now. It was after nine. She was a big woman,
well over six feet tall, well read, and given to conversations that took a
spiritual drift. When I'd first met her, I'd thought—*basketball*. She had told
me that she was considering writing a novel about living an entire life
under the threat of nuclear war. The remains of the night's dinner—

broiled chicken, potatoes, green beans, potato salad, green salad—still lay in the deep pans between the eating area and the kitchen. We ate extremely well. Rikk Kvitek and Diane Carney, an M.A. student from Santa Cruz, came in to eat, and Rikk, who rarely paused for anything, sat for a while and talked. Finally, Dan Reed, a kelp forest ecologist who had recently completed his Ph.D. at the University of California at Santa Barbara, Gordon Robilliard, Bruce Stewart, and I remained at one of the tables. I could see straight ahead through the doorway to the lab. Another of the graduate students, Stacey Kim, was entering the day's findings into a computer. Beyond her at a bench against the far wall, Kathy Conlan was busily cataloguing her specimens. To my left, Trish thumped around in the kitchen.

The three scientists at the table were probing what they'd seen. Gordon said, "In the intertidal community we've got pretty much what we'd expect." He meant that what had not been killed by the initial onslaught of oil was still there, and remained reasonably healthy. This reinforced what the rest of the crew had been seeing in the intertidal communities and put the onus on the massive cleanup effort.

Hunter Lenehan, another of the Moss Landing graduate students, came in and searched the cooler for something to drink. Hunter wore a pair of sweats and a red T-shirt with a black picture of Che Guevera. "I always dive with Che," he'd said. Of all the crew members, it was Hunter who had been the most clearly thunderstruck by what we'd seen at Herring Bay. He'd come back to the *Alpha Helix* cursing, and John Oliver had had to shush him down.

The ship's engines kept up a low, steady growl. Over in the kitchen, Trish ran a mixer, then opened an oven door and bent to look inside. Bruce Stewart said, "The cold water may have something to do with it. In more temperate zones, we'd see things like tumors on the coral."

Gordon said, "Coral is truly stationary, but that sort of thing could still happen here over time. The oil will probably affect the algae and so a lot of the herbivores."

Algae and anemones are nearly stationary. Bivalves, starfish, sea slugs, and crustaceans are less so. The migratory fish and marine mammals— salmon, say—and killer whales are capable of moving great distances. The degree of a creature's mobility, combined with other factors, made them more or less vulnerable to various types of what scientists rather euphemistically referred to as "perturbances."

The more stationary creatures in intertidal habitats that might be washed and rewashed repeatedly with oil would often be the most vulnerable. There are exceptions, mobile creatures such as otters, who have their own peculiar vulnerabilities of physique and habit. It was not clear whether mobile creatures were altogether avoiding the oil or swimming into it. The seals we had seen at North Twin Bay on Elrington Island, popping up, disappearing, and popping up again just beyond the margin of the oil slick, would seem clearly to have been avoiding the oil. Scientists who had observed marine mammals swim directly into the oil from open water, or flocks of birds landing in it, would argue that animals had no such avoidance capability. That such conversations, which presumed the superiority of human sentience, took place in proximity to oil-soaked beaches seemed peculiar at best.

"The point," Gordon said, "is that we're not seeing dead communities. It's going to take a lot of looking before we're sure of anything, but for now the communities are not dead. They've been perturbed, but at five to seven feet below the waterline, we're still seeing communities that have certainly not come back in the three months since the spill. They were there before, and they're still there now."

Because of his experience, knowledge, and his association with Exxon, Gordon's views had quickly become the focus of the conversation. Earlier, he had told me that even the chief accountant Exxon had brought up from Houston had been staggered by the amount of oil spill response money—something on the order of 10 million a day—that was pouring out of the company coffers. Gordon had added that so far as he could see the large-scale cleanup would accomplish two things: it would employ Alaskans, and it would get the deepest pools of oil picked up off the beaches.

Now, Bruce Stewart said, "The other thing would be reproduction rates. The effect of the oil on reproduction would be subtle and hard to track. The clams' reproductive reaction would affect clams first, but we might not be able to see it until it moved farther down the line. Then when we did see it we might not know where it was coming from."

This was the issue that would preoccupy oil spill observers and much of the scientific work for months and years to come. How much damage? What kind of damage? How far-reaching? As Bruce had put it, the issue bore upon the effect reduced numbers in one species might have upon that species' survival, and next upon the effect reduced numbers in one species might have upon another, predatory or otherwise dependent species. It bore upon the lasting effects toxic exposure might have upon survival and genetic make-up, and upon passing toxicity on what is commonly known as the food chain, though the image "chain" evokes in the mind—a linear system of interlocked links—is hardly accurate. It's more like a convoluted, three-dimensional net, the far edges of which are well beyond apprehension. Computer-driven models on the order of Mandelbrot fractals come nearest to representing the ever-widening domain of the net and the simultaneous ever-diminishing, microscopic detail of the linkages.

Butter clams live in fine gravel or sand and feed upon tiny bits of food gathered willy-nilly from the bottom by ciliary action. A primary food source in the sound, these clams may be dug out of the sand, drawn from their shells, and ingested by sea stars. Sea stars range the bottom and rocks for scallops, too, and for urchins, nudibranches, sea cucumbers, dead fish. They will cannibalize other sea stars. Urchins graze the algae for food. Crabs, fish, otters, ducks, and sea gulls eat urchins. They are also a traditional food of Aleut people. Sea stars are eaten by the dominant sea floor species, the tanner crab, and by the less abundant but larger king crab. Larval crabs feed on plankton, diatoms, and barnacle larvae. Juvenile tanner crabs eat diatoms, algae, and hydroids. Juvenile king crabs eat diatoms, algae, sponges, copepods, polychaetes, small clams, gastropods, and sea urchins. In addition to sea stars, adult king crabs will eat algae, mollusks, polychaetes, and fish. Leeches may live and lay their eggs on king crabs. They are eaten along with the crabs by walleye pollock and halibut. People eat butter clams, fish, king crab, and birds. Octopuses eat adult king crabs. Octopuses are eaten by halibut, sea lions, and people.

Otters eat butter clams by the method that has endeared them to aquarium visitors all across the country. An otter dives, scoops up clams and a small rock, returns to the surface, lies on its back and sculls the water with its tail. It places the rock on its chest and cracks open the clam shells by striking them against the rock. Sometimes sea otters develop an affection for a certain rock. After primates, the sea otter is considered the most adept user of tools in the world. It will also tie itself down with seaweed while it sleeps. It is a voracious eater, consuming 20 percent of its weight each day. Killer whales and sharks eat sea otters.

Though far from an exhaustive portrait of the near tidal zone, this may suggest the scope and detail of the exchange, all of which is further influenced from location to location by physical conditions—the density of the flora, the topography of the bottom, the nature of the surface, the degree of exposure, the energy of the wave action. An oil-caused genetic defect picked up initially by, say, clams in polluted sand, or by urchins grazing oil-coated algae, and perhaps reinforced by doses from other sources along the line, might be discovered many steps removed from its source, in a sea lion, say, or a killer whale, and it would then be virtually impossible to trace it back with precision.

Gordon's response to Bruce was measured. "Clams are free spawners," he said. "Even a substantial reduction in reproductive capacity probably wouldn't show up because of larvae recruitment and resettlement from the outside." He was met with silence. After a moment, he said, "Look, my whole thing is community response. In a situation like this, it's either going to be real dramatic in a small area, or else you'll have a small-scale response spread over a large area. But typically, man, creating an oil spill like this, can't touch the effect of something like a hard freeze, or an earthquake, or a change in currents like El Niño."

Some of the bite in Gordon's observations derived from his position. John Oliver, an old friend of his, would later tell me that Gordon, like many of the experts Exxon had brought in, found much of his energy directed at conflict resolution. John would say, "Gordon can't produce truly accurate results because they may not be accepted by Exxon. His work is defined by the conditions of his employment, so as a biologist he mainly finds ways to design research programs that will resolve conflict."

I understood John not to mean that Gordon's findings themselves were inaccurate, but rather the results that followed the findings—this a consequence of conflicts between the findings and Exxon's response to them; with the balancing off of what Gordon found with what others had found; with determining which findings would be shared, and when, and with whom, and how his findings meshed with the needs of other departments in the company and with the needs of individual managers, whose first function was to protect their position; and finally with how it all fit into Exxon's purpose, which was to minimize and resolve its conflict with the state of Alaska, the Coast Guard, the American public, and Congress. A few scraps of information in that context had the potency of a butter clam in a high-energy habitat.

At my side, Dan Reed, who had been quiet up to this point, said, "We don't have any control over freezes and El Niño. To have a disturbance caused by human error is different. For one thing, human disturbances are often recurrent and you have to consider not only the severity but also the frequency. And here, it's really obvious that there's damage."

Bruce said, "But maybe it's impossible to prove longterm damage."

Dan said, "That's a different question. What sort of damage is acceptable?"

Bruce got up to put his plate in the dish bin, then came back and sat down. "I suppose that's the dangerous thing about the research," he said, "that when they're done, they'll have to say it's no big deal."

The research he was referring to had evolved from the original scientific meetings in Valdez. An umbrella organization called the Damage

Assessment Project (DAP) had been formed. It was headed by a board of trustees made up of representatives of the state of Alaska and the federal government, including the secretary of the interior. Federal and state agencies, such as the Alaska Department of Fish and Wildlife, NOAA and its various subagencies, the Department of Fish and Game, etc., sponsored or contracted out research activities by a host of scientists. Frequently a private subcontractor, such as Dames and Moore, was involved.

Among the papers in the briefcase at Gordon's elbow were some 60 scientific Project Files outlining research undertaken under the auspices of DAP. On our first day out from Seward, I had sat at this table with Gordon and John Oliver while John looked through the two-inch pile. As he had moved deeper into the pile, John's initial businesslike approach began to flicker into a kind of wonderment. He sat hunched over the pile with his elbows on the table, looked sideways at Gordon, and frowned quizzically. He began to laugh and, in an allusion to the Mad Hatter's advice to the March Hare, said, "We're buttering our watches." He thrashed through the papers, snapping them down one after another, and looked up again and said, "But it's the best butter." He meant that the quality of the scientific work that had been contracted had little relation to the mechanism to which it was being applied.

At his side, Gordon chuckled. I looked through the files later. Some of the projects were in principle fairly rudimentary, involving counts such as the kittiwake census we'd seen in its initial stages, but many were highly technical and involved both extensive field and laboratory work—tissue samplings, for example, and the numerous water column studies. The projects included studies of flora—eel grass, algae, kelp—and analyses of creatures of all descriptions: diatoms, marine worms, amphipods, shrimp, oyster larvae, herring, salmon, pollock, river and sea otters, seals, whales, migratory birds, resident birds, deer, bears. One not atypical study of salmon (Fish/Shellfish Study #3) proposed to assess survival rates, harvest rates, and the return rates of various species of salmon over a period of years. Another (Fish/Shellfish Study #11) proposed to study the occurrence of herring spawn in oiled and unoiled inlets and to chart lethal and sublethal effects, such as fin erosion, neoplasms, lesions, and the accumulation of hydrocarbon concentrations in bile and roe.

Even the simplest was open-ended, allowing a vent for future study. A relatively straightforward otter mortality study (Marine Mammal Study #6), for example, included a plan to "instrument" otters with radio transmitters so that their mortality and distribution following the spill could be followed. Such provisions made for good science, of course, but they also made for continued funding. The above-mentioned salmon study had a budget of $1,943,400; the herring study, $374,500; and the otter study (with which Chuck Monnett of Cordova finally became involved), $763,000. All those figures were through February 1990 only, and the bulk of the projects were subsequently funded for continuation. As of February 1990, the total allotted for the studies conducted under the State and Federal Natural Resources Damage Assessment Plan came to $35,420,900. Funding was then renewed through March of 1991 for another $37,330,000. In a sense, the entire undertaking was an exact analogue to funding granted otherwise to subcontractors, government employees, engineers, marine equipment outlets, communities, beach workers. It was a maelstrom of money.

At the time we were on the *Alpha Helix* the figures were not known to us, but John certainly read in the level of funding. He bent over the files again, then looked up, wide-eyed, and said, "This is incredible. Everybody is doing something. We're managing the shit out of this spill!"

Gordon rocked back in his chair and said, "A good scientist never passes up a good boondoggle."

Now, in the galley with Bruce, Dan, and myself, Gordon said, "You have to separate the ecological effects from the effect on people—from the economics of it, from philosophy, aesthetics."

By economics, I gathered he was referring to effects like that upon the fishing industry, whose seasons were at times shut down completely, not because the fish they caught would necessarily be hazardous to people's health but because the slightest intimation of the presence of oil on a catch had a devastating effect upon the perception of the market, and so upon prices. By philosophy, I suspected, knowing his predilections, that he meant in particular what he regarded as the sentimentally driven response of the environmentally disposed population. He had already introduced me to the concept of what he called "the Bambi effect," that is, the public reaction to the death of otters, those apparently cuddly creatures who were regarded—usually in a photograph or from the other side of an aquarium glass—as a symbol of the fallen. By aesthetics, he meant the extraordinary ugliness of oil on a beach.

I had to wonder at what point the separation of the appearance of destruction from the measurement of destruction allowed the measuring, or the scientific romance with quantities, to obscure the reality of destruction. The interest of clarity was served well by separating fields of study and thought into categories, but left unassimilated with other forms of knowing, the compartments of science were ripe for misuse by politicians, journalists, private corporations, and true believers of all description, to say nothing of the broken sense of being that living within a fractured world produced.

"If there's a synergism going on," Bruce said, "there's a point where you say this system's maximally perturbed, like a human body with drugs. If the system's lined up just right, or if the addict's chemistry is critically loaded, you can tweak it. If the synergism is on the upsurge, you could knock the system out. If you pollute it only once in a while, maybe it'll be okay. But if it's repeated, there's no question but that you're going to have a disturbance. Sometimes you have to avoid what you can't know for certain."

Dan said, "It's really obvious that there's damage here. That is certain. You don't have to look very hard to see that."

"But you still can't prove longterm damage," Bruce said.

"That's a different question," Dan said. "What level, or what kind of damage is acceptable?"

Although Dan's response was directed to Bruce, the real opposition in the exchange lay between Dan and Gordon. The heaviness of Gordon's bearing expressed the weight of the obligations he carried, and the years of experience and frustration. I liked Gordon and respected the rigor of his mind. I liked his self-containment. After he finished his paperwork in the evenings, he would go out to the deck and stand alone for hours, fishing. A couple of days later, as we approached Cordova, he expressed his disappointment at having to get off the ship and go back to the bureaucrats. He had a feel for the world. He was the type of person who could lay down a hand firmly but gently and make things move. It was the touch of a farmer. When Gordon spoke to you, though, he often looked away, which I took not to be self-effacement but the sign of a sadness he held close to himself.

Dan was filled with promise. I had even heard John Oliver suggest to Gordon that Dan might be somebody Gordon would want to take into his consulting company. When he spoke, he looked you directly in the eye. Dan had qualities equal to Gordon's, but the application of those powers upon the world had yet to break down his idealism. He retained a faith in remedies that Gordon seemed to have lost. I empathized with Gordon, and yet I agreed with Dan and put my hopes in him.

"It's a risk-analysis game," Gordon said. "How much are you willing to pay for the privilege of driving your Cadillac around?"

Dan, holding to his point, said, "The effect on otters and birds is obvious, while the intertidal community is more resilient. That's all."

Bruce, who was playing the role of the trigger in this conversation, said, "Look at DDT. Could you have proved there was a problem before the effects started turning up? There may be an incredible effect happening here that we can't see."

"It'd be a lot easier to track the effects on humans who bathe at sea," Gordon said. "They drown."

Dan said, "Man and society have a responsibility for their effect on the environment."

"Concern has nothing to do with ecological effect. That's a smoke-screen. Look at the newspapers," Gordon said. And again, though it was the subterranean despair that he expressed as contempt for the meanderings of public information, Gordon's point was accurate enough. For all the play the Alaskan oil spill had been given in the media—even bracketing the massacre at Tiananmen Square—and for all the eagerness with which the latest ecological horror stories were lapped up, for all the noise and furor, there were only the faintest indications of any attempt to realistically address the root causes of the oil spill, which might have come in the form of a mass petroleum fast, or the acceptance of, say, a dollar-a-gallon surcharge on gasoline to be used to research alternate energy sources and to effectively police oil production and shipping. Gordon was avoiding the question both Dan and Bruce were putting to him, about dealing with what might not be proven and therefore not predicted but was clearly manifest—the destruction.

"Of course, we've got to stop spilling oil," Gordon said. "Regulations will probably get tightened up. The Clean Water Act will probably become law. Better traffic systems for tankers, double-hulled tankers, etcetera, will be instituted. In the case of the Exxon *Valdez*, though, a double hull wouldn't have made any difference.* It's hard to legislate against human fuckups."

Bruce returned to his tweak theory, which was a version of the final straw on the camel's back—the last ounce of poison that threw a stressed habitat into havoc, or the one confused helmsman who put a tanker from a strained shipping system on the rocks. "So far as error and contingency backups are concerned," he said, "if you get all the conditions lined up just right, something will happen."

"Maybe," Gordon said. "But on the other hand, if they'd had ships from the North Sea and thousands and thousands of feet of boom, maybe they could have controlled the spill. The North Sea has ships dedicated to oil spill cleanup. If you had one of them, and then a way to pick up the oil, you might have been able to get most of it, but then you

---

* Gordon was right with virtually all of his prophecies but wrong about the *Valdez*. Following assessment of the damage to the tanker, experts, including the Coast Guard, reported that a double hull could have reduced the spill by as much as 60 percent.

would still have the economic problems with the fisheries, and the out-cry, and also the tendency of people to become indifferent again. Oil coming out of a tanker, at three to four feet high, then moving over itself downhill, it's a tremendous amount of energy and very hard to contain. The viewpoints need to be balanced in discussions such as this."

Dan still held tenaciously to his point. "Regarding the otters," he said, "first think that they are a separate population, and endangered."

Gordon said, "It's never been clear to me that we have to protect isolated species as opposed to protecting the species in general."

"You have to protect the gene pool," Dan said, "and you have to begin somewhere and stop somewhere."

Gordon said, "One of the problems with an oil spill is that certain species cannot adapt genetically." He meant species like otters, with their near-shoreline feeding habits, their specialized insulating fur, their 670,000 hairs per square inch, their need to constantly groom that fur, their peculiar vulnerability. When exposed to oil as they had been, the effect was mass death. For them, it was like Bhopal.

Dan said, "Right, and if spills are repeated, other organisms will adapt and become over-evolutionized. They'll adapt to oil. This produces a new kind of vulnerability both in those that have adapted and in those that haven't."

Gordon smiled at Dan. "Yeah, as soon as the animals get up on the learning curve, we'll run out of oil. If petroleum were radiation, we'd really be in trouble. Something definitely toxic, both short- and longterm would be very different." Though still shot through with cynicism and irony, it was Gordon's peace offering, a kind of salute to Dan.

Late in the voyage, I would try once again to learn from John Oliver exactly what he and his crew had found. This was two days after Gordon Robilliard had left the ship.

"It's a mew," John said.

He was referring to the emotionally indeterminate sound of a kitten; he judged that the findings would be soft and inconclusive. He spoke of the failure of the federal Fish and Wildlife agency to put scientists in front of the spill to gather what data they could before the oil hit. "Without evidence from immediately before and immediately following the spill, you have nothing," John said. "It's a wipeout. There are no baselines. The evidence is gone."

My mind flashed back to the question that I had carried onto the *Alpha Helix*: What, truly, is the damage? And more specifically for the scientists on this ship: What about the damage to the kelp, the starfish, mussels, worms, and to the shellfish the otters required, what about the effects of the wholesale removal of the keystone predator, the otter, and what about the likelihood of longterm toxic damage to the lower reaches of the food chain? What about the evidence that only science could provide? Although the days spent on the ship had certainly eroded innocence, I retained enough of it to hope that simple persistence might still yield the answers to some of those questions. I had begun spending a lot of time in the company of Dan Reed and had enjoyed the benefit of his positiveness. Dan was with us now at the table. Dan didn't speak. I was stunned by John's answer.

"This is a garbage can," he said. "We've got this garbage can full of shit, and we're playing it just outside the lip. We're no different from anybody else." He was angry, but not at me. He was talking about how scientists get their funding. His anger was in part directed at himself. He stared at me again and waited. Normally, he waited for nothing and nobody. He was usually irrepressible. He loved his work. His life was bound up in science, in the "stories," as he put it, that it told.

Two days before, after a series of dives off the eastern side of Naked Island, we'd beached two Zodiacs on the small Storey Island, the northernmost of the Naked Island complex. A group of us had climbed up a 20-foot rock abutment from the beach and entered a glade. It was morning and light fell in shafts upon the ground. The shadows were dark. In the light, the tall, green grass that grew between the rocks was bright. There was a muskeg, dotted with large rocks. Lichen covered the rocks. Green moss blanketed the lower trunks of the huge spruce trees that grew around the muskeg. There were big skunk cabbages and small, pastel-colored mushrooms—lavender, mauve, and pale yellow. We found a heap of bear scat at the foot of a tree, still steaming in the cool air. It was a strange wonderland, made to seem stranger by the fact that we were well under ten miles from the Exxon *Valdez'* anchorage. John came into the glade, filled with the electricity of delight. He moved this way and that, looking, then nearly running, extending his survey, and bending to look down, and leaning back to look up, then vanishing over the top of a knoll. In a moment, he came back, his eyes gleaming and his face filled with the pleasure of the world he loved.

At this moment in the ship's galley, though, his face was drawn taut, and the rapture had been turned inside out to its equally compelling opposite, disgust. I stared back at him. I had also suddenly become angry, and at him, and I felt a terrible coldness entering my belly. Only afterwards would I realize I had commiserated with him, that the despair he obviously felt over the biological unanswerables was more informed than but fundamentally akin to my own. The outrage he felt over what was perfectly obvious, the wanton death caused by the oil and the sense of self-compromise and helplessness the money triggered, was exactly the same as my own. Though more specifically directed, perhaps, more exact, more confined, he was telling me the same thing that the University of California's Todd La Porte would tell the Oil Commission in August—that the consequences were greater than the value of the lessons, that in this particular scenario we had already passed through the veil to the other side where what we learned didn't matter anymore.

"Look," John said. "We don't want to get too close to the dump. We hold out our cups underneath the rim of the can to catch a little of the shit that's trickling over the top. That's all. We want to get enough of it to do our work. But we don't want to get any dirtier than we have to."

After leaving the Naked Island complex, after I had been on the beach just off Flent Point with Gordon, Peter Slattery, and Kathy Conlan, and had seen the plover and the brown bear, Tom Callahan, eased the *Alpha Helix* up Glacier Bay to within several hundred yards of the face of Columbia Glacier. The ship seemed much closer than that, but as with all things pertaining to size and distance here, the reckoning was tricky. In fact, the front of the glacier was 300 feet tall. Its width was four miles. The ship lightly bumped the growlers and steered clear of the bergy bits, those big ones that might drift out from behind Glacier Island and across the tanker channel. We had come very near to one source of the calamity. The icebergs were blue and white. The front of the glacier was white streaked with blue. On it were huge mounds of black earth. The water was pale blue, laden with cream-colored silt. There was no oil here.

On the icebergs were harbor seals, sometimes one or two on an iceberg, sometimes as many as 20. The seals pup on the icebergs and haul out to rest. One seal, curious, perhaps, or playful, or perhaps running point for the others, swam back and forth in front of the ship's bow. I leaned over the prow to look at it and wondered again about the sentience of animals. Tom Callahan cut the engines and let the ship glide silently. There was the sound of icebergs cracking, like huge ice cubes in a glass. It was as if we were inside the glass. At times, a huge chunk would fall off the face of the glacier and make the roaring sound like thunder. A couple of minutes afterwards, a wave would wash by and the ship would rock.

The entire crew had come out on the foredeck to look, everyone. At first, there was excited talk, but then gradually everyone fell quiet. The ship, a blunt, benign probe, slipped past icebergs that rose above our heads. The seals were dark, as if etched against the ice. They were acutely watchful of the ship. The icebergs came in shapes as various as clouds. Some had ledges for the seals to gather on. Others had tunnels for them to dive through. We edged nearer to the dangerous face of the glacier. The place was still just as it should have been. The sight was eerie and wonderful, the silence, the cracking, the white and blue and black, and light-blue water and pale gray sky, everything huge. The air was cold and white.

II MONEY

Chapter 11

GUESTS

. . . it is to symbols they are reacting when they believe they are acting upon reality. . . . The irrational system rules political life no less. . . . The criterion of maturity: the ability to resist symbols. But mankind grows younger all the time.

—Milan Kundera, *The Art of the Novel*, 1986

On September 28, 13 days after Exxon had officially closed down its cleanup exercise for the year, the *Orca II* came out from behind Glacier Island and crossed the Valdez Arm. As we approached the lee side of Busby and Bligh islands, David Grimes pointed out a line in the water. "Out here," he said. "You can see exactly where the wind chop is and where it isn't." On one side of the line the water had a ragged look. We were in that, and the *Orca II* pitched as it cruised. The water was blue and green and chalky with glacial sediment. On the other side of the line, the water appeared smooth, viscous, and darker, almost like gelatin. We crossed into the calm water, shaped a course around Busby Island and into the Tatitlek Narrows between the mainland and Bligh Island. The navigation charts showed reefs all around the island and a solid bank of them within the narrows. David located the channel and guided the boat along it. It was midafternoon and the three of us—David, Lynn Schooler, and myself—stood in the wheelhouse, looking out. We'd been on the water for five days. We were headed for home port, Cordova.

Following their work on the ad hoc citizens' advisory committee to the Valdez triumvirate (Exxon, Alaska, the Coast Guard), David and Rick

Steiner had traveled to Sullom Voe, a marine terminal on the Shetland Islands that ships 6 million barrels a day of North Sea crude oil. There, in if anything harsher conditions, they found a very different situation from the one at Valdez. Sullom Voe is located just 30 miles south of the same latitude as Valdez, but 6,000 miles to the east in the North Atlantic. Sullom Voe's majority owner is British Petroleum, and Exxon holds an interest in it. Several key Alyeska figures, including its president, George Nelson, and James Hermiller, who was appointed to run day-to-day operations during the summer and would replace Nelson as president in October of 1989—were also BP executives. Interestingly, BP essentially vanished from sight in Valdez, along with Alyeska, following the Exxon *Valdez* spill. At Sullom Voe, where there had been a big spill a dozen years ago, Steiner and Grimes learned there was an oil spill contingency plan in place that looked very similar on paper to Alyeska's. The difference was that it had been put into practice. Unlike the Alyeska terminal, Sullom Voe had reels of boom permanently deployed at sensitive areas, random helicopter surveillance of tanker traffic, full radar coverage, a permanent on-site pollution response team, regular drills, pilots who rode tankers to the open sea, regular inspections of tankers, more tugs used for berthing, and backup assistance for major spills available within 24 hours. Sullom Voe has not had another major spill since instituting its plan.

David and Rick returned with a clear sense that, as David said, "It was the delivery system that was at fault," and the contingency plan in place at Alyeska was "laughable." It was quite evident to them that the oil companies had cut their costs and allowed procedures to become sloppy where they could get away with it, as in Valdez. From there, Rick and David set off on separate but sometimes converging paths to redress the wrong. Their paths would also entwine with those of many others . . . Riki Ott, Marilyn Leland, Jack Lamb, Kelly Weaverling, Larry Smith and Marge Tillion of Homer, John Mickelson of Seldovia.

Rick Steiner finally became deeply involved in a remarkable attempt to resolve the tangle of civil and criminal proceedings by proposing, through a new group called The Coastal Coalition, that damages be settled out of court and be paid by establishing a fund for, among other things, acquiring and placing in trust Prince William Sound timber rights. (In 1990, David joined Rick in this effort.) Following his return from Sullom Voe, David had followed his gift for binding people together and his role as the metaphysician of the spill. He coproduced a documentary video, *Voices of the Sound.* He then acquired the *Orca II* under what he described as an almost magical convergence of circumstances.

He had wanted to put an independent vessel in Prince William Sound—one not bound up with Exxon or the government. Because of the completeness of the vessel call-up for the cleanup, this would make the *Orca II* a rarity, maybe one of a kind. It became known as a "spiritual cleanup vessel." David had said, "Spiritual cleanup was what we needed. Physical cleanup would not address the underlying problems." Although David himself seemed often filled with doubts over his effectiveness, his approach displayed both the artist's vision of the way the sound, the oil, the turmoil, and distant political forces were an interconnected and fundamentally spiritual webwork, and the activist's sense that at times the best way into the heart of trouble would be found by patiently working the edges.

The *Orca II* is wooden, 38 feet long and 10 feet at the beam, with a 115-horsepower Chrysler gasoline engine that rumbles throatily and inspires confidence. A Jacobsen boat, it was built in 1946. Its hull is white above the waterline, trimmed with dark blue. The abovedecks are white trimmed with brown, its masts festooned with flags. Long and low, a double-ender, the boat has a graceful, canoelike profile. It is a pleasure to regard from any position and a pleasure to be within—snug, clean, friendly. Through excellent craftsmanship in the first place and years of meticulous maintenance by several previous owners, it has taken on the quality of a loved thing, like an old family home. By its look and the touch of its wood fittings, the sliding windows in the wheelhouse that open readily when they are pushed just so, the wooden cabinetry in the galley, the lightness of its carriage in the water, its two iron hearts—the Chrysler engine in the hold and the oil-burning cookstove in the galley— it has the power of engaging anyone who enters it.

To this is added the pictures, poems, feathers, beaded things, baskets, notes, and books inside, many left as mementoes by those who had ridden the *Orca II* during the summer. These included David La Chapelle of Juneau, who had been instrumental in finding the boat for David, several Scottish members of Parliament, Earth First! people, Congressman Gary Studds of California, Russians from the Soviet oil-skimming ship *Vaydaghubsky*, the "supersucker," and Charles Hamel, the oil broker James Naughton, the actor Jean Michel Cousteau and several other members of the Cousteau Society, Greenpeace people, National Wildlife Federation people, John McCutcheon, Chris Moscone, the son of San Francisco's mayor, Mavis Mueller, the artist, as well as other artists, musicians, volunteers, and politicians from Prince William Sound and the state of Alaska. A portion of the densely inhabited orbit of activists that formed around the oil spill were transported by the *Orca II*.

We were in the Tatitlek Narrows, cruising easily on the flat water. The three of us still stood in the wheelhouse, looking. Ahead of us, the bald, sheer, rockface of Copper Mountain rose from the mainland. David wears his brown hair in a ponytail and thongs in all seasons. He has a clear, pleasant face. His good manners seemed ingrained down to the bone. Lynn is well over six feet, rawboned and powerful. Thoughtful, more taciturn than David, he is given to breaking his quiet with flashes of insight. He worked in Juneau as a private detective and an expert small boat pilot. David had secured his help when the *Orca II* was first brought up from Juneau. They came through the Gulf of Alaska to Prince William Sound, but out of fear of the pain he would feel, Lynn had then flown straight home without looking at the oil. They had even approached Cordova through the tricky back door at the Copper River flats so that he wouldn't see it. The voyage from which we were returning had been Lynn's first contact with the spill. We were now debating whether or not to stop at Tatitlek. There could be problems of decorum if we pulled in there unannounced.

We decided to put off the decision and to stop first at Ellamar, a tiny waterfront hamlet just west of Tatitlek, and to visit Sylvia Gill and Jon Rush. They had been the first people to see the Exxon *Valdez* on Bligh Reef, and had seen it every day from their living room window for 12 days before the ship was moved to Naked Island. Their house, a fanciful-looking place built close to the water, sits high on the bank. Gabled, four stories, filigreed, turreted, and fronted by a rank of log pilings driven into the beach, it has a commanding presence. Its clapboard is pale and the trim blue. A sign on it reads "Windsinger Haven." On one of the pilings was a large banner made of black petrofabric that had a picture of a hand giving the finger and the words painted in white, "Fuck Exxon." Because of the visual distraction of the house, the banner, and Jon Rush's boat—another, smaller, Jacobsen double-ender—we nearly ran the *Orca II* aground on a reef. Lynn saw the rock shelf first, looming up toward the surface of the water. He shouted. David cut the engines and turned, and then backed out. It seemed an odd incident, alarming for a moment and then funny, an echo on a very small scale of the big one that had happened just around the corner.

We anchored and took the Zodiac to shore. Alerted by our antics with the rocks, Jon Rush had come down from the house to meet us. He was a tall man with brown hair and gray in his beard. He wore blue jeans, a blue plaid shirt, and thick glasses—the consequence of his work with scrimshaw. He'd had to all but quit scrimshaw for the sake of his eyes, he would tell us. He led us up a long stone stairway to the house. Sylvia, a thin, dark-haired woman with a page-boy haircut, met us at the door. We entered a capacious place. The kitchen, dining, and living rooms were open to each other and arranged in a line that led to the big bay window looking out on the water and Bligh Island. The house had the adventurous look of all such self-built places that were lived in and kept as clean as possible while they remained under construction—here the exposed plywood subfloor, and over there a partially finished wall. It had the unmistakable quality of an artist's home, of one who delighted in the visual. There were things on the walls, pictures and artifacts, things knocked into niches and hanging from the beams overhead—tools, odds and ends, a pair of rubber gloves, an old wagon. It was not unlike the inside of the *Orca II*.

Jon and Sylvia sat us down in the dining area. They were pleased to see us and treated us in the manner I had by then encountered again and again in Alaska—with cordiality and generosity. I supposed it was a function of what some would call isolation, the lonesomeness that pleasured in company. I thought of it as a balance struck with the world that allowed for space between people and thus for the proper value to be placed upon exchange and talk. At this time, of course, there was always the one big, readymade subject—oil. The talk sought news of all its convolutions—where it was, where it wasn't, what it was killing now, and what further charlatanry it had provoked. Jon plied us with coffee and Sylvia put a bowl of dried salmon on the table. The three of us had difficulty not devouring the salmon, since by then our food stocks on the *Orca II* seemed to have narrowed to Fritos and salsa. Jon and Sylvia wanted to know where we'd been and what we'd seen. We told them: Knight Island, mainly, Snug Harbor, Mummy Bay, Lucky Bay, Herring Bay. We'd spent a day hiding from a storm at Disk Island. For David, the journey had been the last sojourn of the year in the place he loved, after the cleanup and before he put the *Orca II* up for the winter. We could say all that, but it was hard to speak of the luminous sense we held of water and dark land, of the mountain lake that perfectly reflected the trees and the clouds in the sky, of the way time had turned to liquid.

When we said that the sound looked better than we'd expected, Jon murmured and nodded. He knew David had been deeply involved in the response to the oil spill. For a time the two of them talked shop. Lynn and I sat quietly and listened. Sylvia moved into the kitchen and resumed what she'd been doing before our arrival. She was chopping vegetables with a cleaver. The rhythmic sound of her work formed a backdrop to the conversation.

Jon himself had tried first to join the volunteer brigade of boats from Tatitlek and Cordova, and then to organize a food lift to the Native communities whose beaches had been despoiled, what came to be called the Native to Native Assistance Program. The idea was that other Alaskan Native people would procure food and that it would then be distributed in the sound, particularly to the people of Tatitlek and Chenega. Chenega's shoreline resources had been destroyed, although the damage to Tatitlek remained something of a question. A ribbon of oil had entered the narrows and in the first few days of the spill the fumes had been almost overpowering. The extent of damage to Tatitlek's resources had raised the familiar bundle of claims, counterclaims, and denials from various scientific, political, ethnic, and economic quarters. Jon and Sylvia's efforts in those early days had sprung from the simple desire to do something, the reaction common to others everywhere on the sound and Kenái Peninsula. "But they shot the project down," Jon said. "And then Exxon took it over."

The insult he felt over having his efforts rebuffed was also common, though in my travels I had rarely seen a hurt as strong as his. He failed to get that project off the ground, and then was repeatedly frustrated in his attempts to be taken on by Veco, which had been put in charge of hiring boats and cleanup personnel in Valdez. Jon was told to apply in person in Valdez, but he was delayed by the closing of the channel, and then by a storm. When he got to Valdez, he was told that boats the size of his were no longer needed. He was told it might be needed later. Then he was told his boat couldn't be used because it was uninsured. He couldn't get insurance because the boat had fiberglass applied over the original wood, and when he inquired with other skippers as to how they had insured their similarly fitted boats he discovered that there were many uninsured boats under contract. He said there were people using boats far less seaworthy than his own—plastic boats, pleasure craft. He stayed in Valdez to fight the bureaucracy. He was told that Veco had priorities in its hiring preferences: first to local Area E (Prince William Sound) permit holders, second to Alaskan Area E permit holders, and third to out-of-state Area E permit holders. "But they didn't even stick to that," Jon said. "They lied about that, too. They asked me what fishery I was involved in. I said I was an artist and that we live in shouting distance of Bligh Reef. That was the end of that. They didn't want to touch me at all. They said, 'Tough, we're a big company and we'll hire whoever we want.'"

Lynn, David, and I were listening to a tirade. It had begun because we were here. As guests we gave structure to Jon's pain. He rolled one cigarette after another from his packet of Bugle tobacco as he spoke. At first, he directed his words mainly to David, who had managed to connect himself to the heart of the oil spill response in a way that had not compromised him. David's position, I thought, would seem enviable from Jon's perspective—because David had found a way to take action, whereas Jon had been left here, turning slowly on the spit of his own fury. Judging from the drawn look on David's face, he sensed this, too. It then came out that I was a writer and Jon turned to me. My role, the responsibility I had for translating his pain to the world, tightened the focus on his anger. As he went on, Sylvia's chopping in the kitchen grew steadily louder and faster until it sounded frenetic.

Jon told us how he had proof of instances of graft and payoffs, and how in the midst of the chaos at the beginning of the cleanup operation he'd spent an entire month and a half pursuing some of the hiring people. He also said there was a ploy on Exxon's part to maximize the public relations advantages of aiding Native people. He said that food had been delivered to Tatitlek but not to the Ellamar people, that as many of the Tatitlek boats as they could get had been hired, but not his boat. He said that he was a subsistence person, too, that he hadn't had time to cut his wood for the winter because of the spill. He told us how they'd had to put up with air traffic the whole time the Exxon *Valdez* was on Bligh Reef, and how even after that they found themselves in the flight pattern of the supply helicopters from Valdez. One had hovered right outside his studio window on the fourth floor.

In the kitchen, Sylvia abruptly stopped chopping and said, "We were ready to get a cannon. They all had to detour over here to check our place out."

"Some of my neighbors made a half a million dollars," Jon said. "All I got was a lost month and a half of work and the frustration."

This was the fracturing effect of the cleanup money, the ability it had to turn neighbor against neighbor, and even to come near to splitting entire towns in half. It had happened in Cordova, Homer, Seldovia, Port Graham, English Bay, Tatitlek, and most visibly in Valdez. It was the result of capitalizing the remedy to the spill, of the power of money, which drove the initial impulse to collective, voluntary action into a heavily charged predatory environment. Scruples fell away. The quick, the rapacious, and the well-equipped had the advantage and became what were known as spillionaires. Outsiders arrived. For Exxon, money was not an obstacle. Understanding that the public in the lower forty-eight, especially, had long been accustomed to accepting symbols in lieu of information, the company put its money behind symbology—the otter rescue centers, the machinery on the beaches, aid to Native people. Like all such symbolic campaigns, it had the effect of sweeping negative details away. Jon and Sylvia, who had found themselves out of the channel, connected neither to Cordova nor to Tatitlek, nor to the fishing industry, were negative details.

Jon said he was mounting a massive letter writing campaign. His electric typewriter, in fact, had been disemboweled and was spread out on the floor beside his chair. When we'd arrived, he'd been repairing it for just that purpose. He told us how he planned to go to court to sue Exxon for invasion of privacy, trauma, stress, and loss of reputation. He told us how he'd asked the lieutenant governor of Alaska, Steven McAlpine, if he could expect any sympathy from him, and McAlpine had said, certainly. Jon told us how he'd typed up a bunch of information, and how McAlpine took it and never brought it up with anybody. "I had a shootout with the bigshots," Jon said. "As soon as McAlpine saw he might have to bump heads, he dropped it." Jon paused and looked between his knees at the floor, then said, "It's been an angry summer."

We were quiet for a moment. I got up and moved to the bay window in the living room. Jon, Lynn, and David followed. Jon pointed out where to look through a slot between the dark rocks near the end of the island. Beyond the rocks was an open space of pale water and sky. I imagined the ship in that space, listing ever so slightly, oil spewing from its holds.

"For the first four days," Sylvia said from the kitchen, "it sat there and they did nothing. I couldn't believe how ill-prepared they were."

"The screen got pulled away," David said. "And there was the Wizard of Oz."

Jon told us how he'd been up late working at his bench when he heard the steel grating against rock. He peered out his window toward Bligh Reef and saw the tanker's running lights. The ship seemed much too close. Then suddenly the sky went alight. The shorelines and hills around the reef turned bright. All the ship's lights had come on.

"Actually," he said, rocking back and turning away from the window, "there was no surprise to it whatsoever. We'd been waiting for it to happen. We knew it was a question of time. They've been cutting that corner for years. I was almost run over by a tanker once near Jack's Bay on the righthand side of the lane. He hung a turn and suddenly I was looking up at a steel wall. He'd mistook Jack's Bay for the narrows and turned into it. Can you believe that? Later, I saw the pilot in Valdez and asked him how that could happen. He said it never did happen."

"It makes you feel the oil companies have more power than the government," Sylvia said.

We moved back into the dining room and sat down. "The next thing will be the corruption," Jon said. "Wait and see. Sylvia and I finally ended up playing the role of watchers, not participants. Maybe we were lucky."

"It's economics," David said. In this were shades of what he would eventually become involved with, The Coastal Coalition, the ambitious attempt to knit together the detail of local economy and, in the form of reparation, the resources of an international petroleum superproprietor. "When it comes to economics, we're not really a community."

"That's right," Jon said. "Now, my main concern is how are we going to recover from this thing as a people. The whole thing is warped completely out of shape by the money."

David took a sounding: "What do you think would make you happy?"

Jon thought for a moment, then answered with a cold fury, "Exactly what my neighbors got. Not a penny more and not a penny less. Because I just can't live with the arrogance." He paused again, lit another cigarette, and said, "I debated really hard whether I should even bother with it, or if I should just sit at my bench and do what I always did. I wanted to help and I kept an open mind about what I would do until I ran into the arrogance."

We looked at Jon's paintings. He brought out a box and showed us his scrimshaw. Much of his work, he said, emulated Native techniques. He readily granted that, angry as he was with some of his neighbors in Tatitlek. The root of his outrage, I understood then, and the cause of the fracture in his views came from having been turned against himself by the cleanup money. He showed us a moveable sculpture called *Slow Dancing*. It was close to two feet tall and had a base made of four kinds of wood sanded down and varnished to a shine. Faces were carved into each side of the base. Inside the base was a clockwork. On the base, a man and a woman, carved out of a walrus tooth, made love. Above them was a carved snail shell. The clockwork in the base turned the couple and snailshell one revolution every 24 hours. Over the couple and snail shell was lantern glass, capped with a carved mushroom. The mushroom had a little battery-run spotlight inside it to illuminate the shell and the couple as they made love and turned ever so slowly. It was a wonderful thing, delicately carved, intricately conceived, and mysterious in the way the natural elements played against its mechanics. As we admired it, Jon's mood softened.

He came out to visit the *Orca II*. He and David went ahead in his skiff. Outside the house, Lynn and Sylvia talked for a few minutes about mutual friends and the garden. Sylvia seemed abruptly changed, happy to be out of the pressure cooker of the house. Lynn and I motored out to the *Orca II* in the Zodiac. When we entered the galley, Jon and David were talking. Jon also looked changed, as if he'd shed several years. "This boat's immaculate," he said admiringly. He gazed through a window back toward his house and said, "Ellamar. The community Exxon forgot. But they were over to Tatitlek the first chance they got."

"The people of Tatitlek don't really measure their life in dollars," David said. "If you screw up the environment, you've screwed everything up. If you make a cash settlement, you screw them up."

"Tell that to the kid who bought a Corvette with his cleanup money. What's he going to do with a Corvette in Tatitlek?" He stopped himself, and sighed, then smiled at us. "I've known those people for twenty years and lived next to them for eleven. Some of them are the best people in the whole world."

After he left, we went on our way toward Cordova. As we neared Tatitlek, the face of Copper Mountain loomed higher. Guggenheim mining money had been here, too. The village of Tatitlek had been relocated for the sake of the copper mine. Ellamar had been a mining camp. On a distant shore before us, we could see a swath of bare mountain, a timber clear cut.

Lynn said, "There's a metaphor with Jon, the way the money like the oil goes in some places and not in others. A million dollars on either side of the man who was the first one to see the tanker."

Chapter 12

THE VALUE
OF THE DEAD

War and photography now seem inseparable, and plane crashes and other horrific accidents always attract people with cameras. A society which makes it normative to aspire never to experience privation, failure, misery, pain, dread disease, and in which death itself is regarded not as natural and inevitable but as a cruel, unmerited disaster, creates a tremendous curiosity about these events—a curiosity that is partly satisfied through picture-taking. The feeling of being exempt from calamity stimulates interest in looking at painful pictures, and looking at them suggests and strengthens the feeling that one is exempt. Partly it is because one is "here," not "there," and partly it is the character of inevitability that all events acquire when they are transmuted into images. In the real world, something *is* happening and no one knows what is *going* to happen. In the image-world, it *has* happened, and it *will* forever happen in that way.

—Susan Sontag, *On Photography*, 1977

The storm that struck March 27, the fourth day of the spill, drove the oil slick south and west through the sound. Prevailing currents moved the leading edges past the islands in the southwest and into the Gulf of Alaska. By March 29, the oil had come near Resurrection Bay and Seward on the south shore of the Kenai Peninsula. The town of Seward declared a local emergency.

By April 3, day 11, portions of the slick had moved northward up

165

Resurrection Bay and southwesterly along the Kenai Peninsula off the Kenai Fjords National Park to cover an area of 1,000 square miles. On NOAA maps, the slick was represented as long strips and patches in Prince William Sound and as a large oblong settled just off the ragged shoreline of the Kenai Peninsula. Two days later, the slick widened to cover 2,600 miles, and on April 6, it struck the Chiswell Islands in the Gulf, 35 miles southwest of Seward. The islands were a nesting site for 70,000 migratory seabirds, including auklets and puffins, and a haulout for thousands of sea lions. On April 10, the eighteenth day of the spill, the second major storm hit, and the oil moved ashore at the Kenai Fjords National Park and at the Alaska Maritime National Wildlife Refuge, a place that includes over 700 islands.

Well before this time, the residents of Seward and the towns clustered around the southwestern corner of the Kenai Peninsula—English Bay, Port Graham, Seldovia, Homer—had understood very well what the winds and currents would eventually bring to them. Although some of the authorities, including NOAA representative Hal Alabaster, continued to issue hopeful statements about the powers of wind and wave action to break up the slick, the residents of the Kenai towns thought otherwise and formed volunteer organizations in preparation for the defense of their shorelines. The day after the spill, Alabaster suggested that nature was succeeding in breaking up (or dispersing) the slick where man had failed, which was true enough, in a way, but at the same time chunks of the slick were being driven toward the shorelines. Bill Noll, who was to become mayor of Seward, said, "As soon as we knew a river of oil was headed for Montague Island, we knew damn well what was going to happen. We knew it was first going to hit the gulf and then come back our way. We started by borrowing and stealing boom anywhere we could get our hands on it. We were organized before anybody else got here."

In Homer and Seldovia a rift developed between NOAA scientists and residents who remembered what, outside Alaska, was a little-known incident in Cook Inlet—the 159,000-gallon spill from the tanker *Glacier Bay* in the summer of 1987. NOAA had the data from laboratory experiments, knowledge of previous spills, and the circumspection allowed by scientific distance. But as it turned out, the image evoked by descriptions of the oil breaking up and slipping away from sight somewhere out at sea was quite at odds with the developing reality. The image and the misapprehensions it engendered were due in part to what NOAA's Jerry Galt would later tell me was an overreliance, especially by the press and those in charge of coordinating the response, on "anecdotal data," and to the fact that while NOAA had a good basic fix on the currents of the sound and gulf, not much was known about the winds. "We learned a lot about the winds," Galt would say.

On April 11, the oil moved around the tip of the Kenai Peninsula and was sighted just below English Bay, another subsistence village. By this time the utterly changed and astonishing reality of the spill and of the increasingly complex exigencies of cleanup were coming to be accepted, though in differing ways, by everyone. On the twelfth, Dennis Kelso said, "We are entering a new phase." On April 16, the slick moved up Cook Inlet. On the seventeenth, it finally hit the shores of Seward at the head of Resurrection Bay. On the eighteenth, patches were sited in the mouth of Kachemak Bay near the village of Port Graham.

By the end of the first week of May, oil had been carried across the mouth of Cook Inlet to Katmai National Park, where large numbers of dead birds were sighted. It reached Wide Bay, which is on the mainland behind (west of) Kodiak Island. In some areas, the slick moved at the speed of 17½ miles per day, and it was now more than 500 miles away from the original site at Bligh Reef. By the end of the next week, oil had drifted to Alinchak Bay on the Alaska Peninsula and washed ashore at Homer, Kachemak Bay, the southern and western sides of Kodiak Island, and Chignik Bay in Shelikof Strait.

Fisheries in Prince William Sound, Cook Inlet, and off Kodiak were rapidly being closed or threatened with closure. Over 16,000 dead birds and nearly 700 dead otters had been recovered, and thousands more dead animals had been sighted on and near the oiled beaches. Because of the rugged conditions and the difficulty of spotting oiled animals in an oiled terrain or on oiled water, however, it had become apparent that the majority of the dead animals would never be recovered or counted. They were often seen as black, bubblelike protrusions in the slick. An unknown number of them would sink from sight. Counting fish and other marine life forms was an even chancier proposition. How many sea stars? How many pounds of popweed? The count of the dead was important to the symbology of the spill. Here, where it came to be announced in daily meetings at the Oil Spill Coordinating Office (OSCO) in Homer, the count took on the character of funereal litany. Elsewhere, and certainly in the lower forty-eight, the count took on a cartoonlike spin—violent, powerfully affecting to those predisposed to receive it, and yet remote from the experience of actual violence.

So long as the oil remained mobile, like an alive thing reaching up Resurrection Bay, Cook Inlet, and way back behind Kodiak Island, the story had an arresting effect on the public in the lower forty-eight. Even though the public at large but dimly understood where these places were and what they looked like, the story acquired a libidinous narrative drive not unlike a soap opera or science fiction thriller. Like soap operas and science fiction, it had strong intimations of a morality play. The story was followed in the same way the Watergate hearings were followed during the seventies as they moved day by day nearer and nearer to their final resolution—the excision from office of the villainous one, President Nixon. Just what the resolution of the oil spill story was to be, or should be, however, was unclear. The stripping away of Exxon's assets, the permanent shutdown of the Alyeska Terminal, the permanent closure of future drilling sites in ANWR and elsewhere? Or maybe the public burning of Joseph Hazelwood and upper-echelon Exxon officials? None of these wished-for conclusions would come to pass. During congressional testimony April 6, the same day the oil slick hit the Chiswell Islands and Joseph Hazelwood was released from the Long Island jail, Senator Slade Gorton of Washington suggested to L. G. Rawl that he consider resigning as a result of the spill. Gorton pointed out that Japanese executives often resigned when their companies were involved in environmental disasters. Rawl said, "I don't know if I have to respond to that, but a lot of Japanese kill themselves as well, and I refuse to do that." In this exchange, Senator Gorton, known in his home state as a "moderate" at best, and at worst as an "opportunist" when it came to environmental questions, served as a conductor for the intense public desire for some conclusion to the story. Rawl served as a reminder that the story would never end, that the morally definitive action it seemed to require would never occur.

The pictures of the dead as they appeared in newspapers across the country, newsmagazines, and periodicals devoted to popular science, nature, and the environment at once tended to make the image of death excessively articulate and at the same time to gloss over the fact of death itself. Among the most memorable and common were those that zeroed in on an otter or a bird—often loons, murres, or pelagic cormorants, which were among the most striking because of their long, graceful necks and sharply defined bills. The animals were seen covered with oil and stiff with rigor mortis. Their lower bodies emerged from a pool of oil and their upper bodies were cast in relief against pebbles, sand, snow, water, or sky. In some cases, the animals had clearly been positioned for the sake of the shot. By a quirk of physiogomy, the otters often had their paws crossed near to their chests when they died, and in the pictures this seemed to echo human mortuary practices. Such photographs displayed a studied element of romance in the face of inescapable horror. When I raised this matter with Natalie Fobes, a fine, Seattle-based photographer who spent weeks in Alaska following the spill, she said that she considered it her obligation to get the images of the dead into the living rooms of the nation and to keep them there as long as possible. Hers was an understandable position, and yet in the interplay between the photographer's craft and sense of duty on the one hand, and the public's response to such images on the other hand, lay the danger of what Susan Sontag calls "the chronic voyeuristic relation to the world that levels the meaning of all events."

Such voyeurism, Sontag says, has "a way of at least tacitly, often explicitly, encouraging whatever is going on to keep on happening," and even, or especially, when the event is painful, to continue going on forever without conclusion. Due to the nature of the press, much of its coverage, and due to the necessities of its capital investments, all of Exxon's public relations efforts were devised, first, to keep the story thin and to keep the public in it until the story faded from audibility like a top forty tune on the radio, and second, to prevent the public from conceiving of what had actually happened. In my journeys to and from Alaska, I was struck by nothing quite so much as the lag between what I had witnessed in one place and the versions reported in the other. When I walked an oiled beach, I learned that the dead were not nearly so likely to be found posing for the camera as they were to be discovered as one picked one's way among oil-inundated rocks . . felt through the touch of a footfall upon something too hard to be liquid and too soft to be rock, a pliant thing down there, too solid to be wood or stone, a thing that still had the give of what had been a life and the integrity of lineament, skin, and bone, a thing that slithered away from the boot and when punctured gave off gas. The smell of rot mixed with the smell of raw petroleum. Death was everywhere, twined upon itself and not articulate, a teeming, inchoate crowd, suspended in oil.

Marge Tillion was one of the early community response organizers in Homer. Later, she was a principal member of the Homer Area Recovery Coalition (HARC—also referred to for a short time as SPARC, the South Peninsula Area Recovery Coalition). Later yet, she would represent Homer on a citizens' advisory committee to Alyeska, as Alyeska reformed its contingency plan.

Larry Smith was another Homer organizer and activist, a man of rectitude and yet capable of talking amiably with anyone from any position on the political spectrum. He'd been working for years on forestry and timber harvesting practices in Alaska and had founded what he described as a "profit/not for profit habitat type of thing" called the Kachemak Resource Institute. The institute was located in a low, gray, wooden building on the outskirts of Homer. The building mainly housed an attorney's office and an infant learning program. A set of dilapidated steps led to the deck on which rested a stack of firewood and a filing cabinet with a sign on it that said, "Property of Kachemak Resource Institute." Perhaps most tellingly, out in the chest-high weeds of the front yard was coiled a length of blue oil boom. Later, Larry would move into another building and have, as he put it, "a real office," but when I visited, that was it—the oil boom as memento of the oil wars, the filing cabinet on the deck, and inside a legal secretary who cheerfully took messages for Larry and allowed him to use the phone. It was enough.

Larry had sent me to see Marge Tillion, whom he described as "a formidable character and a hell of a boat woman." Through his interest in the use of timber resources, Larry would also come to be in touch with David Grimes and Rick Steiner. That's how things were. Contacts spun around and jumped out in long arcs.

Joined by highway to Anchorage and by ferry to Valdez and Cordova, built on the northern side of the mouth of Kachemak Bay, Homer fell away to the north and east into plateau country. Out on the edge of town is a group of recent Russian immigrants who follow a communal and conservative style of life. Known as "Old Believers," they came here first from Oregon, and before that from Turkey, and before that from Russia to escape religious persecution under the communist state. More than 300 years ago, they had splintered from the Russian Orthodox. The town of Homer has about 4,000 residents; the greater Homer area, over 11,000. The numbers of actual residents rise and fall according to the season, and over half of Homer's population has lived there less than five years. Fishing is the main economy, followed by government employment and tourism. Timber enterprises are under development. The Homer Spit, which stretches halfway across Kachemak Bay, is the center of commercial fishing operations and also the point of embarkation for tourists and sport fishing.

The town also has a fine small museum, the Pratt Museum, and a first-class public radio station. There is a leftward-leaning activist presence and a strong sense of community spirit. During the summer, there are a lot of strangers around, who are treated pretty well, and a great deal of money in medium-sized denominations pinging to and fro. Although tourism was said to have suffered because of the oil spill when I was there in mid-July, a section of the Homer Spit was nevertheless lined with recreational vehicles. Larry told me that what I was seeing was nothing compared to what it could be, and nothing compared to what it would be when the annual Halibut Derby got under way.

He took me to the spit. We looked at the huge steel ore carriers brought up from Skagway, which were to be used for hauling oiled refuse out to Anchorage. Added to the already boiling controversy over the disposition of oily waste was the fact that the tanks themselves had been found to have been contaminated with lead before they arrived. We looked at the log boom stacked up in a Veco lot. There were lumberyard-sized stacks of logs here and at other locations on the spit. They were ponderous and heavy, affixed with plywood to make a splash shield, draped with petrofabric to make the skirt, and festooned with cable and all manner of metal and concrete chunks to weight the skirts. Now, since much of the boom had been oiled, it presented its own disposal problem.

Originally part of a project initiated across the bay in Seldovia in the third week of April and then taken up in Homer, the boom had become the focal point in the battle between the people of South Kenai and Exxon. As the oil had worked its way toward the Kenai in early April, Exxon and the government agencies were still groping to mount an appropriate response in Prince William Sound. Exxon had concentrated its efforts there, and its expertise, and what equipment it had so far marshaled. The result was that events on the Kenai echoed previous events in Valdez, Tatitlek, and Cordova: the growing public outrage as the oil moved ineluctably in their direction, the town meetings in the Homer high-school auditorium attended by hundreds and during which Exxon representatives, notably Wiley Bragg, would take public verbal beatings, the community frustration over the lack of action, and the confusion over what action to take and how to pay for it. As the time between the day of the spill and the arrival of the oil was wider here than in the sound, so too was the lag between "official" recognition that the oil was indeed coming and mobilization. Because of the lag, the sense here that Exxon and the government had given up trying to prevent it from washing ashore grew ever stronger. The distinct impression was left that Exxon still hoped the oil would disappear, or that ignoring it would somehow magically reduce its impact, although in all fairness it should be said that at this point Exxon's resources and its organization were so overtaxed in the sound that it was virtually impossible to catch up and mount a response elsewhere appropriate to the problem.

On April 14, the Coast Guard had approved Exxon's initial cleanup plan, but as the oil spread along the Kenai and toward Kodiak, the plan became instantly obsolete. Included in the plan was the creation of a Shoreline Cleanup Assessment Team (SCAT). The SCAT team passed its recommendations back to Exxon's Valdez office. From there, revised recommendations were passed to multiagency coordinating groups (MACs, which included representatives from the community, the state parks, the Forest Service, and at times other agencies), who made site-specific recommendations and passed them back to the Coast Guard. Included in the process was the issuance of permits by such agencies as the EPA and the Department of Fish and Wildlife. The Coast Guard approved (or disapproved) the recommendations and sent them on to Exxon, which then implemented them by sending word to their regional representatives. By the time the crisis was hitting the Kenai, this was the form Admiral Yost's plan to cut through the BS and "kick some butts" had taken. In the meantime, the Exxon crews had cleaned less than two miles of shoreline in Prince William Sound.

What hit the Kenai people was the same contradiction seen elsewhere. On the one hand, they expected Exxon to get here and do something, even to do the impossible. On the other hand, they resented the presence of Exxon once it did arrive. What emerged for a time was another public effort by residents of Seward, Homer, Soldotna, Port Graham, English Bay, and Seldovia. The Homer MAC was at first headed by Loren Flagg, a fisheries biologist appointed by Burough Mayor Don Gillman. The group sought to channel efforts and expedite communication, supplies, and money, but not surprisingly found the system close to immovable. For two weeks, very little got done. Moreover, Exxon seemed once again to be trying to impede efforts, repeatedly telling the Homer MAC that commercial boom in quantity was unavailable. Marge Tillion began to make her own list of suppliers and outlets and, incidentally, of fishermen and boats willing to fight the spill. In 48 hours she had 100 boats signed up. The Homer MAC put in an order for 5,000 feet of boom and had it within two days. It was a prime example, Loren Flagg would say, "of our frustration with Exxon's lies. They hadn't tried to get it. They deceived us."

Because of the almost complete absence of commercial boom, at first, and then because the quantities on hand remained insufficient, the log boom project went on. The boom was intended to be used to protect the most critical shorelines of the area—notably, the state salmon hatchery at Tutka Lagoon, English Bay Lagoon, Dogfish Bay Lagoon, and other spawning grounds and prized wildlife habitats. Boom experts from the outside advised that log boom would not be as effective as commercial boom, but the volunteers procured logs, at times cutting, limbing, skinning, and hauling them themselves. Various designs were tried. Crews worked through the night to build the boom, and finally thousands of feet of it were floated and hauled to critical sites. In some cases it alone was deployed. In other cases, it was augmented by commercial boom. In many situations, it didn't work especially well. In certain other situations its heaviness was thought to make it superior to the commercial variety.

Although Larry Smith acknowledged that the boom hadn't always worked, he was proud of the project, and of his part in it. His skills as a carpenter had been put to use. He pointed out how this material was scrounged up from what was available—a piece of iron, say, cut out of a crab pot—and how this type of skirt had worked and how that one had not, how the logs were joined with cable and weighted to prevent them from rolling. Once again, the project spoke well of the capacity of Alaskans to take action, of the meaning of action when it sprang from the root of a community, of the variety of talents and capabilities that could be called forth, and mainly of the profoundly different effect upon the spirits of people such an approach had in comparison to the alienating effect of the approach emanating from the Valdez headquarters, and at times from the borough mayor's office in Soldotna.

What followed, and what caused the deepest frustration, was the invasion of Exxon, implemented mainly by its contractor, Veco. I talked to Ken Broginoff that night on the Homer Spit. He was a partner in a fishing fleet and head of operations for a packing company, and so had been in a position to command an impressive array of resources—a warehouse, 78 fishing boats, supplies, and the distribution contacts that go with an outfit of that size. He said that he knew the oil was going to come to the Kenai, so he figured that his best course would be to start a cleanup effort. Exxon told him that it wanted his yard and building and fleet, and so he became a Veco subcontractor. Dark-haired and spare, Broginoff has a melancholy aspect. He sat behind a desk in the warehouse office and leaned back in his chair as he spoke. He struck me as an admirable man who had found himself in a position to make himself useful, but as often as not in ways that were objectionable to him. He had little respect for Veco, and detested the fact that local people had been put out of work by what he called the pipeline syndrome. He'd had to lay off all his regular workers because they weren't union members. He worried about the effect Exxon welfarism would have upon the people. He said, "As soon as Veco got into the log boom business, five chain saws disappeared. For two weeks, no groceries were delivered . . . where they went, I don't know. The paperwork is incredible, but I'm keeping accountability with everything that's come through here. If there's a pump out there, we know where it is."

He was worried about sinking oil, which at the time I spoke with him—mid-July—had become the dominant controversy on the Kenai Peninsula and at Kodiak. Science said that oil couldn't sink. Broginoff, who had worked previously at Prudhoe Bay as an engineer and project manager, said, "The oil gets heavier and heavier and eventually sinks. It gets stuck on gear. You pull a shrimp pot and it's oiled, and you can't figure where it came from. It sinks because of the shearing effect of currents. At one point," he said, "there was no progress on the oil spill. It disappeared. It was shearing, then all of a sudden it popped up at Chugach, and at Kodiak. As fishermen we're skeptical of fishing. We don't want to contaminate our plant. If they find one oiled fish, they can close the whole area and our plant could be quarantined.

"The people running the operations are good supervisors from Texas, but they don't know a thing about our beaches. We're putting a hundred-ton crane out on the barrens tomorrow," he said. "It's a bird sanctuary. The barrens have maybe the highest bird mortality of any place. They're planning to hand-clean the north side and use the crane on the south side. I've told them, but they won't listen. The crane's going to sink on that beach."

After talking to Broginoff, Larry and I went out to the docks and watched John Glidden, a DEC inspector, examine a salmon catch as it was unloaded from a seiner. The silvery fish were lifted from the boat to the dock in large plastic totes. The totes are loaded to the brim. From the tote, they went into a large steel container, but first Glidden spot-checked them for oil. The rule was "zero tolerance" on oiling of the catches, taken from what areas were allowed to open.

Larry and I moved nearer to the edge of the dock. Glidden would select a fish, stroke it, peer closely into the gills, and then check the anus. He would squeeze the fish and examine the offal emerging from the anus. Our presence seemed to make him nervous. He glanced over at us, and then back behind us at the notebook I'd left on top of Larry's car. Its pages fluttered in the breeze. Glidden's face took on an alarmed look, and in an expression of the wariness many of the government people had over being watched, he said, "You're not taking notes, are you?"

From Marge Tillion I heard another version of what had become the main story told and retold by lower Kenai Peninsula people—the shock felt when Exxon and its contractors came to town. I sat on a couch in

Marge's living room and she sat across from me on an easy chair. She and her husband are fishermen. She is also a fireman and licensed emergency medical technician. Her father-in-law, Clem Tillion, was an old-time Alaska legislator and close associate of former governor Jay Hammond. Marge has dark, short hair and flashing eyes and is deeply tanned by the outdoors. She is articulate and, as Larry had said, formidable.

She'd become involved with the response four days after the oil spill. "My immediate thought was that they were going to need boats to help them," she said. "I made a data base by feeding in the lists from fishing organizations." She got up and left the living room, then came back with a three-inch-thick stack of spread sheet–sized computer printouts, set it down on the floor, and ranged through it, looking down at it at times as she spoke and then over at me. The data base had grown fast, she said. People began calling to get their boats and equipment on it. For its range and sheer voluminousness, her data base echoed the other lists that were everywhere. Hers included storage tanks, hydroblasters, shovels, five-gallon buckets, people, showers, skiffs, airplanes, and 800 boats.

Right away, she said, she and the other local volunteers arranged to use the high school as a Bird Rescue Center and the junior high swimming pool for the Otter Rescue Center (later moved to Jackolof Bay near Seldovia). The high-school teachers encouraged their students to help with the effort. An Exxon representative called from Valdez to ask if he could get access to her data base. She had so many calls that she added five telephone lines to her house, and a fax and photocopy machine. By the first week in April, her house had become the Oil Resource Center, and then she suddenly discovered that she was up to her nose in politics.

The people were calling from Valdez and Cordova, warning about inflated prices, housing problems, the press, lawyers, the ruthless take-over of the towns. "I worked for hours begging our mayor not to let them bring Veco in," she said. She wanted a local organization to work with Exxon. She remembered what had happened in Valdez when the pipeline came in. "I had the clearest picture of what was going to happen here. But I still wasn't paying close enough attention. I still didn't believe that we wouldn't be able to do something to stop it. I picked up the first two Exxon people at the airport and pleaded with them—'Please don't bring Veco in.' I showed them my data base. They assured me all they wanted Veco for was to do the accounting. I worked for two or three weeks without a contract, just to watch them because I had a gut feeling they were not being straight. Sure enough, Veco came in and started up with the accounting. During a storm, I heard Veco was hiring skiffs to go out in heavy seas to pull boom. Suddenly it hit me that somebody might die out there and that if they did I might be liable, too, and I told the Veco people, and they said, 'You shut up. You do what we want you to do, and say what we want you to say.' "

She moved back to the chair and looked at me. "I will not be bought off," she said. "A guy from Exxon blocked off my car one day and said, 'Hey, what do you want? Six, seven thousand a day? We'll pay you.' I said, 'I can't work with you. This is my data base and I want control of it.' It was a tough spot. I wanted to take my data base out of there, but at the same time if I did I'd set the whole effort back several weeks."

At that time, the Homer and Seldovia volunteers' log boom project was well under way. Marge said that Exxon went back on its word and turned the entire Kenai Peninsula cleanup operation over to Veco. "Everything went bad then," she said. She said that Veco inflated figures, including counting boat people twice—once as a boat crew and once again as cleanup crew—in order to increase the margin on its "cost plus" contract. Marge, like many others, had become distraught and decided to go out with a science crew to "cool out." When she returned she found Larry Smith and John Mickelson, the Seldovia MAC representative, had secured a million dollars from Exxon, which was to be channeled through the borough to run an independent cleanup crew. It was at first thought to be a replenishable million, that is, a million-dollar balance that would be sustained by Exxon, but as it turned out, by the time the million ran out the entire operation had been taken over by Veco. In Marge's view, this was how Veco took the town over—by gradually encroaching upon agreements and filling in all the gaps until it had control.

In the meantime, an 18-man crew had been hired and put to work. In an echo of some of the Cordova efforts, it picked up between four and five thousand gallons of oil a day. But then they were left out there, awaiting tankerage to take on their oil. When the money ran out, Marge tried—and, but for one boat skipper, failed—to get her crew taken on by Veco. The entire operation was stalled, she said, while the new manager, a real estate agent, took two weeks to develop a company to handle his business. At the same time, oil was appearing in Cook Inlet. When it was reported, it took between two and three weeks to get anybody to look at it. She claimed that the Veco workers went to absorbent pads for cleaning because the crews were always green, and anything else was too complicated for them. She said they hired 40 crew members, flew them to the beach to perform for a film crew, and then when the filming was over, let the entire crew go. "We don't hold it against them that they don't know how to clean beaches," Marge said. "What we do hold against them is that they refuse to use our expertise. They could have benefited from us and at the same time left us all feeling good about oil companies by putting us to work.

"Salmon is my whole income," she said. "They gave us ten thousand for the Cook Inlet Drift Net Closure, and that may be all I'll see. In the meantime I can't leave, I can't get a job, and I can't fish. I've got three kids, and one of them is going to a school in Seattle for dyslexia. The contract for our tender boat makes two-thirds of the payments on the boat, and we've got to find the other third somewhere or lose the boat." Her voice had begun to shake. She paused, and then told me I should get Larry Smith to show me the bird-burning video. Eventually, I saw it at his house. Rough and grainy, strictly amateur and not attempting to be anything else, a kind of accidental document, the video carries more of the weight of death than any of the professional photographic records I have yet seen.

Marge's disappointment, and her desire to do something, to be engaged, along with similar feelings by others, led to a project sponsored by HARC. A beach cleaning project, it came to be centered at Mars Cove, not far from Gore Point on the southern side of the Kenai Peninsula—a heavily oiled area that Exxon had essentially abandoned to the elements. The project proposed to rehabilitate one beach. It would raise all its funding through contributions, apply the strictest methods of accounting, and employ an all-volunteer labor force. Begun in early July, and initially using shovels, buckets, and absorbent pads, the project later used a rock washing machine invented by a young man named Billy Day. The process involved digging up a small section of oiled beach at low tide, running the rocks through a system of high-pressure hoses, vacuuming off the oil from a catch pond, then replacing the rocks. The project was begun in late August and ran through September, after the Exxon cleanup operation had pulled out. When the volunteers were done, a small patch of the beach was clean.

Larry Smith lives about 20 miles outside Homer, in a house he built. Between the house and water are several hundred yards of dense growth, out of which Larry's son, Liam, and a friend abruptly emerged one evening with a moose hot on their heels.

We watched the video in Larry's kitchen one night. The television and VCR were balanced on top of the refrigerator. The video had been taken by Drew Scalzi, a boat skipper employed by the Department of Fish and Wildlife. He and the beach crew had gathered 676 seabirds at Gore Point, and then awaited instructions for what to do next. They contacted officials in Homer and requested permission to destroy the birds. Their request was denied. They waited, and then, wary of the fact that the birds would soon begin to rot, and mindful of their job description, which was, as Scalzi put it, "to get this stuff out of the food chain," the crew took it upon itself to burn the corpses. Scalzi made the videotape, he said, in order to prove he wasn't trying to destroy evidence against Exxon. Marge Tillion had told me that she thought the action had the elements of a protest.

The tape, which has become an underground classic of the oil spill, was often blurred and ragged. Shots veered wildly from one subject to another. The heavily oiled birds were first laid out in a long line on the beach like death camp victims, and photographed. The crew then made a seven-foot-high pyre out of driftwood, ignited it, and began carrying the birds one-by-one to the flames and throwing them in. There is a nervous boisterousness on the part of the crew near the beginning of the video. However, as the tape continues, as the birds mount on the pile, their attitude changes. The initial buoyance dissolves. The joking ceases. The movement of the crew members, carrying bodies to the flames, grows more and more ponderous.

The tape is true cinema verité. The person holding the camera is a participant in the action. As the tape proceeds, the shots grow longer. The lens seems as close to the eye of a human as a camera might get. The tape is run without break, and the occasional dipping of the camera suggests the cameraman's own fatigue. The imagery becomes less and less trivial. The movement is toward complete involvement, an emotional sinking in. The line between the disengaged bureaucratic view of the world and being in the world is inescapably crossed.

The Department of Fish and Wildlife wanted the bodies for the sake of the numbers. Scalzi and his crew wanted, quite reasonably, to remove oiled carrion from the beach. Scalzi was fired by the department when he returned to Homer. When he showed his video, he was reinstated. For Scalzi and his crew, the value of the dead resided in the weight it transposed to those who came to be intimate with it. For those who merely counted, the dead had no intrinsic value.

The dead were important to institutions likely to be involved in litigation—Exxon, Alyeska, the federal government, the state of Alaska, and the various environmental organizations. Counting the dead meant money, although there would always be argument over how much the dead were worth. Estimating the dead meant argument over the validity of the surveys by which estimates were achieved. A year later, the dead that had been gathered would still wait in refrigerated trucks for litigation to commence.

In their article "Assessing Damages from the Valdez Oil Spill," A. Myrick Freeman and Raymond J. Kopp point out that in accordance with "provisions of the Clean Water Act of 1972 and Alaska State law, both the federal and state governments can sue 'potentially responsible parties' to recover the economic damages sustained by the publicly owned natural resources of the affected region." In a courtroom, the damage to resources lost (or not harvested) due to fishery closures may be relatively easily established, though never to the complete satisfaction of all parties. Similarly, the damage to chartered sports fishing or hunting may be approximated. The damage to subsistence villages or to the visual beauty that might attract tourists becomes rather more complex because in the first case the material value of, say, urchins, sea cucumbers, or fish is tied to community and spiritual values, to a way of life. In the second case, the majestic appearance of a place is tied to something like spiritual values, as well, or at the least to a commonly held romance. It was the rupturing of this romance, which takes the place of religion in our country, that caused much of the outcry in the lower forty-eight. John V. Krutilla, covering similar ground in his article "Conservation Considered," suggests that any "grand scenic wonder or unique and fragile ecosystem . . . [is] a significant part of the real income of many individuals." Such individuals, Krutilla says, "are the spiritual descendents of John Muir . . . to whom the loss of a species or the disfigurement of a scenic area causes acute distress and a sense of genuine relative impoverishment."

Freeman and Kopp also discuss what economists refer to as "lost non-use values," that is, intrinsic values that might be said to affect a large group of individuals who have no direct involvement with the place or thing of value. "The origin of these values," Freeman and Kopp say, "may lie in a desire to preserve the natural environments for the enjoyment of future generations or from a simple expression of stewardship. Economists generally place diminished non-use values on an equal footing with diminished use values and argue that failure to account for lost non-use values will understate the damage suffered by society."

Krutilla speaks of the values of potential use, such as the potential usefulness (or benefit to the world) of maintaining diverse gene pools and unique habitats, and the usefulness of a resource that might be employed more efficiently in the future. Many oil fields presently under use, including Prudhoe Bay, are producing because of previously undeveloped drilling technologies. Attempting to measure such values, though they are again certainly real enough, is so speculative as to put them functionally in a category like non-use values.

The method of measuring non-use values is referred to as contingent valuation. It's a curious term: contingent upon what? Freeman and Kopp point out that the contingent valuation is based on surveys used to gather data to determine society's willingness to pay. Gathering the data involves not only economic theory but the psychological and statistical sciences. The answer to the question has to be: contingent upon itself, upon the very concept of economic valuation.

The notion that those who purchase cheap fuel and so sustain the system of production or even reinvent the validity of that system every hour of every day—that is, all of us—should bear a substantial portion of the cost of both cleanup and future prevention of oil spills is correct (and inescapable, through taxes and petroleum prices). Yet the entire economic and legal procedure for determining the value of the dead or of lost or damaged habitats is caught in a loop that finally sails crazily away from the matter of death and loss. The system is attempting to measure the immeasurable—that is, what Marge Tillion, Drew Scalzi, and Billy Day felt, what caused them to take action; and what those who worked in the otter and bird rescue centers felt, no matter, given the general picture of destruction, how futile their efforts would be; what the people of Chenega and English Bay felt had been sundered when their subsistence resources were taken away.

The system of measuring non-use values is another venture at pushing the elements of rationality—quantifying, counting, numbering—into utter, infantile irrationality. It is interesting, though, that in the summer of 1990, Rick Steiner and others (including Alaskan Natives, environmental groups, commercial fishermen, tour operators, recreationalists, and biologists), joining in the Coastal Coalition's proposal for a comprehensive settlement of all resource damages from Exxon used the concept of "contingent valuation" as a basis. As of August 1990, the coalition had a simple solution. Drop all litigation. Free the dead from refrigeration. In return, Exxon would establish a two-billion-dollar Alaska Restoration Fund to underwrite continued restoration of oil-damaged areas, research, education, economic development, and, most importantly, the acquisition of resources equivalent to those damaged, such as timber rights—that is, adjacent resources.

Chapter 13

SELDOVIA

On July 20, I took a Homer Air flight across Kachemak Bay. The 20-mile hop carried me from one place, Homer, made accessible to the world by the road from Anchorage, to another place, Seldovia, accessible only by air or water. In a rough sense, the two towns have a relationship rather like that of Cordova to Valdez. Like Cordova, Seldovia is built on the mainland but has the feel of an island community. Seldovia is a much smaller town than Cordova. Its population is around 500, and by virtue of that and its nearness to Homer, it tends to fall rather more into the gravity of Homer's orbit than Cordova does to Valdez. This is a source of some resentment in Seldovia, but again, because Homer lacks the singular presence of anything like the Alyeska Terminal, Seldovia's edginess toward the richer town seems subdued in comparison with Cordova's to Valdez.

As communities, Seldovia and Homer share a vulnerability created by the movement of chemical and oil tankers to and from Anchorage and the Drift River Oil Terminal. Also, the two towns and other towns on the Kenai Peninsula had already been through the spill from the tanker *Glacier Bay*, and the politically divisive controversy over offshore Kachemak Bay oil leases. In 1973, leases had been sold in Kachemak Bay, but following pressure from local groups and fishermen, and a timely accident with a jack-up oil rig stored in the bay which resulted in a diesel spill, the state legislature bought back in the leases in 1976.* After the oil spill, the two towns would experience the collective alarm triggered by the eruptions of the volcano Redoubt during the winter of 1990, and the danger the flooding Drift River and ensuing mudflows presented to the Cook Inlet Pipeline Company's Drift River Terminal—yet another precariously situated and ill-defended oil installation. The terminal is located across the inlet from the town of Kenai, not far north of Homer. The mudflows threatened to undercut the foundations of holding tanks, and so to spill millions of gallons of oil into the inlet. Finally, the tanks were drawn down, the terminal summarily closed by the DEC, the mudflow diverted, the waters protected, and the people, as if they needed it, reawakened to the danger of oil. Such circumstances of location may explain the degree of cooperation Homer and Seldovia forged during the Exxon *Valdez* crisis. They also fall under the same borough government.

There were three of us in the six-seater Cessna—myself, the pilot, and a solid-looking man in a white shirt and suspenders. The two rear seats were folded down to accommodate our luggage and the overflow of parcels the flight was delivering to Seldovia. The pilot circled before landing, a common practice hereabouts. It is a good idea to check for obstructions before putting down, for vehicles, pedestrians, other planes, moose, or, in the case of English Bay, where I would land several days later, the logs that the sea regularly deposits on the runway. The crosswinds buffeted the Cessna. I took out my notebook to record what I saw: the town built up just off the runway, and just west of town the long, five-mile finger of water, Seldovia Bay, and running northward through the trees near the shoreline, a narrow road. The Cessna dropped precipitously and landed neatly on the strip. I was seated next to the pilot and got out first. As we waited beside the plane for our luggage, the other passenger turned to me. Up to that moment, we had exchanged nothing more than pleasantries, but he said, "I hope you write something about how this has changed everybody. We knew twenty years ago it was going to happen. But we didn't know what it would do to us."

He had known that I was a stranger. The notebook must have told him the rest. He said, "We'll never be the same again, and the others need to hear."

I thought about that as I walked the mile or so from the landing strip.

---

* Using the same line of reasoning, and following the 1989 spill, Alaska Governor Cowper would urge Congress to buy back the Bristol Bay oil leases that the government had sold in 1988. Bristol Bay is the site of the richest salmon fishery in the world.

I had regularly experienced the sense of expectation the oil spill writers created in the Alaskan people and had felt the weight of an almost overwhelming sense of obligation to them. The roadway took me along a lagoon, the Seldovia Slough, where kids were fishing, and then into the trees and out again and down a slope to the town. It was a warm, sunny day and the sea air felt luxurious. The buildings in the main section of town seemed equally divided between strictly functional and quaint. The quaint addressed the tourist trade. The town otherwise addressed the bay and docks.

Frank Monsey, Seldovia's fire chief, found himself in a position rather like the one Marge Tillion found herself in over in Homer. Frank had a high regard for Marge. Of her troubles with Exxon and Veco, he said, "Nobody has a male ego problem like a bureaucrat. Here we had more women than men in leadership positions."

Frank is trained in the Incident Command System (ICS), an emergency management structure that evolved from fire fighting. On paper, the system is represented as a series of boxes, each of which describes a duty and which as circumstances arise may be broken up into more boxes, or eliminated, or replaced. At the heart of the system is the emergency manager, Frank's position. The manager's responsibility is simply to facilitate the response. The system's emphasis is on decentralization of structure, and autonomy in the various positions. Since it was designed to handle situations in which sudden change occurs, such as a fire moving overnight out of the hills to a suburb, or an oil slick, the object is to maintain basic structure and at the same time maximize fluidity. Ideally, it addresses the objective, which is to quell the emergency, and nothing else. When the emergency is over the structure shrinks or even vanishes.

Frank Monsey waxed eloquent on this subject, and on Exxon's and subsequently Veco's inability to take control, which he ascribed to their centralization. "Exxon has all the managers, but everything is always falling apart on them because it's all so centralized. The first people they send out are the PR managers and the lawyers. Usually, they have no idea where they've come to, so they can't make a decision without routing it back through headquarters. If they'd had the correct people out here, and organized it right, and given those people authority to deal directly with us, a lot of the oil would have been cleaned up. They don't have their shit together. The company is running itself. It's a juggernaut.

"And then you get the agencies, and Veco, and you've got one huge cluster fuck. For Veco and Exxon, this is an industrial cleanup. For us, it was our life. Exxon's first concern is PR and Veco's managing the money. For us, the main thing became, first, be ready for anything, and second, never believe the assholes. The Coast Guard couldn't get Exxon to move. The Coast Guard supposedly has all the power, but they haven't used it. The Coast Guard keeps saying, Exxon has the resources, but the Coast Guard's job is to lead and manage, according to the law, and while they're screwing around, not cleaning up oil that could be cleaned, federally protected species are dying out there."

Frank stopped and settled back. We were inside the fire station, sitting in folding chairs on opposite sides of a steel table. To one side stood a red fire engine, next to it another engine, and stored all around and hanging from the walls were firefighting supplies. I guessed that Frank was in his early sixties. He wore a red cap, a gray pile vest, and an aquamarine-colored shirt. The strength of his language notwithstanding, he was actually soft-spoken and affable, a grandfatherly type. He was given to smiling and, judging from the upwardly curved lines around his mouth and eyes, had been so for a long time. He'd lived in Alaska since he was three.

Frank Monsey had put his finger on something, what for me was a piece of the puzzle. It had to do with the government's and Exxon's inability to mount a structure of response sufficiently flexible and sufficiently direct to deal with a disaster that had the unpredictability of an oil spill. Something like the Incident Command System—the contingency plan—had existed in an underequipped, understaffed, and poorly maintained state at the Alyeska Terminal. The state-mandated decision matrix for the use of dispersants had a flexibility analogous to ICS, but with a fatal flaw—no provision for expert decision making at high speed and very little provision for the use of local expertise. The Exxon system of management as it came to be instituted was hierarchic, and so structurally contrary to ICS. To it was added the state's involvement, the sometimes politically motivated state and federal agencies, and the Coast Guard, and the introduction of Veco and other contractors whose primary interest—making money—was at odds with controlling an oil spill. In addition, I would learn, the Kenai borough government had imported its own two ICS teams (one from Anchorage and another from Denver) which as often as not were at odds with Homerites and Seldovians. It was as if the system that arose had been designed for conflict rather than the reverse, and then for the inevitable decay through adversarial relationships toward the approval loop that made decisions ever more remote from the communities and their necessities. The failure of that system to respond to the oil spill raises serious questions about our capacity for dealing with another type of disaster, one, say, that might threaten human life on a massive scale.

Before I left, Frank sallied into a tirade. I had heard the like repeatedly, but it seemed the more surprising coming from a man of his demeanor. "The basic problem," he said, "started with Exxon's inability to see the world. They're concerned with PR, not cleanup. The little people getting screwed over by these companies have to start thinking big. Arrest the whole damn company. Run an air force strike on the Exxon offices. Organize a boycott. Block the channel. Hell, block the Suez Canal. Think big. We have to protect ourselves with power, otherwise the financial harassment will go on forever."

Frank looked down at the table, then took off his cap and ran his fingers through his gray hair. He looked up at me and chuckled softly. "Now see? I'm all excited again."

Others recounted for me the events in Seldovia. They included Annie McKenzie, owner of the Annie McKenzie Boardwalk Hotel, Tim Robertson, who with his wife, Debbie, was the owner of a lodge outside town, Sandy Elvsaas, who in July had become Veco director in Seldovia, and John Mickelson, Seldovia representative to the Homer area MAC and later a leader in the volunteer group the Oil Reform Alliance. On day six of the spill, March 29, the townspeople—like the people in Homer, and the people in Seward, like the Park Service people at the Kenai Fjords National Park—realized that the oil was headed their way. When contacted, however, the Exxon office in Valdez disputed the likelihood. If anything, the situation was worse at Kenai Fjords, an 1,145-square-mile tract with a series of deep fjords and over 40 glaciers. Located on the southern, gulf side of the peninsula it was more in the track of the oil.

Park service people had been told previously by a NOAA representative that no more than 50 barrels of oil would escape Prince William Sound. As with the Department of Fish and Wildlife, there were intimations in that case, too, of the upper echelons of the park service in Washington, D.C., trying to minimize the severity of the threat and deliberately stalling action. Eventually, Anne Castillina, the superintendent of Kenai Fjords, bucked authority and took action on her own by ordering boom through the Seward MAC, deploying it, and retrieving oiled animals.

In Seldovia—as in Homer, Seward, and a little later, Kodiak—the townspeople set out to organize their own response. They put the ICS into action and set out to design, fabricate, and then deploy log boom at the mouth of Seldovia Bay, even though they had doubts about whether or not it would be effective. Between two and three hundred people became involved, or, as Tim Robertson would put it, "the entire adult population of the town." The high school closed its doors. Logging people donated logs and equipment. Volunteer food and childcare services were set up. Exxon's Wylie Bragg promised to send technical help for boom construction, but it never materialized. Money was promised, but it came in amounts insufficient to cover the supplies, and it was initially earmarked, the Seldovians were told, to fund setting up an office, not to purchase boom material. While they were building boom and trying to secure materials, the Seldovians reached a point, according to Annie McKenzie, where they realized that booming the bay was going to cost half a million dollars and that they only had $15,000.

I talked to Annie in her hotel apartment when she was preparing to fill out the claim forms needed to secure compensation for the loss of business she said her hotel had suffered during the summer. It was nearly four months after the spill. The forms, scattered across her desk, filled her with anger and frustration. They were the bitter tailings—money, financial exigency; and then there was the memory of what Annie called "the thrill" of being a part of the community's initial mobilization. Annie became Seldovia's first oil spill coordinator. Formerly a women's rights activist in Washington State, she is a pretty, vivacious woman in her forties, her dark hair speckled with gray. As we spoke, she several times nearly broke into tears. "But for a solid week," she said, "we worked at a peak. We really produced, and it made us realize what our capacity was. We'd get mad at each other once in a while, but the intimacy among us as a group was exquisite."

That was the first week of April. The next week, Veco, operating out of its base in Homer, came into Seldovia, and brought with it Exxon money and the expectation that it would manage the response both for Seldovia Bay and outlying areas. There was confusion over the dispensation of funds to the volunteer effort—whether or not to route funds through local city or borough government. There were suggestions of graft that turned on the city's use of Exxon funds to order items that many believed had nothing to do with the oil spill—a computer, for example. A proposal, supported by the mayor, Jerry Willard, was floated to rebuild an old logging road through Native property to Port Graham, which by the extended access it created, it was hoped, would have tied in Seldovia more firmly to cleanup money. In Annie McKenzie's view it was an attempt to gouge Exxon, and to create an avenue for future logging development, which in itself was a controversial matter. The money tended to do that, to move out laterally and find pockets it could fill, and then to exponentially increase confusion and distraction. After Veco's arrival, the log boom project continued. It still needed supplies, such as industrial drills. Annie said she convinced the area Veco supervisor, Ray Springer, to order drills, and as he did so she heard him say over the phone, "Yeah, the chipmunks are running." She took it to mean that the community effort was being patronized.

Fishing and tourism are important to Seldovia. Even setting matters of environmental principle aside—which most Seldovians decidedly did not—it was inevitable that local people would be concerned with waterways and shorelines beyond their immediate environs. Simultaneous with the boom project, action was undertaken to protect fish, wildlife, and shorelines by collecting oil. Tim Robertson, who was to become a new city councilmember and then, for a time, acting mayor of Seldovia, and who I had met previously in Anchorage, was instrumental in putting together the plan for oil collection.

Tim has a master's degree in fisheries biology and had worked six years for the Alaska Department of Fish and Game Wildlife and eight years as an engineer for a North Slope service company. He took a rather more benevolent view of Veco supervisors, such as Ray Springer, than others did. Tim believed that the real problems were in the higher echelons of management and that the local supervisors were left in the difficult position of managing the cutting edges of controversy. Ray Springer had felt, according to Tim, that he had no problem with Seldovians. Springer had hired eight of the original volunteers as foremen, among whom Annie McKenzie was not included. Annie had told me that she preferred to operate as an independent voice. "But in Seldovia," Tim said, "we became Veco."

As it turned out, the oil never entered Seldovia Bay in quantity. The oil collection operation, however, performed in collaboration with Homerites, met with the same type of frustrations that all locally based operations did. Tim said, "Once we saw that oil wasn't coming into Seldovia Bay, we started preparing to go out and get it." The group secured and modified boats, and then Exxon called and ordered that the operation be shut down. Senator Ted Stevens intervened and the group went back to work. They had secured a float plane to spot oil. When they were ready to take off, a storm stopped them. By the time they did take off, according to Tim, Ray Springer himself had grown frustrated with Veco and resigned. The group had Veco funding, but they were running at cross purposes with the system. The new supervisor, Bob Warren, called the group on the radio and said that Exxon had ordered them back. The group refused, and, having located oil, began to deal with the technical problems of recovering it on their own. They couldn't pump it because it was too thick. They finally used modified dipnets and buckets to gather it, techniques that would also be used at Kodiak. Two people, Tim said, could pick up 200 gallons an hour.

For their first load, the group captured 8,000 gallons of oil and oily debris, but then they had nothing to do with it. A tankerage ship had been in their vicinity for ten days, but the ship had been given orders not to take their oil. The group towed their oil and debris to the ship, the *Alaska Husky*, but when the ship threw its pumps into it, the pumps plugged up immediately. Tim said, "We told them, 'We've got thirty-five guys with shovels and buckets. Where do you want it?' They said, 'Wait a minute. This is a union boat.' " Robertson's group, still intent above all else upon getting oil out of the water, no matter how tedious the process, did shovel the oil into the *Alaska Husky*. The boat, which had a 30,000-gallon capacity, took off, and the group had to find another for their next load. Tim said that they made three trips. "But each time it got more frustrating. We went down to pump it and found that you have to physically move it. We were worried about the toxicity. I asked for help with that and a guy said he would come out. He never made it. All the time, there were helicopters everywhere. Exxon and Veco were in control and they are not efficient. Fishermen aren't like that. They just go to it. They have the heart to get a job done."

Tim came to the same conclusion that Billy Day and Marge Tillion had, that it was better to go independent. At the time I spoke with Tim in early July, he, Mei Mei Evans of Homer, Marge Tillion, John Mickelson, and others were working to get their beach-cleaning project off the ground, and Billy Day was putting his rock washing machine together.

Sandy Elvsaas was the Veco director in Seldovia in July. Veco had taken hold but had placed her, a local person, in charge. She managed 17 boats and 63 people who were rotating in and out of Picnic Harbor, the Barren Islands, and Port Chatham—all down around the corner of the peninsula. She also had a Veco boss, an Exxon boss, and five other people checking on her all the time. Her predecessor as Veco director, Jennifer Dilley, had left her position in a fury that was tied, in part, to the lack of support given to the oil collection enterprise. Sandy Elvsaas is a fisherman. Her husband, Fred, an engineer and fisherman, is president of the Seldovia Native Corporation. Sandy seemed to have a circumspect view of events in Seldovia.

She knew that there was bitterness in the town and was frustrated by the failure of cleanup in her area. She felt that Exxon still hoped the oil would break up and disappear and that compared to Prince William Sound, the Kenai Peninsula had been given short shrift. "If we hadn't screamed and hollered," she said, "we'd never have gotten anything. And it's true that if they'd let us go our own way, just funded us, we'd have got the job done better than they did." She disliked the peremptory way orders came down to her from her superiors. Earlier on the very day I talked to her, Veco people had come in and fired six of her workers. "This morning there were four people in this office," she said. "Now there's one. Me. I wish they'd allowed me to pick the six people, and prepare them and lay them off myself."

Her inclination, though, was to emphasize the positive. "Good things happened," she said. "Long-lasting alliances have been formed in Seldovia. Incredible things were accomplished, but now there's a letdown. Basically, everybody's tired. People need to refocus on the great things they did because you're never going to get all this oil out of here. The women designed the fabric to make wave skirts for the log boom. They helped build the boom. We had ten thousand feet of it. We shoveled oil off the beach and deployed the boom and felt really protected.

"And a lot of new technology has come out," she said. "We developed some things ourselves. The scientists are developing a fertilizer to break down the hydrocarbons in the oil."

She was talking about bioremediation. She said they were working on it at the NOAA station just down the road, where James Payne was.

This was the same James Payne, the oft-quoted expert I'd heard of in the science meetings in Valdez. I'd been trying to reach him for months. It was his work that had been cited in the early science meetings as a corrective to Exxon's figures for the evaporation rate of crude oil. He knew as much as anybody about the nature of Prudhoe crude and how it interacted with a marine environment. Over the last several weeks, the controversy over "sinking oil" had picked up energy, mainly because oil seemed to be arriving off Kodiak from unknown places. The issue was acquiring mythical proportions. Fishermen there and in Cordova claimed that oil was coming up with their nets. Frank Monsey had talked about sinking oil. Tim Robertson claimed that on one of his flyovers during the oil collection project, he'd seen a patch of oil sheer underwater. Back in Homer, Ken Broginoff had claimed that oil sank. Marge Tillion had said that oil had come upon anchors from four fathoms down at Picnic Harbor and that divers' bubbles pushed up oil near Home Cove on Nuka Island. Lee Glenn, the head Fish and Game biologist in Homer, had acknowledged the possibility of underwater oil. To discount these claims and questions, James Payne's research was always cited, principally by NOAA. The question of whether or not oil sank had become critical for one central reason, which carried with it all the usual political, economic, and legal baggage: if it sank, then its toxic effects would be expanded in area and extended in time, and the numbers of affected creatures would be enlarged.

John Mickelson agreed to drive me out to the NOAA lab at Kasitsnu Bay. We set out in the evening in his pickup truck and drove along the same narrow gravel road I'd seen from the Cessna before I landed in Seldovia. The lab was located about 15 miles away, halfway between Seldovia and the otter center at Jackolof Bay—where holding pens had been constructed at a place to care for and then retain healthy otters until a decision was made as to what to do with them.

Besides being deeply involved with all phases of the oil spill response, John worked as maintenance supervisor for the city of Seldovia. He is a tall man, powerfully built, and wears a baseball cap all the time. He is outspoken, passionate, friendly, and there is something in his bearing that suggests dangerousness, as if of a pirate. On the way to the lab, John recounted his story of Exxon, Seldovia, graft, greed, intrigue, and oil. He drove with one hand draped over the steering wheel and leaned toward me, talking as the stiffly sprung pickup lurched and swung through the potholes in the road.

As maintenance supervisor, John had begun at the heart of the action. As Seldovia's representative on the Homer MAC he remained at the heart for the duration. He had practical knowledge of equipment and of the channels of local government. He told me that by mid-July the city budget had a $300,000 surplus, while before the spill it had been running a $60,000 deficit. There had been an 8 percent increase in the city budget due to purchase orders run through the local store, and to such things as dock fees and leases for Veco offices. Port Graham, John said, had done "even better" than Seldovia. He said that with irony, though his voice remained even.

John's main complaint, as with many in Seldovia and Homer, was not so much with Veco as with Exxon, with Exxon's continued focus upon Prince William Sound, where the white lights of the media were trained, and its failure to respond to the presence of oil on and off the Kenai Peninsula. Exxon's slow response was compounded by its policy of shifting supervisors in and out of position. Exxon had a furlough system by which many of the supervisors and managers working on the oil spill would stay in a position for several weeks, then rotate out. The approach worked well on remote drilling sites and made some sense here in terms of the personnel themselves, who in many cases had left homes and families behind in the lower forty-eight, put in long hours, and were subjected to high stress.

In Homer, where the Exxon office was located, public appearances by Exxon's Wylie Bragg, John Dean, Dan Jones, and Dean Peeler, were sometimes occasions for merciless barrages of criticism from all quarters—citizens, local leaders, state and federal agency representatives. The furlough system further aggravated the situation and for local people heightened the sense of Exxon's colonialism—a foreign power that had pushed its way into a locale through foolish-looking representatives. The newly assigned Exxon people often had very little familiarity with the area to which they had come, and less than adequate familiarity with oil spill procedures as they had evolved. Everyone who came in had to "get up to speed," and it was not uncommon to see Exxon supervisors being educated by agency representatives or reporters. Because of the bureaucratic decision-making "loop," supervisors were encumbered with paperwork and also had very little real authority. Finally, everything was further exacerbated by the fact that the oil spill remained a rapidly shifting, quirkily evolving reality, or what Exxon's Dan Jones referred to in early May as "a moving target."

Public and private meetings in Homer produced tangles of contradictions and raised emotions to the boiling point. Back in the first week of May, for example, Dan Jones, then the newly arrived chief spokesman for Exxon, had asserted that boom was not being sent to the southern Kenai because headquarters kept diverting it to Prince William Sound, where, presumably, it was needed more. He had been contradicted by several MAC members, including a Coast Guard commander, Richard Asaro, who said he understood that Exxon's decision not to send boom to Homer was based on cost-saving considerations, not on environmental ones. On the lower Kenai, commercial boom was still needed at that time to replace the log boom that was in position at several critical locations. Jones had also said that boom and other support need not be sent by Exxon to boats in Port Chatham—a bay near the southernmost tip of the Kenai Peninsula that was acting as a catch basin for passing oil—because that was not an Exxon operation. In fact, however, boats under contract to Exxon had been anchoring at Port Chatham every night.

Jones had said that there would be no more skimming off the Kenai because at that time oil was not present in sufficient quantities to justify the procedure, and then two days later he had reported that that very day, the fifth of May, had seen the best skimming day yet on the outer peninsula. He had said that federal and state agencies put the brakes on Exxon's offshore work at Gore Point—the narrow, heavily oiled protrusion of land just east of Port Dick,* not far from Mars Cove. He had said that prior to an April 26 memo from Vice Admiral C. E. Robbins, the Coast Guard ruled that Exxon should not clean up outside Prince William Sound, and that that was a cause of much of the delay, but representatives of the state Department of National Resources (DNR), the DEC, and the Coast Guard stated that mechanical cleanup had been requested at Gore Point long before April 26, and that an Exxon official previously in Homer, John Dean, had said he couldn't order cleanup because Exxon headquarters had directed him to stay off the Gore Point beaches. Jones had also asserted that Exxon had not anticipated that shoreline cleanup would be necessary at all off the Kenai, this in contradiction to the advice of fishermen and to projections for the course of a major oil spill in the sound that were in existence long before the grounding of the Exxon Valdez.

These meetings in May took place while the retrieval project with which Tim Robertson had been involved was still under way, about two weeks after the bird-burning incident at Gore Point, and two weeks after a high-level delegation that included Alaska Representative Don Young, Alaska Senator Frank Murkowski, and Secretary of the Interior Manuel Lujan were presented with oily pom-poms and bottles of oil by Larry Smith as proof that oil was indeed in Kachemak Bay, contrary to Coast Guard reports and Exxon assumptions. The May 5 meetings were held three weeks after Marge Tillion resigned her volunteer capacity as a community liaison to Exxon and Veco, a full month after the oil had washed ashore at Kenai Fjords National Park. During this time, the various government and private parties continued to jockey for control, including control over the groundswell of effort and anger. Vice Admiral Robbins several times publicly chided Exxon for lack of action and state and federal officials repeatedly attempted to establish a clear chain of command. For a while, reorganization of the response was a weekly ritual.

Also during this time, the crews stationed on the beaches, some of

---

* Gore Point also became the locus of yet another controversy over Exxon's manipulation of information that Marge Tillion had first told me about. On May 19, a *U.S.A. Today* production crew filmed cleanup efforts at Gore Point for national broadcast. Two hours before the production team arrived, as many as 53 workers were shuttled to a Gore Point beach and then filmed as they industriously mopped and shoveled the heavy oil. After the production crew left, the workers were shuttled back out. The next day 40 of them were laid off.

whom were assigned to shovel oil into plastic bags, were complaining about fumes and lack of support. Some fell ill. They lacked tankerage for oil and storage for oily debris. They lacked facilities for cleaning themselves up at night after wallowing round all day in oil. Back in town, John Mickelson and others, still using Marge Tillion's lists, were locating boom supplies for Exxon and generally trying to deal with the confusion. At its essence, it was a recapitulation of events in Prince William Sound during the first weeks of the spill, but in slow motion. It took more time for the oil to get to the Kenai, and, it should be granted, there was rather less of it and it was somewhat more weathered. The command structure in Valdez was preoccupied with Prince William Sound and even more hopeful that the oil would disperse and disappear off Kenai than it had been in the sound. It certainly didn't want to face a second front nor a third, Kodiak.

While the command structure was attempting to handle the Kenai, it had also rigidified. The response from within the Kenai communities was more organized, but so was the political infighting. Exxon money was more clearly a factor from the outset than it had been in either Valdez or Cordova, and therefore more of the Kenai people, including local politicians, were prepared to chase it. The subcontracting companies were more firmly established. The result was that, if anything, the local people were left even more out in the cold and more subjected to bureaucratic machinations than they had been in the sound. The fracturing was more immediate and more brittle.

"Ultimately, the truth is that we couldn't have done it," John said. "There was too much oil for fourteen people with shovels, or even ten times that many. The log boom didn't really work. It was all too heartbreaking to consider. Fourteen people on the first offensive. Two boats. But I told Wylie Bragg, 'Look, the people need to do something. We gathered a hundred thousand gallons of oil and Exxon didn't know what to do with it.' He said there were no barges. So, we went back to the boom again. We found them twenty thousand feet of boom and then some storage tanks, and said, 'Here it is. Just get it off the damn beach.' But nothing happened.

"Finally, I got fed up with the whole goddamn deal," John said. We were continuing in the pickup along the road toward the Kasitsnu Lab. The sky was beginning to darken, and the woods along the side of the road deepened. "The Exxon people cared less about what we said, though they were always pleasant. They just kept luring us on." John veered to avoid a pothole and my body swung inward and then back against the door. "I went into the legal library and started jerking books," he said. His voice had softened and the power with which his presence seemed normally to bristle had diminished. He'd allowed the pickup to slow down. "I wanted to make a citizen's arrest of Dan Jones. I found federal code thirty-four ten. It was illegal to knowingly convey false information with reckless disregard for human life.

"We were just playing this fucking game," he said. "I got a declaration of arrest from the police. I arrested Jones, then I tried to get a park ranger to take him into custody. The ranger called the attorney general. I ended up talking to the attorney general [Doug Baily], who tried to talk me out of it. I had called the networks. I'd loaded he MAC meeting with everybody I could think of. The bottom line of the deal was that the networks never showed up and the attorney general instructed the ranger, Roger MacCampbell, not to take the guy into custody. So, then I understood that the government would refuse to enforce its own laws."

We turned off the road and John goosed the truck up a steep, deeply rutted lane. We came out in a parking area nestled between sturdy, well-kept buildings. He parked and we sat there for a moment. I felt a great sympathy for John's daring, perhaps misguided action, and for the sense of loneliness with which the failure left him. He had tried to enforce the letter of the law in a situation in which the very arms of the law were entwined in a lawless dance. It was on May 5 that he'd done it, the same day as the chaotic sequence of meetings described above. It was an existential deed that expressed the engulfing perversity of the power that had gathered around him. He had tried to take one perpetrator into custody, to make him stop.

As we sat there, staring through the windshield at the wall of a building, he said, "Later that night they had a party at the Homestead Inn. I went up, but somehow hearing them all in there laughing, the Exxons and the Coast Guard, and all your agency people, and some of our own people who were making money hand over fist, all the permit people making jokes out of things that were crucial to the guys on the beach . . . it turned my stomach. I refused to go in and have a beer with them. The next day they had another party and invited everybody but me."

Chapter 14

THE TRUTH
ABOUT OIL

Outrage animated the oil and transformed it into myth. As myth, the actual multifariousness of oil was reduced to a single, all-encompassing thing, an overwhelming pestilence, a horde, like the mythical plagues of locusts, snakes, and bees, or like the film versions of all-consuming forces of devastation, such as hoards of birds, man-eating ants, or uncontrollable magma as in *The Blob*. Natural occurrences of geology and weather, such as floods, earthquakes and tsunamis, and volcanic eruptions carry many of the same qualities—utter inescapability and wanton destruction. In natural disasters, the acceptance on the part of survivors that mankind is incapable of countering the force of nature is not unlike the stage of acceptance that terminal cancer patients reach. It grants the presence of a power beyond one's own control.

Marauding armies, particularly when they are considered barbarian, or subhuman, acquire the character of myths of pestilence. Coincidentally, in the American mind these armies have come as often as not from oil-producing states like Iran and Iraq. They are sometimes linked to visions of Armageddon and seen as emanations of the overriding sentience of God. If any sentiment was universally expressed by those close to the oil spill, no matter what their persuasion, it was this: "We brought it on ourselves. We let down our guard." In the early days of the spill, much was also made of the fact that the oil spill occurred on Good Friday, 25 years after the Good Friday earthquake. Such sentiment is seeking a reason and tacitly acknowledges a source of wisdom behind the event, but in the case of the oil spill it was complicated by the fact that the spill was a quintessentially twentieth-century scourge of human nature, and so a small-scale model of the ultimate scourge—the atomic searing of all the earth. This made it difficult to look to God for the lesson behind the teaching.

Perhaps the human inclination to use symbolic thought as a way of giving pattern to the inexplicable is necessary. The shapelessness and devastation of the horde as it is represented in film and literature is a barely defined version of the true, meaningless, shapeless thing we carry in our subconscious, death. Our feeling for this thing is confirmed at times by events. In the ninth chapter of Revelations, a recurrent Middle Eastern scourge, the locust plague, is transformed into an instrument of revenge that strikes only the ungodly. Following the sounding of the Fifth Angel, the locusts come, shaped like horses with gold crowns on their heads, hair like women, teeth like lions, and tails like scorpions. They have the ability to hurt men for five months. It's a powerful, beguiling, and fanciful vision, but hardly more fanciful than heaping all of the blame upon Joseph Hazelwood's head, or transforming the oil into a plague that carried in its wake men with briefcases, Stetsons, and Texas boots, hauling carts loaded with money and commandeering and equipping an army of 11,000, 14,000 vessels, 80 aircraft. . . .

In what must be the ultimate prodevelopment fraud, James Watt, President Reagan's first secretary of the interior, had used his purported belief in the Second Coming as a means of justifying the pillaging of resources—quickly, before the final scourge arrives. His vision was animated by greed. In a similar manner, but with the animating force of despair, or fear of the future, many environmentalists use their belief in the motherly beneficence of nature (the Gaia hypothesis) or presumed natural patterns as a means of leaping to "preservationism." In its extreme forms, it's an impossible position to hold.

Often enough, seeing the oil on the beaches and the machinery devised to make it go away, I thought I'd been dropped into a hell of endless death. To see it that way made it possible to hold it in the imagination even when I did not understand it. It is necessary to have metaphors, at least, to guide conduct, but the metaphor must be as closely aligned as possible with the reality, as best that can be perceived. John Oliver and others on the *Alpha Helix* had told me something about the true nature of Prudhoe crude. Riki Ott of Cordova had told me more. Now, Dr. James Payne led John Mickelson and me into the NOAA lab— a clean, amply lit place decked out with long benches, computers, and exotic machines, and overlooking a bay that was visible through a line of plate glass windows.

Prudhoe Bay crude, like all crude oils, is a complex mixture of organic (carbon-based) and inorganic (noncarbon-based) compounds. The chemical make-up of crude oils drawn from different sites, or even from differing locations within one formation, may vary widely. Due to processes during petroleum formation that result in what is called molecular scrambling, crude oils contain thousands of different chemical compounds. Each variety of crude oil carries the traces of specific plant or animal precursors. Each bears individual molecular markers, or fingerprints of a sort, by which its source can be identified. One of the tasks performed at the Kasitsnu lab was to check samples of recovered oil to determine whether or not it came from the Exxon *Valdez*. There were other possible sources of spilled oil in Cook Inlet and the sound.

Of the types of molecular compounds in crude oil, hydrocarbons are the most abundant, varying from 50 to 98 percent of the whole. In Prudhoe crude, hydrocarbons constitute a little over 60 percent. The hydrocarbons are the concentrated residuum of the detritus of life that entered the formation and made the oil. It's a remarkable substance, crude oil, the chaotic, chemical essence of the North Slope's chaotic biota. Through their use of oil, humans have entered into an exchange with their own natural history that extends back through the millennia. This makes for another disconcerting metaphor, the notion of consuming our natural history faster than it can replenish itself, and as we do so pressurized compounds previously contained in geologic formations have been released back into the world in the form of fuel and sometimes dangerous molecular junk, such as carbon monoxide and carbon dioxide.

The inorganic compounds are grouped into six classes, including sulphur, nitrogen, oxygen compounds, and trace metals. The organic compounds, or hydrocarbons, fall into two categories, or fractions—the aliphatids and the aromatics. The aliphatids are nontoxic, biodegradable, and do not persist in the environment. The aromatics come in two types—single ring compounds (they include BETX: benzene, ethylbenzene, toulene, and xylene) and multiple ring compounds. Single ring compounds have low molecular weights. They are light, highly soluble, and acutely toxic. They dissolve and suddenly evaporate. Multiple ring compounds persist in the environment. These are not acutely toxic but are longterm mutagens with the capacity to penetrate deeply into the food web, to enter on the cellular level, to be carcinogenic, to warp DNA.

The aromatics may otherwise be known as light ends, which refers to the relatively low temperatures at which they reach boiling point. In the process of refining, crude oil is heated and the compounds, based on their differing boiling points, are separated, or "cracked." The components made into fuel (gasoline, diesel, kerosene, etc.) are composed primarily of hydrocarbons and, of course, are highly toxic and explosive.

The refining process provides a rough picture of the rate at which the various compounds partition into what are termed the natural compartments—the air, the water column, the sediment, and the organ

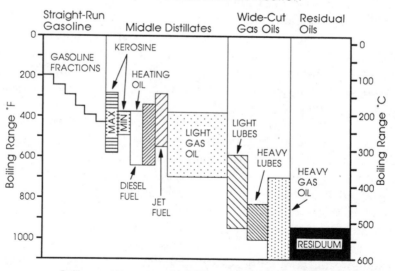

FRACTIONAL DISTILLATION DISTRIBUTION

Boiling point range of fractions of crude petroleum.

Source: John H. Steele et al., *Oil in the Sea: Inputs, Fates and Effects* (Washington, D. C.: National Academy Press, 1985), p. 27.

isms. In the last category, organisms, there are potentially as many sub-compartments as there are species within affected areas. Through feeding interrelationships the hydrocarbons (especially multiple ring) lodged in bodies pass from one species to the next. This is the way in which persistent compounds have chronic effects upon life, and such effects are most likely to occur in places that are repeatedly exposed—the Port of Valdez, Galveston Bay, and New York harbor. The words used by scientists—"partition" and "compartment"—imply an orderly process, as if of pantries and cupboards. In fact, the leading edges of molecular exchange are quite disorderly.

Generally speaking, compounds with boiling points below 488 degrees Fahrenheit, the light ends, are the only ones subject to partitioning into the atmosphere (evaporation). This process caused much of the first, acute wave of marine mammal mortality: animals, especially otters, inhaled the fumes and developed respiratory failure. The fumes also caused sickness among beach workers. Some of the compounds are the same as the ones we inhale when we put gasoline in our tanks. They go right into the lungs. They are also the most subject to rapid dissolution in the water column.

As I had already learned, the single most obvious and most compelling fact about crude oil in its relation to water, and one that James Payne emphasized, is that it floats. Its specific gravity is less than that of water. This is a truth, and therefore a thing to be held closely. In the racket of claims and counterclaims, even among scientists, even concerning the behavior of oil, there were precious few things that could be said with certainty. Everything else seemed to plummet in the direction of paradox. But it is certain that oil floats. All matters connected to the oil spill are derived from this truth: the visibility of oil on the surface of the water, the visibility of affected animals, the propensity of oil to ride the tide to the shorelines, the possibility of retrieving it, or burning it, dispersing it, or biodegrading it. It would not sink unless enough matter, such as sediment, adhered to it to make it heavier than water, unless it was driven temporarily beneath the surface, or unless it stuck to something beneath the surface. These derivatives of the true nature of oil are important as things that happened in various places, but it remains true that crude oil floats on water.

Once crude oil is introduced to water, it immediately begins to weather. In all its peculiarities, weathering is also a function of the fact that oil floats. It occurs in several different ways, including spreading and drift, evaporation, dissolution, dispersion, water-in-oil emulsification, adsorption onto suspended particulate material, and shoreline interactions.* It should be noted that in no sense does weathering mean that oil disappears, but rather that its components are transferred into one compartment or another. Matter does not cease to exist.

Once oil has entered the sea, it spreads. Its lateral movement is affected variously by forces of gravity, inertia, friction, and surface tension, and by its own volume and the rate at which it is spilled. Eyewitness accounts of the Exxon *Valdez* spill reported that the oil came out of the ship so fast that it backed up on itself. Even presuming that the surface of the water is relatively calm, as it was in Prince William Sound on March 24, the oil will spread in an infinitely random combination of thick and thin patches. This is due in part to the chemical interaction between oil and water. It has not yet proved possible for laboratory scientists to model in detail the pattern of spreading.

Drifting occurs independently of spreading and is controlled by wind, waves, and surface currents at all levels of intensity. The center of an oil slick moves at roughly 3 percent of wind speed, with a 20- to 30-degree shift to the right due to the Coriolis effect. These forces and others that occur simultaneously—the perturbation of secondary currents, the obstruction of land masses—add new factors to the already scientifically unpredictable destiny of oil. Both spreading and drifting increase the surface of the slick and therefore enhance transfer through evaporation and dissolution.

Evaporation is the most important process of weathering during the first 24 to 48 hours following a spill. This is the most acute phase in terms of damage to wildlife. Over a period of 12 days, between 15 and 20 percent of the total mass of the crude oil may be lost through evaporation alone. The rate of evaporation, however, is affected by such things as air flow, and air and water temperature, which in south-central Alaska tend to be low. Ultimately, Prudhoe crude loses between 21 and 22 percent of its mass through evaporation.

Dissolution of hydrocarbons into the water column generally does not represent significant numbers in terms of the overall mass of an oil spill, but again the biological effects are potentially very damaging because of the propensity of light end hydrocarbons to partition into organic compartments and thus to enter the food web. Most dissolution occurs

---

* These categories and explanatory material are largely derived from conversation with James Payne and from his and G. Daniel McNabb's report "Weathering of Petroleum in the Marine Environment." My presentation, of course, is far less detailed than is Payne and McNabb's. Two additional categories mentioned in the report but not covered here are the weathering effects of ice in arctic environments, which had little or no application to the Exxon *Valdez* spill, and photochemical oxidation, about which little is known.

within 8 to 12 hours after the release of oil to the water and then falls off exponentially. Dissolution is heightened by the spilling energy of oil into the water and by wave action, which stirs the oil into the water.

Dispersion is the tendency of crude oil to break up into droplets within the water. This increases surface area and allows further dissolution and evaporation of the light end hydrocarbons. Although most of the dispersed droplets will return to the surface of the sea, some will be ingested by organisms at depth, then redeposited as fecal pellets and enter the food web as a chronic source of toxicity. This phenomenon, in addition to the presence of toxins in chemical dispersants themselves, which speed up the natural process and for a time increase the amount of hydrocarbons in the water column, was the source of the controversy over the use of dispersants immediately after the spill. Science remains genuinely divided over the use of chemical dispersants, and particularly their longterm effects.

A side effect of natural dispersion, dissolution, and evaporation is that the proportion of waxes and asphaltics in the oil that remains will have increased dramatically—in 12 days from 34 percent to approximately 50 percent. The formation of water-in-oil emulsions, or mousse, depends upon the presence of these materials, and Prudhoe crude happens to have them in high levels to begin with. Within a short time (following the first storms) much of the oil spilled from the Exxon *Valdez* had formed a mousse composed of up to 55 percent water. This made it impossible to burn off the oil and seriously compromised other strategies, such as skimming. Also, the formation of mousse, because of the sealing effect of water, significantly impedes evaporation, dissolution, and microbial degradation. Therefore, emulsified tarballs that appeared at shorelines on, for example, the Kenai Peninsula and Kodiak Island (they continued to do so at various locations for months) tended to retain toxic compounds at serious levels. The transformation of the original oil slick into mousse following the initial period of calm weather and the failure to either mechanically retrieve it (the most desirable first scenario) or chemically disperse it was one of the most critical developments in the history of the oil spill.

The adsorption of oil onto suspended particulate material, or in other words the tendency of oil droplets to adhere to the surfaces of minute particles suspended in the water, creates the possibility of oil sinking to the bottom because of the weight of the object to which the oil has adhered. Again, Payne's findings suggested that this process was not significant in terms of the total mass of crude oil but potentially significant in certain locations, usually those heavily hit by oil, or hit repeatedly through tidal action. In such places the load of oiled particulates could transport itself on a massive scale to the bottom and affect the food web. Although John Oliver and the *Alpha Helix* science crew reported very little apparent damage to life systems in the intertidal habitats they surveyed, their work was done in early June, and so they were looking at first effects. Longterm damage would not have been evident yet.

The final category—shoreline interactions—was easily the most serious development from the Exxon *Valdez* spill, and one for which nobody was prepared. The near-shore waters received many of the unpredictable variables of other means of weathering, such as adsorption and dissolution, and the shorelines themselves added their own unchartable complexities: plant life and sediment to which the oil might adhere, surfaces of varying degrees of porosity through which the oil might sink to varying depths, and tides that delivered the oil sometimes repeatedly, sometimes forming asphaltic mats. More than any other compartment, it was at the shorelines that crude oil in its complexity assumed the proportions of an out-of-control pestilence.

As he spoke to us, James Payne deemphasized the effects of oil at sea. His view was of the whole of the slick. If you took all the water from Valdez to Port Graham, a distance of 400 kilometers, he said, then went offshore 200 kilometers, and assumed for the sake of argument that the water was 100 meters deep (a low estimate), the oil concentrations would be three parts per billion, and effects on fish larvae will probably not occur until concentrations reach ten parts per billion. His point was that the water column concentrations were extremely low. He also deemphasized the likelihood that oil could have sunk in appreciable quantities—the controversy into which his work and his name had entered. Contrary to much of what I had heard about him, however, even from other scientists, he did not downplay in the least the seriousness of either the adsorption of oil onto particulates or the interaction of shorelines with oil, nor did he deny that oil might submerge. He said, "Oil could be entrained into a rip, but it would be a transient, short-lived phenomenon. Reports of submerged oil had yet to be confirmed in the samplings."

That was clear enough. It was science, and it depended upon evidence. Later, I asked Dexter Chan, a NOAA scientist stationed in Homer, about sinking oil. He looked at me warily. Since he worked out of the Homer OSCO office, he'd been receiving his share of the brunt of the controversy. He said, "Every instance of sinking oil is in the intertidal areas. There's nothing in deep waters."

Some time after that, in late July, I spoke to Robert Tworkowski, a Woods Hole geologist working for Alaska DEC in Kodiak. He regarded the sinking oil question as unresolved because, as he put it, "of the complexity of the water systems off Kodiak." He said that he could see oil still washing up around Kodiak, and that the question was: How was it getting there? He offered underwater channeling, underwater eddies, and a huge underwater reservoir as possibilities.

Later yet, in November, still puzzled by the question, I spoke to Jerry Galt in the NOAA offices in Seattle. Galt had worked on the oil spill. He had a certain exasperation, even a disdain for the question. He said, "You can't repeal the law of gravity. Oil floats." Of Kodiak, he said, "Of all the oil that got there, the amount that might have been entrained would be in the one percent range." Throughout all that time and extending into the spring of 1990, fishermen reported oil showing up on their lines, crab pots, and anchors. Jerry Galt referred to such reports as "hearsay."

James Payne was far more willing to grant the possibility of exceptions and variations. Trim, with something of the bearing of an assured surgeon, he has eyes as clear as any I have ever seen, like water. He spoke forcefully and rapidly, in the manner of one accustomed to holding forth. The company with which he was associated, Science Applications International Corporation (SAIC), had begun testing Prudhoe crude for NOAA back in 1981 with the 2,100-liter flow-through tanks located outside. They were designed as models of marine conditions. It was through his work with them that Payne had arrived at most of his conclusions concerning the behavior of oil in water. He was careful to have us understand that SAIC had never done work for a private company, including the oil companies. In the political climate of the time and place, this was a matter of significance.

There were certain things, he said, that he couldn't tell us. The court-ordered rule of silence placed upon scientists connected with any oil spill litigation included all research activity supported in any way by Exxon or state and federal agencies. It included the 60-odd projects I'd seen among Gordon Robilliard's papers. The effect, since so few independent scientists (of which John Oliver was one) came into the oil spill region, or could afford to (Oliver and his crew came in on a National Science Foundation grant), was that beginning several weeks after the spill virtually no scientific information tied to damage was available to anyone. The order had provoked an outcry. It fueled the perception of science as an arrogant fourth estate and raised serious questions about the privatization of science and the apparent willingness of government agencies to allow themselves to be levered into joining that privatization. It raised the same kinds of questions associated with government-sponsored science generally—that it would be politicized. It raised questions about the validity of the scientific work itself, since all of it had become litigation connected and put in the hands of lawyers. Being secret, it was not subject to open review. Science is merely data and not science at all if it is not reviewed by experts.

Millions of dollars were being spent on science: the $72 million so far budgeted through state and federal agencies, and the additional millions Exxon had budgeted to counter the government findings. Within the adversarial attitude toward information were more loops from which the public was also excluded. Riki Ott said that Exxon had tried to contract all the private scientists. "So who does that leave as the public defender?" she asked. "It's the EPA," she said. "But through the Technology Transfer Act, the EPA and Exxon have a joint agreement to share patents." These patents included new dispersants that were being tested on the oil spill. Another effect of the secrecy, Riki and Heather McCarty of PWSAC pointed out, was that information critical to determining the condition of released salmon fry from the hatchery system was not made available. "It's creating tremendous problems for PWSAC," Heather McCarty would say. A part of the truth about oil was that the court system has so far not permitted those who know the most about it to speak. James Payne declined to offer an opinion on the gag order.

In the NOAA lab, James Payne and I stood before a long bench where one of the lab's two gas chromatographs was located. The chromatograph is a machine designed to calculate the compounds present in oil samples. It takes the fingerprints of oil and measures the quantities of compounds, including hydrocarbons, that remain in the samples. The cost of such a machine, the computers, and the facilities at the NOAA lab generally were one reason why independent scientists were so rare. John Mickelson had wandered off, and I'd glimpsed him in a side room, talking to someone. The gas chromatograph abruptly went into action, as if by its own volition. It was loaded with tiny vials rather in the manner of a slide carousel. The vials contained samples. They rotated around the machine, and one by one an armature picked them up and entered them into an aperture. The contents spat into the machine for measuring. Next to the machine, a printer fed out the results in graph form. The results of the measurements the machine was making were one of the things Payne could not talk about.

Payne brought John back and showed him the machine in operation. He explained to us how it worked. He explained again how few of the aromatics remained in the oil, how little of the oil there was on the open water, how unlikely it was that the oil would travel underwater. He knew who John was, and he wanted him to understand. John stood still, listening.

Payne said, "Water column processes are not a concern. We knew this from other oil spills, and what we're seeing here so far is confirming it. The beach processes are another matter. It's a two-dimensional problem, as opposed to a three-dimensional one."

Some would disagree with Payne's inclination to deemphasize water column processes. Riki Ott had questioned it all along, and she would tell me later that water column samples taken in the sound at five different depths by Exxon scientists showed hydrocarbon readings of 16 to 28 parts per billion. "You didn't get a reading like that until after the spill," she said. In April two marine scientists, Usha Varanasi and Byron Morris, reported finding rockfish, a bottom-dwelling fish, with evidence in their viscera of sublethal effects of hydrocarbon poisoning.

Payne went on talking about the two-dimensional problem: "The subsistence people have real troubles if it's their beach that's been hit. It's the same with the fisheries. All the aromatics are essentially gone. You're not going to be able to measure them. It's all the people walking around the salmon beds that are messing it up. Skimming doesn't work. The booms don't work. The futility of the cleanup exercise is awesome. They should have focused on protecting certain places at the beginning."

John Mickelson still didn't speak. There would probably have been little disagreement on Payne's last point, though, from John or anyone else. Riki Ott would have added, however, that the problems went beyond the mere presence of the gruesome stuff, the machines, and the footfalls. They also included those hydrocarbons that were persistent in the environment and that over a period of time could reduce the reproductive capacity of organisms. The metabolism of aromatic hydrocarbons can result in their activation to toxic. They are then in the food web. The existing literature almost universally states that the longterm effects of oil upon organisms are unestablished but that, from such spills as the Amoco Cadiz in France, there are definite indications of mutations.

Payne went on to tell us about the work they were doing on what he termed microbiological degradation, or bioremediation, the process by which microorganisms assimilate oil. Payne said that they were seeing microbiological degradation at a rate five times higher than what naturally occurred—up to one part per thousand. They were fertilizing the oil by adding nutrients to it. It was an augmentation of a natural process— another speedup mechanism, but maybe a good one. The project was being cooperatively pursued by Exxon and the EPA's Office of Research and Development (ORD). It was the same project that Sandy Elvsass had talked about back in Seldovia. It was probably the single most promising development from the oil spill. Even Riki Ott would say, "It's a great technology."

By way of explanation, James Payne said, "Oil is the result of bacterial degradation of living matter to begin with."

His was the circumspect view, taken from the vantage point of distance, and of definite advantage—his high-tech machines, his staff, his respectability—and yet there was a definite touch of the cosmic to that statement. Bioremediation was almost a form of alchemy in which the natural tendency of a prime matter to turn back into its own circle was merely accelerated. The leading edge of one disorder met another. This was the metaphor I had been seeking.

John Mickelson held his silence, and stood there impassively with his arms folded across his chest.

Chapter 15

CRAPS

Never in the millennium of our tradition have we thought it possible for the water to die. But it is true. We walk our beaches. But the snails and the barnacles and the chitons are falling off the rocks. Dead. Dead water. . . . We walk our beaches. But instead of gathering life, we gather death. Dead birds. Dead otters. Dead seaweed. . . . We are in shock. We need to clean the oil, get it out of our water, bring death back to life. We are intoxicated with desperation. We don't have a choice but to take what is offered. So we take the jobs, we take the orders, we take the disruption.

—Walter Meganack, Sr.,
Port Graham village chief, 1989

The barge was about 70 feet long. Near its stern and mounted side by side were two 5,000-gallon tanks used for water exchange. One held clean water. The other held dirty water, and between them was a filtration system. This was a cleaning barge, set up to wash boats, skiffs, nets, and fish totes in accordance with Exxon's policy of zero tolerance—no oil whatsoever released to the water. Near the center of the barge were engines and a compression system hooked up to the tanks and pressure hoses, and next to that was a container from Korean Shipping Lines, used as an office and storage space. The barge itself was licensed in Portland and leased out to Veco, Inc.

Toward the bow was a large pile of absorbent pads, bale upon bale encased in plastic, and drums to hold waste, and then an open area at the bow where the fish totes were cleaned. Off one side of the bow a wooden dock was attached, into which the boats could be pulled. Over-head lights illuminated the barge. In the time I was there, the better part of the swing and graveyard shifts over three days, no oiled boats or skiffs appeared, no nets, and only a few totes. The entirety—barge, docks, buoys, and skiffs—was surrounded by two rings of boom to hold in any oil that might be spilled.

During only the first of shifts that I visited was any work done at all, and that meticulously—a stack of a dozen or so totes left by a fishing boat that departed just as I arrived by skiff from the Native village of Port Graham. A villager named Martin worked the totes over with great care. He scrubbed with large scouring pads, steam cleaned and rinsed them, then spread out absorbent pads to soak up the oil from the deck. The pads went into the drums. He rinsed the deck and skimmed up the oil off the water with a fine net. Martin is a fisherman with a reputation for being a highliner, the best commercial fisherman in the village, but since the fishing was closed he was working on the Veco barge. There were three other crew members on board, three young women from the village, as well as the barge's night supervisor, George Hiller, and Paul Katroscik, who worked for the Environmental Pollution Claims Service of the Crawford Insurance Company. Exxon had brought the Crawford people in to monitor cash flow.

The three young women sat on the bales of absorbent pad and talked as Martin worked. Occasionally, one got up to spray while Martin scrubbed, and even more occasionally one helped scrub. There wasn't enough work to keep one person busy for long, and Martin seemed content to carry that small portion. I fell into conversation with the women. Just beyond the line of boom were two otters. Periodically, one or the other would dive, then reappear in a different spot. One of the women, Anna Sue, was pretty and talkative. She said that the pair of otters had recently moved into the bay. "They came away from the oil around the corner," she said. By around the corner, she meant down at the southern extreme of the peninsula where the oil was heavy.

"Now, they're eating the shellfish. They eat all the big clams," she said. "We eat every animal except the otter."

When I asked her why, she said, "The meat is bad."

Struck by her answer, I later asked the same question of another, older woman from the village, Fiona Sawden, who said, "We don't like them because they eat our seashells. But we don't eat them because they're our brothers."

*   *   *

The village of Port Graham is located southeast of Seldovia, on the next fingerlike bay down on the peninsula. The bay goes by the same name, Port Graham. From the barge, anchored halfway across the bay, I could see the village. At the beginning of a shift it was visible as a line of lights backed by a dark space, and then another, more distant line of lights. The dark space is a landing strip around which the better part of the village presses like a doughnut. As the night shift on the barge progressed, the lights of the town went out, and early in the morning they came on again. On the barge, evening dwindled to twilight, and there would be a pause in which the overhead work lights would be surrounded by dark. Soon, the light in the sky started back again.

At the western edge of the doughnut is a cluster of houses extending to the woods. Beyond the houses, a small hydroelectric project was under construction. The project was a source of pride, the cause of greater self-sufficiency. Just to the north were the recently constructed Port Graham School and the old Russian Orthodox Church, a carryover from the Russian fur trading days. All the old Native villages and many of the predominantly white towns on the Kenai, in Prince William Sound, and out on the Aleutians, as well, have Russian churches. They are plain on the outside—white with blue roofs—and filled with elaborately framed portraits and gold icons. Services are at once heavily ritualized and casual. People wander in and out. Children are attended to in mid-service. The churches are the vestiges of another imperialism, and yet they are a part of the grain. They've been here for nearly 200 years. They have replaced shamanism but now exist side by side with the old ways of subsistence living.

From the church, a narrow road drops down to the town store and the cannery operated by the Chugach Native Corporation. Everywhere, lying in the yards or standing in the road, were large, rawboned dogs. At the intersection of the narrow road and the main road that encircled the landing strip live the village chief, Walter Meganack, and his wife. At all times during the day, it seemed, either he, his wife, or both of them were outside their two-story house, sitting on the porch, working in the front yard, or conversing with neighbors. They maintain a watch. Their house overlooks the main roadway, the narrow road that leads down to the store, and the landing strip. Walter is a tall, imperious man in his seventies, a man of reputation, known by Native people throughout Alaska, proud, conservative, and at times uncompromising. At no time did the presence of oil on the water and of the money that pursued it seem so revolutionary as when it was cast against Walter Meganack's figure.

Off to one side from the Meganacks' house stand the remains of a dwelling from the old days, a small, chest-high, elliptically shaped dug-out. It has sod walls and a corrugated tin roof. The rough typology of the village's history runs this way: dugout and tin roof, and then elsewhere the cannery, landing strip, the store stocked with all manner of supplies—food, paper goods, tools, hardware, clothing, fishing gear. In every driveway stands a three- or four-wheeled ORV—Yamahas and Hondas. The ORVs buzz up and down the road, scattering the dogs. Behind the houses are fishracks. Not far from the town is a natural coal seep that had been a signal to early white arrivals of the potential mineral riches in this part of the world. From the village, I could see the barge out in the water, encircled by its two loops of boom. Walter Meganack had said, "We fight a rich and powerful giant, the oil industry, while at the same time we take orders and a paycheck from it. We are torn in half."

In June, Elenore McMullen, the village health aide, had said, "Veco came in one day and literally took over the country. It was really strange. Telephone people were here putting in telephone lines. People were everywhere. It was unreal. Our people are very excited about going to work, but there also was a lot of fear about losing our subsistence. And we have. We haven't been able to collect our clams, seaweed, herring roe, halibut. . . . This is something that has affected us emotionally, and I expect it will affect us physically. It has affected us spiritually. Our spiritual leaders have gone off to work on the spill, making $16.69 an hour. . . . I don't know if Port Graham will ever be the same. People don't have time to visit. They don't have time for tea. They're too busy. Even the children look lost."

Cleanup work was done around the corner at Windy Bay, a large indentation at the bottom of the peninsula, cut into the landform and placed at such an angle as if designed expressly to accept the oil that floated by. One young villager, Neal Hedrick, told me that he and a co-worker had cleaned a square yard of beach one day on Windy Bay. "The next day," he said, "we cleaned the same square yard again. We were working the shovels. The third day we were given trowels instead of shovels because we were going too fast."

Another villager, who asked that his name not be used, told me that he'd made over $10,000 in two months on the beach crews, and that the only workers who'd survived much longer than he were the ones who didn't speak out. "If you work hard, they tell you to quit working," he said. "As soon as you feel like you've started to do something, Exxon shuts the crew down. You fill your bags with debris, then sit around for three days because there's no tape to close the bags with. The only time they want you to work is when the helicopters are coming. 'Incoming.'

That's the command to get busy, and then when the helicopter leaves, everything goes back to normal."

Such stories were so common everywhere on the Kenai and in Prince William Sound that they became undeniable. They were the most wrenching when told by people who cared deeply for the natural world and would have worked for nothing to restore it. Walter Meganack had said, "The land and the water are our sources of life. The water is sacred. The water is like a baptismal font, and its abundance is the Holy Communion of our lives. Of all the things that we have lost since non-Natives came to our land, we have never lost our connection with the water. The water is our source of life. So long as the water is alive, the Chugach Natives are alive." Out of the hell of oil on the water had come the assignment of the people to a Sisyphean circle, where the penalty for their innocence was the ceaseless, meaningless labor of shoveling, troweling, and wiping, what Robert Engler described in The Nation as the spectacle of "hundreds of young people wiping oil-soaked rocks with absorbent pads . . . like a scene from a mental institution."

I was in Port Graham nearly a month after Meganack's remarks were delivered to the Conference of Mayors. By then, Exxon had already begun dismantling its Cleanup effort, and it grew increasingly clear that the company was placing its hopes for the future on bioremediation. Though it was not stated publicly, all signs seemed to indicate that the company regarded further efforts at mechanical or manual cleanup as an exercise in futility. Considering the circumstances as they had evolved to this point, such an attitude was understandable. The cleaning barge at Port Graham was but one indication of a futility that had passed across the line from despair to ludicrousness. At first, I'd had difficulty understanding why the barge was there at all, way up here, so far from the action. Relatively speaking, only moderate amounts of oil remained in the waters of Port Graham itself, and there was no sign of continuing beach cleanup. Neil Hedrick's father, Larry Hedrick, had taken me around the bay in a skiff. There was evidence of oil, but not a great deal of it—enough to justify watchfulness so far as food supplies were concerned, but probably not enough, considering the standards of futility by which such things had come to be measured, to have maintained a serious cleanup effort. Some of the villagers here had resumed fishing and gathering, avoiding the bad places.

Fiona Sawden told me that at first the barge was to be stationed on an island out near the gulf, but that the people complained that they would get sick if they had to travel so far out to sea. This suggested that the purpose of the barge was, first, to employ villagers, and secondly, to serve in the cleanup effort. George Hiller, the barge's night supervisor, said plainly that Exxon had "set up the Port Graham Barge so that the people would get something." He said that he and Jim Perry, the day supervisor, "were sent here for PR." George also echoed Gordon Robilliard's assessment when he said, "The time to make money is when there's chaos." Later, I told Dean Peeler, the Exxon spokesman in Homer, that I'd been on the barge and that virtually nothing at all was happening on it. A tall man, Peeler smiled down at me and said, "So, now you know."

What I knew was that the barge was stationed there for reasons quite apart from the cleanup itself. At that stage in that place, cleanup mattered only to those who lived there and yet who had given over what powers they had to execute the cleanup to outsiders. In return, they received money.

Port Graham is a transitional community—not as faithful in its adherence to traditional life as English Bay or Chenega but more strict than the urban villages located within Seldovia, Seward, or Cordova. There was a story making the rounds in Port Graham about an initial meeting between Exxon representatives and the villagers. When Walter Meganack entered the community hall, he found the Exxon people stationed at a table in the front and otherwise poised along the walls and near the doorways. Meganack immediately directed that the chairs be rearranged into two groups and that the Exxon people sit on one side of the room and the village people on the other side. He took his place at the head of the room. The story was told to me by George Hiller. He said, "It was a master stroke. It completely changed the dimension of power in the room." It's an exemplary story, at once indicative of Meganack's wisdom and canniness. The money spilled into Port Graham, nevertheless.

Exxon's solicitous approach to Native communities stemmed from several causes. No doubt there was genuine concern for those whose resource would be most directly and immediately affected by oil on the beaches. Exxon must have been aware, also, of the intense sentiment felt by a large portion of the American public in the lower forty-eight for Native people—the hazily formed romance of the "noble savage." From Exxon's perspective, such strong, potentially inflammatory sentiment must have posed a distinct PR hazard, and so put Native people almost in the same class as sea otters. The best way to snuff out such a hazard, Exxon seemed to have determined, was to inundate the victim with money. Most importantly, probably, Exxon managers were aware of the potential power Native people held as collective owners of 10 percent of

Alaskan lands, including lands in which oil wells might yet be sunk, or across which more pipelines might yet be built.

In the view of Carl Pulliam, whom I spoke to only a few days after his resignation as the Veco area supervisor for Port Graham and English Bay, Exxon's plan had been "to buy out public relations in the villages and to divide the villages from Homer and Seldovia by creating tension between them." As time passed, Carl said, "the first idea among the people of cleaning up as much oil as possible changed to the idea of making as much money as possible."

Carl and I had met early one morning in his mobile home on the edge of the town of Seldovia. It was a few days before I traveled to Port Graham. Carl was still feeling ragged from his tribulations as Veco supervisor. I sensed that he also felt compromised by his role in an enterprise that had become loathsome to him. Even speaking of it made him uneasy, but we sat in his living room and spoke softly for two hours, his children and wife, a Port Graham native, asleep in adjoining rooms. Carl is a tall, lean man who fishes commercially and teaches high-school science and basketball. He spread out a navigation chart on the floor and sat next to it, hugging one raised leg. He leaned over the chart occasionally to point out the places of his former domain as he spoke: Windy Bay, the heavily oiled site of controversy over failed cleanup methods; Koyuktolik Bay, just down the peninsula from English Bay and, in Carl's opinion, the westernmost of the heavily oiled locations, the point from which the current spun off and carried the oil toward Kodiak; the Chugach Passage, where Exxon had ordered out the oil capture crew that Carl had felt needed to be stationed there to intercept as much oil as possible before it worked its way around the peninsula; and Perl Island, where some Exxon people had maintained what he considered basically a party house. He'd seen the stacks of beer cases outside, a direct contradiction of Exxon's stringently worded policy on the use of alcohol.

Carl spoke of the difficulty of accomplishing anything because of the competition that developed between the villagers and townspeople, between Veco and another subcontracting company, Martech, between Veco and Exxon because of Exxon's inefficiency and its refusal to listen to local people. "When Veco came in back in the spring," he said, "greed entered the picture. We were doing things that didn't make any sense. We'd send a boat with a six hundred-gallon water tank to water up a boat with a twelve hundred-gallon tank. We had a boat that needed a part. It took a week to get the part because Exxon refused to let boats cross the lines between Veco projects and Exxon projects. There were two sets of contracts. Exxon paid three thousand for a thirty-two- or thirty-six-foot gillnetter, while Veco paid fifteen hundred. We were always getting caught trying to work for one or the other, and they'd envy each other. One group got steaks. The other got beans. There'd be disputes over hours. Sometimes a crew would get paid for eighteen hours even if they only worked six. While I was working, I saw probably two hundred thousand dollars in wasted wages."

"It was like Cinderella. Everybody knew the story. But we all got thrown into Cinderella's part, anyway. We believed we were Cinderella, coming out of the ashes, but at the same time we knew there was never going to be a ball at the end."

At about eight o'clock on my second night in Port Graham, Paul Katroscik and I took a skiff from the village to the cleaning barge. We unhooked the first line of boom and motored inside it, then waited for a skiff from the barge to pick us up. When it came, as a safeguard against releasing the virtually nonexistent oil that might be inside we stepped from one skiff to the other over the interior loop of boom.

Once on the barge, Paul and I moved to the edge of the stern where the fishing poles were kept and a picnic table had been set up. Paul checked a tide chart to see when he should do his work, which consisted of working through the barge's inventory sheets and filling out his reports, and when he should fish. Since he had so little work to do, fishing was the first priority.

Paul owns a roofing and rain-gutter business in California. A friend from his Vietnam days had arranged for him to be taken on by the Crawford Insurance Company. At about that time, Crawford monitors had begun to turn up everywhere in the oil spill region. I would see one in Exxon's Homer office, a Bartleby-like figure surrounded by heaps of papers and ledger sheets, and several in Cordova, in Valdez. . . . They wore dark blue peaked hats with gold scroll work and the name of their Crawford division. They commanded instant respect. Paul said he shouldn't talk to me at all, but he did. He said that Crawford was there to check for graft. "There is graft," he said, "such as people turning in duplicate work sheets with overtime." By that time, this was not news to me, but it was interesting to hear it coming from one whose job was to ferret out such mischief. He told me about a young woman who had hooked up with a man in one of the offices and had arranged to work overtime in two different places at once. When I told him what Carl Pulliam had said about the $200,000 in wasted wages, Paul said, "No doubt. Exxon's been taking a beating." Nearly a year later, in the late spring of 1990, the towns would begin to buzz with rumors that information gleaned by the Crawford monitors, among others, was to lead to suits brought by Exxon against local persons and businesses. By summer, but for a couple of cases, the rumors had not been realized.

Seeing that the tide wasn't to come in for a while, Paul went into the office to do his paperwork and I moved toward the bow of the barge, where I'd arranged to meet Jim Miller, the community alcoholism counselor for Port Graham and English Bay. He was also working on the barge. Jim is a Native from southeastern Alaska, married to a woman from Port Graham. He was the board president of the "other" church in Port Graham, an unaffiliated charismatic church, the Church of the First Born, that had grown up after the Baptists had left seven years previously. The Russian Orthodox Church tended to include the more traditional element in the village, Jim told me. "Our church is strict. It's language, food, and religion that makes you an Aleut in this village. If you don't do those, then you're not a real Aleut. But even Walter," Jim said, "has to admit that we're a sober bunch."

Charismatic churches, I understood, had become common in Native communities of the area, and they were especially attentive to matters of sobriety. In that respect, they were forward-looking. Drugs and alcohol were a problem in the villages, and Jim was worried about it, now. We sat at the edge of the big stack of absorbent pads, looking off the side of the barge toward the mouth of the long bay. Slowly, the light was fading. To our left, several clean fish totes stood on end. So far as I could tell, they were the same ones Martin had cleaned the night before. Jim has a short crop of dark hair and a bony face. He sat still and spoke quietly. "My feeling is that the money will finally cause more problems than it'll solve, especially with the alcoholics and addicts. We have some of those. Exxon money accentuates the spill, and this'll take effect in the winter because of the depression. We'll have more suicides than usual.

"At first, we were really scared," he said. "The people were afraid to eat anything. And they didn't know what to do, because in the annual cycle the spring and summer are the time to do all the work. So they were lost for a while. But now they're gathering again. Financially," he said, "the villages are much better off than they've ever been. For people who use the money wisely, it's good. They can find a self-respect out of being self-supporting. But the anger from the oil, and then the pride, jealousy, and greed that comes from the money, it all comes from the spill and it affects the spiritual world of the people. That's not a good thing. There's a real take 'em for what you can get attitude. Spiritually, it's not a good thing."

Jim is a young man. He'd been educated differently than most of the

Port Graham people, he told me. He'd been to college. He was independent, personally hopeful, and prepared to enter the world outside. His preference was to take the shares he'd received through the Alaskan Native Claims Settlement Act of 1971 and sell them so that he could start up his own business. This touched upon a controversial question among Native people. Besides converting Native claims into the 12 Regional Corporations and over 200 village corporations, ANCSA also included a provision by which individuals received share allotments that could be sold. Some people felt very strongly that ancestral claims should be held collectively for the sake of future generations.

Jim's wife didn't want to sell her shares, he said. That was fine with him because then their children would inherit her shares and they could use his money. He said, "I like being on a boat, but I don't like fishing. There's a lack of opportunity here. I'd like to relocate and start a business. Someday I'd like to write a book. I want land, but I want to buy it when and where I want. I had a chimney cleaning business for a while. I can't picture myself ever being out of work. It's become very clear to me that my people can't rely on world systems for their security."

Inside the Korean shipping container that served as the office on the barge, Paul was teaching the game of craps to Fiona Sawden and two other older women who, along with Jim Miller, made up the work crew. Paul and the three women were clumped around one end of a long bench that stretched most of the way along a wall. The office was a dense place. In the open space past the end of the bench, two rows of folding chairs faced each other from opposite walls. At the far end of the bench, George Hiller, the supervisor, was organizing papers. There was an attached storage room loaded with supplies and snacks. On the bench was a coffee pot. Above the bench, the wall was plastered with photographs of the crews, and warning and safety posters and regulations—what to do in case of a tsunami, drug testing procedures, Coast Guard regulations, alcohol regulations, emergency procedures, emergency numbers. On all the cleanup vessels safety had become the number one priority. Zero tolerance for additional spills of any sort was the second priority.

Paul had a notepad on the bench, and he was explaining the rules of craps to the women. One of them would roll the dice, and he would explain what the roll meant. They were intensely interested in the game, particularly Fiona Sawden. They played a few mock rounds. One rolled and they all looked at the dice, then over at Paul. They laughed softly, rocking in their chairs as he explained how they might have lost or won. Paul told them how the game was played in Las Vegas. Fiona had been to Reno. Paul worked the odds of the rolls on the pad of paper, making an elaborate chart for them. There was an intriguing heaping up of elements in the scene . . . the bunch of us pressed into the Korean container, its walls loaded with regulations, and the container mounted on a barge from Portland that did no work, lying still here in the bay, put here to quiet the villagers, and the Crawford monitor whose job it was to dig out graft teaching the women how to play craps.

I learned that Fiona, a plump, attractive woman in her fifties, was a bilingual teacher and had been involved with translation. When I asked if I could speak with her sometime, she said, "We can meet in the banya."

Not understanding that a banya was a bath, a steam house, I said, "Where?"

"In the banya," she said, leaning back and laughing. Everyone in the office looked at me and laughed at my foolishness.

I talked to her the next day in the living room of her home. It is a comfortable place with a thick carpet, a sofa, and easy chairs. On the walls are pictures, family photographs, and Russian orthodox icons. Her husband was out working and her two grandchildren were there, visiting from Los Angeles. Their father, she said, was up on the Kenai. Occasionally, she would get up and tend to one of the children. "The oil didn't have much impact here," she said, "except for making money. At first it scared the heck out of us. There were a lot of dead salmon fries on the booms, but we won't know about them for three, four years. How long is Exxon going to be around? If I don't smell the oil, I'll eat the food. We've been eating birdarki [chiton], and now the clams and cockles are starting to build up. A couple of weeks ago we got birdarki, built a fire, cooked them, and ate them. We didn't get sick.

"But now there's not much fishing because of the working," she said. "I'm working on the barge to make money. I'm just as greedy as the next person." She smiled. "If they want to make money, I want to make money. It's the greed Exxon is bringing out in us. The greed is bad. Families are fighting amongst themselves and nepotism is going on. A lot of families are not taking care of their kids. They're working, or if they're home, they're too tired. And we're worried about what the money will do to the people this winter with the drinking. The winter is long."

One of her grandchildren, a boy of three or four, had snuggled up next to her on the sofa. I asked her about the Church of the First Born, and she smiled again and said, "The trouble is they can't sin. The Russian Orthodox don't have such rules. The born agains can't dance, and now our kids don't know what a dance is. We have masking in our church. It's all that's left from the old days before the Russians came. It comes during Christmas. We have to wash the masks each year to purify them. The traditional masks were burned."

Fiona was a part of a movement in many Alaskan villages to rediscover and record their own history so that traditional languages and values could be preserved for the young and serve as a buffer against white culture and extractive economies. "My great-great-grandfather was a Russian priest from San Francisco. Before the Russians, Shaman was our religion. I learned that at the bilingual conferences," she said.

After the shift change at midnight on my second and third nights on the barge, Jim Miller and the women went home and the younger crew came on. Paul Katroscik and I then fished off the end of the barge deep into the morning. We were fishing for halibut, a bottom feeder. We caught nothing, but sat there, baiting and rebaiting our hooks, reeling them out and reeling them back in. An older man from the village came and set a line and tied it off on the barge, and came back every half hour or so to check it. He caught fish.

I thought about Fiona, about how impressed I was by her bearing, her calm, her humor, her acceptance of herself. I thought about the distinction Thomas Berger made in his book on the Settlement Act, *Village Journey*, between the Native regard for the earth as inalienable and the white regard for it as endlessly alienable. For the one people the earth was never a stranger. For the other, the relationship was one of estrangement. It seemed to me that the grace with which Fiona and others like her had positioned themselves in a world loaded with contrarities came from a deeply felt sense of her own inalienability. The capacity to contain the contradictions of the world and human behavior and yet to act with grace, to not suffer the defeat of a complete change of heart, seemed to be the measure of character the oil spill had mounted.

On the third night, Martin and Anna Sue were out at the stern for a while. They had a ghetto blaster and played a Dolly Parton tape. For a while, they jiggled around voluptuously to the music. They knew what a dance was. Slowly, the light began coming back into the sky. Martin and Anna Sue went into the office to watch television with the others, and Paul's and my place at the stern fell silent. The hump of the landform across from us took shape against the pale air. The tide ran hard and the loops of boom were drawn almost to a point on the high side of the barge. White jellyfish floated slowly by in the dark like flowers. Paul told me the story of his lost love, a woman he was going to marry when he was 29. She was killed in an automobile accident a few days before they were to move into a new house. The story was perfectly told, filled with emotion and yet devoid of self-pity. The oil spill seemed to do that to some people, to carry them to the edges of themselves and to open them to the seams of the world.

A year later, Walter Meganack told me that Port Graham was still not normal. "Some people used the money they made wisely," he said. "They are doing good. The others have a problem. Some of them now have income tax problems, especially the ones that worked on the barge. The fish did not show up this year. We are waiting for them. There are good reports and bad on the shellfish, and we don't trust the reports, so we don't use the shellfish."

Chapter 16

MASKS

In July, I went into the Homer Exxon office in hopes of meeting Dean Peeler. I was told by the receptionist that he was not in, but that his assistant would meet with me. I gave her the letter from my editor that I carried with me in lieu of a press card. The receptionist disappeared with the letter down the hall, then she returned. She was a friendly woman whose telephone rang constantly. Behind her on the wall was a long poster that read, "Hip, Hip, Hooray, for the Gang Away . . . From The Folks You Left Behind." Beneath the poster was a photograph from the *Anchorage Daily News* that showed a smiling woman holding an otter pup. The caption to the photograph read, "One tough pup beats the odds." The poster was laced with the signatures of those who had left; only a few of the Exxon people had been here continuously from the beginning. The poster and newspaper photograph were an expression of team spirit, at a time when the local firestorm of criticism was just beginning to wane. I waited 15 or 20 minutes. Waiting was a part of the game.

Several times, the receptionist walked down the hall, then came back, and each time she told me that someone would see me in a minute. I began to get the feeling that my letter was being checked out. Eventually, the assistant, a young woman, did come out. She led me down the hall to a back room and introduced me to Dean Peeler, who I had been told was not here. He led me into yet another room, deeper into the complex of offices. He offered me a Coke and a doughnut. I understood that it was admirable that graciousness could persist under these circumstances and also that it meant nothing. Peeler is a large man, tall, bearded, young, and friendly. He is from New Orleans and speaks with a soft accent that gently rounds off the edges of his words. More than once, I had heard the oil industry people switch from flat accents to the most beguiling of South Atlantic and Gulf Coast drawls. Peeler wore a white striped shirt, pale blue denims, and white Reeboks. Had I not already seen him at the Homer MAC meetings cutting a community representative to the quick,* had I not seen the iron under his gracious surface, I would have found it impossible not to like him. We sat across from each other at a table and he affably informed me that he could not answer my questions, that instead he had questions for me. He wanted to know what I was interested in.

I told him—the barge in Port Graham, the state of the cleanup in his region, the continued use of dispersants on shorelines, bioremediation, the local controversies over the Exxon and Veco presence, the sinking oil question, the otter recovery center at Jackolof Bay, the disposition of archeological materials members of the Shoreline Cleanup Advisory Teams had been finding, the structure of Exxon management, and the matter of reliable information. He said he'd been on the phone to Valdez. That was what indeed had been going on while I waited in the lobby. Peeler had been getting his directions for dealing with me. He said that what I needed was a briefing, that if I went to Valdez they would answer all my questions. What information he then was willing to give me came in an indirect form, such as his remark about the barge at Port Graham—"So, now you know."

He did have something he wanted to show me, a portion of a videotape. It was the *U.S.A. Today* show on the oil spill. It included segments from the notorious, staged cleanup operation at Gore Point and a cutting from the equally notorious Marilyn Monroe ad. The ad was part of a campaign developed after *Alaska* magazine devoted its June 1989 issue to the oil spill. The magazine's forthright portrayal of the damage resulted in the withdrawal of all advertising by the Alaska Tourism Marketing

---

* The discussion concerned whether or not Exxon would approve and fund Billy Day's rock washing machine. The heated discussion turned not on the merits of the rock washer but on what had happened to the memos that had traveled the loop back and forth between the Homer MAC, the Coast Guard, and the Exxon headquarters, and where the rock washing machine was.

Council, which represented a major portion of the magazine's advertising. The editor of the magazine, Ron Dalby, stood his ground. Exxon gave 4 million dollars to the state tourism division, citing the urgent need for image enhancement. The state tourism division gave the money to the Alaska Visitors Association, which was associated with many of the same parties as the Alaska Tourism Marketing Council. The Visitors Association* spent some of the money to retain a public relations firm that also represented Alyeska. Under the guise of supporting the worried state tourism interests, Exxon was funding its own image enhancement. The result was the Marilyn Monroe ad, which appeared nationally in magazines and on television in the lower forty-eight and was shown to Exxon shareholders.

Marilyn Monroe was presented as Alaska. Her famous mole had been airbrushed from her face. The absent mole represented Prince William Sound, without which, the ad implied, Marilyn and Alaska were equally beautiful. Naturally, the wished-for response to this video image required a regard for Marilyn and her absent mole as an image only and a complete ignorance of Alaska.

Dean Peeler looked at me and smiled. We were to enjoy this man to man. In his expression, however, there was a hint of apology, a slight crack in the mask, as if to inform me that he understood I was not so stupid as to not know what a fraud the ad was. "It's a great idea, though," he said. "I really admire the person who thought that up."

In between my time in Homer and Valdez I had communicated several times with Exxon's Valdez headquarters. They asked for my list of questions, which I revised and sent on. I was assured that the proper persons to answer my questions would be provided. I could expect an encounter with a battery of experts. When I arrived in Valdez on September 19, Karsten Rodvik came out and asked if I could come back a few hours later. I agreed to do so. Rodvik introduced me to another spokesman, Joe Ferguson, with whom I had talked previously, although Ferguson insisted that we had never spoken before. The fact that he had forgotten me, considering the numbers of people who had been through those offices, was hardly surprising. It was his emphatic denial of a meaningless lapse of memory that seemed curious. Surely, it was not important, and yet the inclination of Exxon people to protect themselves

* The Alaska Visitors Association is the same organization that sponsored another advertisement run on network television (notably CBS) during the early fall of 1990. This ad invited would-be tourists to come to Alaska, and in particular to Prince William Sound, where they would "see its pristine shoreline nearly recovered now from the oil spill."

against often nonexistent threats tended to draw attention to them. Each of the men looked tired.

When I returned later that day for my appointment, I waited for 45 minutes or so in the small lobby and watched two construction workers just outside a window. I had seen them earlier. They were setting sono tubes to make footings for what would be a covered walkway to the building. As it happened, there was a controversy in Valdez at the time over what would happen to the building when the Exxon headquarters moved to Anchorage. Questions over its disposition would continue through the winter into the next summer. It was a steel-sided modular building with a well-appointed interior. It had been hauled in on trucks and thrown up to make the Valdez headquarters. Exxon had refused to commit itself to leaving the building behind when it moved but left open the possibility that it would be knocked apart and shipped back out.

Valdez wanted the building. Everything considered, it was a minor question, an isolated fulcrum point in the chaos that had overrun Valdez. The city's normal population of about 5,000 had swelled at one point to over 11,000. Carol Smith of the city's community development department told me that through most of the summer the population was in excess of 7,000. There was not anything approaching sufficient housing, or sufficient office space. There was no available storage space. Subcontractors, such as Norcon and Veco, threw up trailer and container camps just outside town. Workers lived there, or sometimes in tents in campsites. The drug trade had exploded. The bars were loaded. The city jail ran out of space. The court system and police department were overtaxed.

The shortages continued into 1990, well after Exxon and its subcontractors had pulled out of town, because of continued increased employment there for government agencies and Alyeska's upgraded system. Alyeska added 125 oil spill response positions. At the same time the established stores and businesses had difficulty finding employees because so many had made so much working on the cleanup. The counseling center had been stretched beyond its capacities. The hospital found itself left with a huge operating debt as a result of unpaid bills stalled in litigation that was connected to claims. All through 1989 and 1990 the city services, including the development department, were run ragged. Since Valdez does not have a sales tax, the city treasurer, Don Gill, was unable to estimate the total amount of money that came into the city. There was a little over 2 million dollars, Gill said, in expenditures by the city directly connected to the spill and cleanup presence. It went for things such as extra snow removal, extra employees, office supplies, overtime, police, campsite construction, remodeling. Those expenditures were funded by Exxon. Because of litigation, Exxon itself would decline to estimate for me the money it spent in Valdez or any other community.

As I waited in the lobby of the Valdez Exxon headquarters, the guard at the podium next to the door asked me if I thought the workers were making any progress. Earlier, we had talked about the walkway. I had observed that the sono tubes had been set below the frost line. If Exxon took the building out, some pretty good footings were going to be left behind. It seemed to be Exxon's way. Driven by codes, regulations, insurance, and bad feeling, the company threw money at construction, supplies, equipment, safety regulations, testing procedures, research, and personnel while the real question of what would be done with the building or, more generally, about the oil, remained unanswered.

So far as I could tell, in the time between early morning and now, about 1:45 in the afternoon, the workers hadn't moved the work forward an inch. They were still standing around, occasionally fooling with their tape measures and string lines. The guard looked around to make sure no one was in hearing distance, then said, "They're paid by the hour, too."

I learned that I was not to speak with Rodvik, nor with Joe Ferguson, but with yet another man, Bleu Bethard. Since Bethard was a senior staff adviser, I had apparently come up a bit in the world. He met me in the lobby and led me back through the hallway to his office, offered me a Coke, then sank into the chair behind his desk. A middle-aged, slightly overweight man, he appeared extremely tired. His face had a gray cast and there was a heaviness in his carriage and an almost paralyzed deliberateness in his movements. He leaned on his elbows and looked up at me briefly, then back down at his desk, and said he wanted to find out what interested me. I replied that I had already sent on a list of questions and subjects. He said, yes, that he was looking at it. I straightened up in my chair and peered at his desk. He stared fixedly down at the surface. There was nothing there between his arms, no paperwork at all, and I had an eerie sensation, but then Bethard slowly revolved his head to the right and stared at the computer screen mounted there.

He began to speak in a monotone, and for a long time did not look at me at all, shifting his gaze between the computer screen and his desk. The usual slippery friendliness had fallen away to reveal something nearer to a death mask. Every once in a while, he reached out and touched a key on the computer keyboard. I presumed he was scrolling the material on the screen, that my questions and whatever other information Exxon had about me were stored there. I was in there made out of electricity and amber light. It was like a Platonic ideal, cast on the wall of the cave. My true reality was in there, while the other me, whose presence the reality of the file could probably find to be a mistake, merely sat there in the room and breathed the air.

Bethard said he would answer what questions he could, and apologized for his failure otherwise to provide me with the information I wanted. He said that because of the withdrawal of the cleanup machinery and forces, they didn't have the time to do many interviews, and that if I could come later, perhaps even a month later, after they had moved to Anchorage and things had settled down, they could set up a series of briefings for me. When I said that that was what I had come here for, Bethard again expressed his apologies.

"We've given the press complete access to the scene," Bethard said. "We ran the press out in helicopters. We had two flights a day for weeks. We told the pilot to take the people anywhere they wanted to go."

I said nothing. His statement was true in a way. It was also true that at times it took the persuasion of a national network to get the press tours to move, and that such tours were compromised twice over— first by Exxon sponsorship and then by network agendas, their obsession with photo opportunities. The labors of the cleanup crews as they were depicted in the national media did not jibe at all with the stories told by workers: the stories of graft, goldbricking, senseless assignments, discouragement, and speedups when incoming flights and boats came near. For those reasons, I had taken little interest in Exxon-sponsored press tours.

Bethard told me about the numbers of workers Exxon had employed, and the number of boats it had leased. "Exxon had zero employees here four a months ago," he said. "Now they have four hundred Exxon people from round the world, and contracts with another ten thousand. Our main camp has support for seven hundred people. We serve them four meals a day, including one at midnight. The speed with which we did this," he said, "is unbelievable."

Perhaps this was true, but it hadn't worked.

One of the questions I had sent in had to do with the gag orders attached to the contracts Exxon had first issued to fishermen who leased out their boats. Bethard said, "When you work for Exxon, you agree that you don't speak for Exxon. That's all."

I said that that wasn't exactly what the fishermen in Cordova had reported.

Bethard looked up at me briefly. It was a glimmering of contact, but then he looked back over at the computer, stared at it fixedly, and said, "The story that we were paying fishing skippers not to talk to the press is not true. We have tried to be open and we've given a lot of access to the press."

This was not exactly correct. The initial contracts the fishermen received did contain an explicit stipulation that contractees not speak to the press without permission.* What this would have meant in practice was that only fishermen willing to speak favorably of Exxon would be allowed to speak to the press. It was also not exactly correct in my experience that openness was the common practice—access, maybe, according to Exxon's guidelines, and obviously in accordance with Exxon's schedule, but openness only when the questions were the ones Exxon wished to answer, which was not openness at all. It was common for Exxon to refuse to answer questions, particularly when they touched upon specific matters of finance, science, and law. I was interested in breakdowns on projected expenditures—how much for research, animal rescue, reimbursements to communities, how much paid to cleanup workers. Bethard said that they didn't have those figures. I was extremely interested in scientific findings, but because of litigation they were unavailable. I was interested in corporate structure as Exxon had implanted it here on the shores of Prince William Sound because of the obvious incompatibility between the structure of response and the reality of oil on the water.

When I raised the question of corporate structure, Bethard said, "Oh, you mean an MBA type thing."

I was interested in language, in the way Exxon (and, incidentally, government agencies, as well) used language not as a means of transporting information but as a kind of veil dance that always promises but never reveals. The Exxon press releases were filled with such vaporous stuff:

> One of Exxon's top concerns was working with fishing groups to identify critical areas for deployment of the first available containment booms.

> From the onset, "helping people help themselves" has been Exxon's way of operating.

> The mammals most impacted by the oil spill were the sea otters and Exxon's response to their plight was swift.

* Clause #8 of the contract offered to fishermen read, "Contractor agrees to avoid unnecessary publicity and to make no statements, admissions or representations on behalf of EXXON or purporting to be on behalf of EXXON. Further, all press releases and/or contacts with the press, television, radio or other media discussing the services performed hereunder shall require the prior written approval of EXXON before being released." Bethard's point is true for the first part of the clause, but clearly not for the second part.

Within the first few days of the spill, Exxon invited the Tourism Bureau and the Alaska Seafood marketing Institute to make suggestions on how Exxon might help alleviate their customer concerns. The dialogue led to an Exxon grant of $4 million to the Alaska Visitors Association for an immediate advertising campaign.

Exxon deeply regrets the oil spill, has acknowledged responsibility, and accepts the obligation to mitigate its impacts.

. . . current plans and schedules indicate that all significantly impacted shorelines will be treated prior to September 15, 1989.

The massive effort undertaken during 1989 was successful in significantly improving shoreline and water conditions in Prince William Sound and the Gulf of Alaska. The resulting stable conditions minimized the likelihood of harm to the area's wildlife, while the extensive activities provided a foundation for natural forces to accelerate the cleansing process during the harsh Alaskan winter.

The half-truths in the statements are evident: Exxon worked with fishermen only after the fishermen took action on their own, and in many instances Exxon submarined the people's efforts to "help themselves." The response to stricken animals was forced upon Exxon by the Department of the Interior and the public. Exxon's interest in tourism was also one of alleviating its own bad reputation; most of the 1,090 miles of oiled shoreline had been in sufficiently treated. Even more troubling in my view, however, was the resort to vagueness, the flimsily cast words: concern, dialogue, mitigate, obligation, significant, stability, minimize, likelihood, cleansing process, and the most overused buzzword of all, impacted, which in a previous life I had thought referred to a tooth lodged in the jaw. Such obscure language muddled the issues. Because there was so little in it to hang on to, it prevented examination.

I found it impossible to establish a ground upon which Bleu Bethard and I could discuss the matter of language. The question he did want to answer had to do with bioremediation. "It's working better than we thought it would," Bethard said. "It's a great follow-up tool. We also think Corexit is a net benefit for the environment. We wanted to use that on some of the areas that have oil stuck on the rocks. Corexit is even faster than bioremediation. We've got environmental studies going. We'll probably have more information than anybody in the U.S."

I asked about the availability of that information.

He said, "It's not in our nature to put out preliminary results."

He went on: "We'll never get it completely clean. Maybe we'll get all the oil off some of the shorelines, and some off the rest of them. We've cleaned some sections five to ten times. We have scientists working for us and we're not paying them to tell us fairy tales. Some of the beaches, you wash again and again and you can't get it all out. We'll get it off to varying degrees. We will not leave a shoreline where it'll be an environmental threat to birds and otters and sealife. I hate to say Mother Nature will help, but it's true. We have both high and low energy shorelines, though. Some of the oil will be absorbed in nature, and then we'll have to decide—now what do we want? More people on the beaches?

"We've spent eight hundred eighty million so far, and there's another four hundred million in insurance that we expect to be added to that. This doesn't include litigation, which will probably go primarily to the fishing industry.* I'm just a PR man," he said. "I'll be perfectly happy if I can get the public to understand what we have done and nothing more. I'd be happy if we can just tell the facts well."

I didn't interrupt him, but thought that the "well" part of that statement was the rub.

"One of our problems," he said, "is that the state of Alaska is perceived as an independent party, and it's not. It has a vested interest. If people would scrutinize their opinions as closely as ours, they'd see that."

Bethard had begun to look at me a little more often. His gaze now seemed about equally divided between computer screen, desk top, and me. We'd been in close physical proximity for well over an hour. Despite myself, I'd begun to feel a sympathy for him. He was easily the least slippery and most credible of the Exxon PR people I had spoken with. His face remained gray, his voice soft and expressionless. The mask remained fixed, but out from under it came glimmers of character. He told me that the Exxon employees here had mental health counseling, that there was a fishing boat to take them out on the water for relief, that it was not uncommon for them to work past midnight, that some of them had had to be sent home. He paused and glanced out toward the hallways where there was a bustle of activity, then looked back at me. "We have a lot of pride in Exxon."

"Pride" seemed to me to be the most dangerous buzzword. It repre-

---

* A month later, when I talked to Exxon officials in Anchorage, I found them surprised to learn that I had those figures. By late fall, the total had climbed to 1.4 billion. By winter, it was predicted to be in excess of 2 billion. Ultimately, I suspect, the cost to Exxon will be well in the tens of billions.

sented the screen behind which the Exxon people could hide their own questions.

Bethard said, "And now suddenly we're the object of national scorn. Many of us think it's the worst thing that's ever occurred."

A woman came into the room, and left a stack of papers on Bethard's desk. His face brightened. The woman went out. She was young, blonde, and attractive. Bethard told me that she was from the Valdez city offices. "She's always pleasant," he said. "She always has a smile." In a moment, the woman returned and stood just outside the doorway, talking to someone else. Bethard had to go to a meeting. He began talking to the woman near his doorway, then got up from behind his desk. There was a spring in his step, as if he were about to be freed from captivity. Suddenly, he moved through the doorway, forgetting me completely.

Chapter 17

NO ROAD

This damn town has been smeared with money.

—a Cordova fisherman, 1989

Besides Exxon and Veco, the full complement of the national and international press came to Cordova, and came again and again. A Cousteau Society team, filming an oil spill special, had come to town several times. The heads and representatives of environmental organizations came and went. State politicians came and went. Agency heads came. Agency representatives established a semipermanent presence. Oil observers from foreign countries came. Coast Guard admirals came. Members of Congress had been here, and so had Vice President Quayle, sealed up tight in an envelope of security. For a while, it was thought that President Bush was coming. But he didn't, preferring to hold the same distance Exxon chief executive officer Lawrence Rawl had held. The singer John McCutcheon came. John Denver gave a benefit concert. James Naughton, the actor, appeared with Chuck Hamel, the oil broker, and there was a buzz about a Paul Newman–financed feature movie. Economists came to study the contours of economic windfalls made in a small community. A group of social scientists from North Carolina came to study the effects of disaster.

Mental health researchers came to watch the course taken by delayed stress syndrome, which a striking number of Cordovans would eventually suffer, the consequence of a violent alarm over the threat to the very substance of their life, and the long hours spent battling that threat as it stretched into months, and then the precipitous dip in energy, the confusion over the simple details of daily life, and the depression. In August, John Crowley, who worked in the mental health outpatient division of the local hospital, said that the number of cases had increased fivefold, but he also said, "Each case has had a history of fragility that the spill itself, the destruction of nature, or the financial stress triggered." It was a reminder of the tweak to a system that Dan Reed had talked about on the *Alpha Helix*. In these cases, the tweak was to a psychic system.

Back at the end of May, the town had rolled out the red carpet for the crew of the Russian supersucker *Vaydaghubsky*. The largest and most effective skimmer in the world, the ship had an oil storage capacity of 670,000 gallons and a recovery rate of 200,000 gallons per hour, but it was far too large to negotiate the narrows and shallows near the shorelines. By the time it arrived at Resurrection Bay on April 19 (following yet another bureaucratic snarl, this one with the U.S. Customs Department over the question of allowing a Russian vessel to enter U.S. waters, which was finally resolved by having it fly both Russian and U.S. flags), the oil had scattered and formed mousse. Attempts to modify the ship's machinery proved only marginally successful, and ultimately very little oil was collected. If a ship like the *Vaydaghubsky* had been on the scene during the first few days of the spill, it would have made a difference.

The people of Cordova, understanding that the supersucker was anchored off Knight Island, doing nothing, invited the crew to town. The ship moved to Nelson Bay just up the coast from Cordova and the townspeople ferried the crew and themselves back and forth between town and the ship, threw a five-hour party with food, music, and dancing, and so entered the realm of foreign relations.

Money came into town, too. By June of 1990, the Exxon money that had entered through the city government in the form of grants totaled $740,000. From this, $196,000 was devoted to various means of rectifying the housing shortage during the summer, $18,000 was devoted to childcare. The remainder, or some $530,000, was devoted to reimbursements of various types, including to the Cordova Oil Spill Disaster Relief Office (COSDRO).* Unlike Valdez, Cordova has a sales tax, and revenues generated through it were the best available measure of the effect of the presence of outsiders and of income earned by Cordovans, including fishermen who worked for Exxon. Sales tax revenues increased by 22 percent. In June, Dale Daigger, city finance director, said that at that point

* COSDRO was the more strongly community-oriented equivalent in Cordova of the MACs in Seward and Homer.

further reimbursements from Exxon or Veco remained, as he put it, "under discussion."

PWSAC, upon which the fishermen relied heavily for its hatchery system, had received by June a total of 8 million from Exxon. The bulk of this money was channeled through a containment and management company called Spill Tech, which was hired soon after the oil spill to protect the PWSAC hatchery system. Besides management costs, money went for the actual purchase of boom and related hardware, boat charters, people, and overtime work in the PWSAC offices and in the field. PWSAC had also instituted a permanent storage system for boom and other protective gear at the hatchery sites. This was a part of Alyeska's new contingency plan.

Cordova District Fishermen United had received a payment of $250,000 from Exxon in mid-April 1989, and it was gone by the following September. According to CDFU Executive Director Marilyn Leland, the organization's budget was normally $50,000 per year. When I talked with her in June 1990, she told me that CDFU had projected that its oil spill–related expenses would reach the $350,000 to $400,000 range and that they anticipated no difficulty in obtaining the additional money from Exxon.

The Cordova Science Center, a new project modeled upon Woods Hole and the Moss Landing Institute in California, was established early in the summer. Under the acting directorship of John Harville, the founder of Moss Landing, the science center would soon appear to be well on its way to success. It was the crown jewel of the city's response. It received a total of $100,000 from Cordova in the form of a loan. Another $250,000 awaits action in the U.S. Congress. In addition, $85,000 had been received as donations from various organizations and individuals, including Cordovans. According to Nancy Bird, who began as a local volunteer, worked at COSDRO, and then became the coordinator of the Science Center, the degree of support given by the city was made possible by the presence of Exxon funds. The energy to implement the long-planned-for center was triggered by the alarm of the spill during the summer of 1989.

The large and small doses of capital that passed through Cordova fed into all the interstices of daily life—in the restaurants, grocery stores, the liquor store, through the extra flights to Anchorage, to Seattle, to Hawaii, back and forth between Cordova and Valdez, in the long-distance calls, newspaper subscriptions, boat purchases. Marilyn Leland told me that CDFU went through 20 or 30 cases of photocopy paper in a year as opposed to the usual four or five. Close on the heels of the paper came the maintenance of copying machines, copying fluid, and wages for additional help and overtime to run and maintain the machines, to file the copies, or to find copies in the files. Such expenditures were in part a result of the work being done by CDFU itself and in part because photocopying services were made available without charge to everyone in town. Paper was a primary tool of the intense community effort.

In mid-August 1989, I met with Brenda Guest, COSDRO deputy director. She had replaced Susan Ogle, who had worked as a volunteer. Brenda, a young woman, had come to Cordova from Anchorage, fell in love with the town, and remained amazed by its spirit, by the complete involvement of the people in the crisis. She said people had walked into the COSDRO office and read letters to Exxon off the computer. As arrangements were being made for the visit of the *Vaydaghubsky*, she'd gone around securing supplies for the party, and local businesses had accepted purchase orders with very little idea of how they were going to be paid, or by whom. "These people fought to get what they needed. Ultimately they've done really well," Brenda said.

At the time, I was trying to sort out where outrage ended in Cordova and where adventurism began. I asked her what she thought the heart of Cordova was. She paused a moment, then a light came into her eyes. We went outside, got into a pickup and drove along the old New England Road that passes by the house filled with Filipino cannery workers, past the canneries themselves, the Veco boat cleaning lot, the ferry terminal, and toward the old New England cannery since taken over by the Chugach Native Corporation.

We stopped first at what some referred to as Hippie Cove. Its proper name was Shelter Cove. It was a shallow inlet on one side of the road and on the other a creek drainage, backed by a steep slope. Brenda showed me a sauna, built at the base of the slope. It had mystic symbols and a sign that said anyone could use it so long as they brought their own wood and left it clean. Just above the sauna, almost hidden in the foliage, was a small, handbuilt house, and then above it another house. Brenda said there were several houses up there. She led me 100 yards or so along the edge of a pool in which a lone, spawning salmon struggled to enter the creek bed. We climbed the slope, winding our way through the dense woods to a string of campsites and dwellings built out of wood salvaged from a wrecked ship down below. No one was in sight, but left in the campsites and shelters were suitcases, bags, and cooking gear. Higher up on the hill, Brenda said, were better-built dwellings. She said something about how Gene wasn't here, and I wondered if it was Gene we were looking for, or if what she'd already shown me, the semipermanent and strictly temporary dwellings, made her answer to my question.

From there we drove to a set of campsites COSDRO was building to help accommodate the overflow of people in town, then went on toward the Chugach Corporation and found Gene walking along the road. He was Gene Rosellini, Brenda told me, a member of a prominent Washington State family and now the unofficial spokesman for Shelter Cove. He wore a ragged pair of black shorts and a ragged brown shirt and had a pack on his back. The pack was filled with rocks. It was his practice to carry rocks in order to keep what he referred to as his "primary means of transportation" in condition. He had carried building materials up the slope at Shelter Cove. His brown hair was cropped short. He had a weathered face and eyes nearly as clear as Dr. James Payne's had been. Behind a strap that passed across his chest was wedged a tiny, plastic prescription bottle filled with water. It was just enough water to sustain him on his walk, in accordance with his principle of no excess.

He spoke with difficulty, as if he wasn't used to talking. He and Brenda were negotiating. Brenda was making arrangements to move a trash bin and two Porta-Potties to Shelter Cove and to build a fire ring there. The reason for such "development," again, was the influx of people. Gene approved of the Porta-Potties and the fire ring but not of the trash bin. He didn't want trash removed from the sites. "Besides, there's a new theft problem," he said. He meant that on general principle he didn't want people getting the idea that things could be either taken or thrown away. "I can't leave anything valuable in my cabin, anymore. I have to carry my money with me."

Later, as we drove back to town, Brenda told me she was surprised that he had money. She said that some time before Gene had gone to the police chief, a man revered in Cordova, to inform him that he would be appearing in town a little more regularly now, that he wanted to prepare the police for that. "The children love him," Brenda said. I now understood her answer to my question: it was the campsites, spartan, exquisite, and built with Exxon money as it was routed through the city of Cordova; it was Shelter Cove, for years a refuge for those in transition, for many who came here seeking their future, such as Heather and Max McCarty; and it was Gene Rosellini, the offspring of wealth in the lower forty-eight come here to drop out completely, way down to the bottom, but who by the trust of the town placed in him and by the duration of his presence in Shelter Cove, and by his labor, had become the spokesman who negotiated the most extreme and thinnest tailings of Exxon largesse. Porta-Potties and fire ring, yes. Trash bin, no. It was a good answer.

Clearly, one of the more unsettling aspects of the spill was the uses to which the Exxon money was put. In Cordova, as elsewhere, there were instances of graft, nepotism, and profit-taking. In the early days, rifts developed over the assignment of boats by CDFU or the Prince William Sound Aquaculture Corporation (PWSAC) to the cleanup or hatchery defense. Prices in some public establishments were jacked up. There were tales of a Veco supervisor who skipped town with funds. Some residents billeted out their homes at exorbitant rates. There were spillionaires, and with that came the envy, bitterness, and isolation. The money was incendiary and in the later stages of the year of the spill threatened to undo the old solidarity and split the town in half.

The instances of graft and outright greed were not representative of the town's fundamental response. The problem here was more the position that community groups and institutions that received funding found themselves put in. Some of these, such as the Cordova Science Center and COSDRO, which sponsored the *Vaydaghubsky* party and ultimately paid for it with Exxon money, were created after the spill. Others, such as the Cordova District Fishermen United and PWSAC, had been in existence long before the spill. To those who preferred to walk the moral high road, the use of Exxon funds for any purpose not connected strictly to cleanup and reparation was wrong. Such people came from both ends of the spectrum: those who hated Exxon and wished to have nothing to do with its money, and those who applauded Exxon's cleanup efforts and wished to prevail no further upon the company's indulgence. Among the remainder, and particularly those adept at managing money, were some for whom the presence of Exxon capital in large quantities presented the opportunity to extend the meaning of reparation. The Cordova city government came to lean in that direction and COSDRO was its arm.

At the beginning, the oil spill frightened many Cordovans, including then City Manager Don Moore, into thinking that economic diversification was necessary as a defense against the unknown effects of the spill and of future spills. Cordova is completely dependent upon the fisheries. A professional business consultant, Mead Treadwell, was hired to head COSDRO. Treadwell was a member of an old entrepreneurial Alaskan family, a graduate of Yale and of Harvard Business School. He had been associated previously with Walter Hickel's venture company, Yukon Pacific Corporation. Hickel, a former Alaska governor, was secretary of the interior in the Nixon administration and had been instrumental in establishing the Alaska pipeline.* Treadwell had also been associated with the economic futurist Robert Theobald.

As the summer wore on into August and then into September, it gradually became manifest that Exxon would indeed have its cleanup forces out of the sound by September 15. The Cordova claim offices were also slated to be closed. The presence of state and federal agency representatives would be reduced. The population of observers and hangers-on would melt away and Cordova's brief, high-velocity stint as a weird sort of disaster-fed company town would soon be over. It also seemed that the Prince William Sound fisheries might be all right for the time being, although doubts over the condition of the salmon fry released from PWSAC hatcheries earlier in the season remained unallayed.

A new Alyeska contingency plan that would be more along the lines of the one at Sullom Voe in the Shetland Islands was being instituted. From Valdez, tankers were now escorted through the sound by two tugs and one of three new emergency-response vessels, each carrying 4,600 feet of boom. They had storage capacity for 4,000 barrels of oil. Barges, skimming vessels, and 200,000 more feet of boom were on standby at various locations. Pilots guided vessels past Bligh Reef. Captains and crews were submitted to alcohol tests before departure. True to form, the Cordova CDFU and groups from other affected communities had had a part in this and would continue to do so, but the question remained as to whether or not any contingency plan would be worth the paper it was printed on in the event of another big spill.† It would be a very long time before Cordovans rested easy on the matter of tanker traffic. Work was being done to lobby the Congress and the state legislature to pass stricter regulations and to limit further Alaskan production.

The town otherwise found itself hung between returning to something like what it had been before the spill (a complete return was patently impossible) and putting the best face on the changes that had

---

* In the fall of 1990, Hickel made an eleventh-hour entry into the Alaska gubernatorial race. He financed his campaign with his personal fortune, and ran as an independent on a prodevelopment platform. He won the race by carrying the principal Alaskan cities, Anchorage and Fairbanks, but lost everywhere else in Alaska. The cities are both tied to development. In the view of some, his election may also reflect voter dissatisfaction with the traditional political parties. Although Hickel has expressed a soft spot in his heart for Prince William Sound and has vowed to pursue restoration, what the meaning of his strong leanings toward extractive industry will be to the state remains to be seen.

† As of February 1990, the new Alyeska contingency plan included this statement: "Alyeska anticipates that in many circumstances spills of fewer than 1000 barrels (42,000) gallons can be substantially controlled and recovered. There will be few circumstances in which a catastrophic spill (over 4.2 million gallons) can be substantially contained."

come to it during the spill. "Exxon," Mead Treadwell told me, "keeps saying that they don't want to pick up garbage that's not theirs." From Exxon's perspective, garbage referred to a range of things that ran from trash left by others on the beaches and oil from other sources (which James Payne was checking for in the Kasitsnu Bay lab) to mental stress and economic dislocation stemming from causes unrelated to the oil spill. "But my attitude," Treadwell said, "is go jump in the lake, guys. You certainly won't be able to pick up all your own garbage. This city is trying to recover from an economic disaster, and I don't see anything wrong with trying to mount a deeper keel to stabilize the city." What Treadwell was talking about was the municipal equivalent to "contingent valuation" of damaged resources.

The "deeper keel" he referred to included community development projects. One of these was the Science Center. Another under consideration was a deep water port, which was tied to the interests of the Eyak Village Corporation. Yet another was the road to Anchorage and Fairbanks. All three projects had been longstanding concerns in the community. But again, those who took the moral high ground said that any such project had nothing whatsoever to do with the oil spill and that even to pursue them with Exxon funding was a form of gouging, and so of capitulation to villainy. Others said that the oil spill necessitated such considerations, and with the help, among others, of Treadwell and the future mayor, Bob Van Brocklin, a local businessman with a background in economics, the city entered into economic projections.

Treadwell is a resolute young man with an air of ambition and drive. He is East Coast, and at first glance seemed an odd leader to place in a community of rough-talking fishermen. In another way, though, since the fishermen were also businessmen in their own right—smart and independent—Treadwell was perfect. According to Treadwell, the city government remained worried about the potential longterm effects the spill would have upon fish processing in Cordova and upon the number of boats for which Cordova was the home port. Both the boats in the harbor and the canneries (through a raw fish tax that brought approximately a million dollars annually into the city coffers) had a direct effect upon the economic and social fabric of the town. "Twenty-nine families have left town because they made so much money on the cleanup that they had no reason to stay," Treadwell said. "It's what's called a pattern dislocation in our economy and Cordova will be feeling it for years." Treadwell stayed on. In October 1989, a full month after the Exxon pullout, the Cordova city council appropriated another $180,000 to carry COSDRO through April 1990.

*   *   *

Some would argue that the Cordova airport—the best in the sound—made a good reason for Exxon to use Cordova as a staging ground for 1989/1990 winter cleanup and for future oil spill response, and that Exxon should be courted to this end. One of these was Connie Taylor, a member of the Oil Response Committee (an advisory arm of the city government) and president of the Cordova Chamber of Commerce. Earlier, the Cordova business community had split between the old-line Chamber of Commerce people, led by Connie Taylor, and a newer, more aggressive group, "Main Street Business," led by Bob Van Brocklin. A bitter rift developed between the two groups that stemmed from the question of who represented Cordova businesses to Exxon and the state government. In the October municipal elections, Taylor was elected to the city council and Van Brocklin was elected mayor. The rift deepened through the following year, culminating with Taylor bringing suit against Van Brocklin and councilmembers R. J. Kopchak and Jeff Hawley for holding secret meetings in her absence in violation of the Alaska Open Meetings Act. In turn, Taylor was accused of channeling information from council executive sessions to Exxon attorneys (one of whom represented her), including information connected to future possible suits for reparation from Exxon. The city council appropriated $75,000 to defend Van Brocklin, Kopchak, and Hawley against Taylor's suit. As I write, the suit is in progress and the bitter division divides the town.

In August, Connie Taylor had told me that she objected strenuously to businesses that take advantage of the turmoil in town for their own gain. She said, "I've worn two hats through the whole thing, the Chamber hat and the Oil Response Committee hat. I have a hard time with people who are angry with Exxon. Exxon has done what it could. Nobody forced Exxon to open up two offices in town to pay claims. Exxon could have said, Here we are in Houston. Come sue us."

She felt that Exxon was making every possible effort to clean up the spill and to route business through local banks and businesses. She felt a sympathy for the Exxon people, which was almost unheard of in Cordova. "What about these guys from Houston?" she said. "They were jerked out of their normal lives and sent up here. It doesn't make sense not to treat them decently." She favored encouraging an Exxon presence in town. The other side wanted the suits for damages to serve as a basis for making permanent the city's independence from Exxon. The anxiety over future additional drilling sites adding to the flow down the pipeline and to further possible spills ran very strong.

This fallout from the spill and the continuing promise of available money occasioned a seemingly endless sequence of disruptions that by the winter of 1990 would virtually paralyze the city council. A rift developed on the CDFU board, too, over the questions of lobbying and the appropriate level of cooperation with the new Alyeska head, James Hermiller. CDFU publicly recognized Hermiller for his accomplishments in improving communications with fishing concerns at the same time that CDFU board member Riki Ott was lobbying for stricter oil spill legislation in Juneau. Ott, who was lobbying on behalf of the Oil Reform Alliance, of which she was president, and on behalf of CDFU. She felt her efforts had been undercut. By the early summer of 1990, Ott, ever buoyant, said, "Crisis brings unity, but then in unity there's the division as different perceptions begin to split off. What we have going on here is a revolution. As revolutions are won, you evolve."

The road debate had been an issue during the October 1989 election. Connie Taylor was pro-road. Van Brocklin was anti-road. The lack of a road, some would argue, was part of the reason the town had been passed over as a winter staging ground. Therefore, less money came into town. Some, of course, would just as soon no Exxon money had ever come in. Others wanted as much of it as they could get. Proponents wanted the road built for the sake of future opportunities. Most typical were the fishermen who were stunned by the destruction of Prince William Sound, and who then grew increasingly outraged by the ever-deepening bureaucratic tangles attached to righting the wrong and in which they, in order to survive, came to be required to participate. First they had to get somebody to do something about the oil, and then do something about it themselves under Exxon's payroll. They had to collect their fishing claims, watchdog Alyeska's new contingency plan, and generally adjust their lives to changed financial realities. Finally, a lot of them simply wanted to see Exxon shut up, pay up, and get out. The results of the October election and of ensuing council action suggest that the majority of the voters remained opposed to the road. Treadwell, the COSDRO director, told me afterwards that though he continued to work assiduously on other diversification projects, he "wouldn't touch the road question with a ten-foot pole."

The disaster that struck Cordova and the other towns is markedly different from most natural disasters. Rather than one catastrophic event, it became a persistent sequence of events that disrupted and threatened to continue to disrupt the normal conduct of life. It left people with the sense of having lost control. The effect of environmental destruction on the level of the oil spill upon the lives and minds of people is not always immediately evident, especially among those who make a speedy, active response, such as Connie Taylor, Van Brocklin, Riki Ott, Heather McCarty, Marilyn Leland, Tom Copeland, Kelly Weaverling, and many others.

The town's roadlessness and the PWSAC-administered hatchery system seemed most emblematic of the contradiction Cordovans were forced to confront. The lack of the connection by road to the outside makes a contradiction that is lodged deeply in the town at large and in the imaginations of individuals. One part of the imagination wishes to keep things just as they are. Another part wishes to expand endlessly outward. The midground between the two extremes would be to protect, probe, and nurture what lies at hand. It's a hard line to find, and to hold the edges on either side of it in the proper measure of disorder requires a diligent, gentle touch.

For the hatcheries, the egg selection must not weaken gene pools, and so PWSAC has a program for renewing wild runs and for replenishing the genetic diversity of its own stock with wild-run eggs. The fry and the eggs especially must not be subjected to pollution, as both the fry released in 1989 and the spawning run of 1989 were. As it happend, the 1988 pink salmon brood, released as fry in 1989 following the spill, produced the largest return on record (an estimated 43 million pinks). One result was an immediate barrage of press releases and advertisements from Exxon claiming that the oil spill had hardly damaged the ecosystem. What the 1990 pink salmon return validated, however, was what had been observed in the weeks following the spill—that the all-out effort to protect the hatchery stock had been successful and subsequently that the fingerlings seemed to be making it out beneath the oil. It said nothing of the multifariousness of factors that might—for better or worse—affect a run at sea, of the effects of oil pollution upon the spawning run of 1989, of longterm sublethal effects, or of the fact that 1990 was not the year biologists expected to see the effects of the spill. Also, the 1990 returns in the lower Cook Inlet, which was still recovering from the 1987 Glacier Bay spill, were very poor. There, the pink salmon return was less than 50 percent of the 30-year average, and the chinook return was one of the lowest on record.

As a matter of course, the hatchery system comes with built-in hazards: die-outs at sea, disease, the practices of high seas drift-netting, which may ambush large proportions of a returning run, and the effects of the marketplace, which is 80 to 90 percent Japanese.* These are the typical dan-

---

* Due in part to anxiety over oil-tainted fish, the price for Prince William Sound pinks collapsed in 1990, thus effectively offsetting the high returns.

gers of monoculture, or of converting salmon fishing into something a little like dairy farming. Among other things, the sameness of the stock creates vulnerabilities. Unlike oil, however, and minerals and timber harvesting, the hatchery system, with luck and wise management, can provide an annually renewable resource indefinitely and sustain the lives of an unusual group of people. The oil spill accentuated the trickiness of fishing, but for all its trickiness, the hatchery system has become indispensable. It cannot be set loose, and it must stay tricky.

Chapter 18

GHOSTS

Boone's genius was to recognize the difficulty as neither material
nor political but one purely moral and aesthetic. Filled with the
wild beauty of the New World to over-brimming so long as he
had what he desired, to bathe in, to explore always more
deeply, to see, to feel, to touch—his instincts were contented.
Sensing a limitless fortune which daring could make his own, he
sought only with primal lust to grow close to it, to understand it
and to be part of its mysterious movements—like an Indian.
. . . taciturn in his demeanor, symmetrical and instinctive in understanding, Boone stood for his race, the affirmation of that wild
logic, which in times past has mastered another wilderness and
now, renascent, would master this, to prove it potent.

—William Carlos Williams, *In the American Grain*, 1925

I'd first heard of David Grimes's boat, the *Orca II*, in July
1989 at Mavis Mueller's cabin near Homer. Larry Smith had
taken me to meet Mavis, an artist, and at that time involved in organizing
the Geo-Textile Banner project through which large banners would be
hung in Kodiak, Homer, Seldovia, Valdez, Cordova, Anchorage, Fairbanks, San Diego, and Tijuana to protest the spill and commemorate the
arrival of the Exxon *Valdez* in San Diego for repairs. Mavis's cabin had
barely enough room for a kitchen and a bed, and yet there were six or
seven of us in there—Larry, Mavis, myself, and a group of Earth First!
people, whose arrival had caused a kind of panic among the police and
Exxon people. The FBI had come to Homer, I'd heard. Most of the Earth

Firsters were from California. One young woman who happened to be from Homer had just been arrested and then released for chaining herself to the doors of the Exxon offices in Valdez.

Mavis, whom I came to know, was solid, committed, and funny. She described herself as a "deep ecologist," one who believed in the kinship of all living things. The Earth Firsters struck me as being surly and a bit puffed up with themselves. They had the "they" lingo down pat, the use of the pronoun which usually meant Exxon but also served as a catchall receptacle for vaguely defined forces of evil. As it turned out, the Earth Firsters eventually went to work on the Mars Cove volunteer effort. A part of the story of the oil spill was the constant presence of activist elements, a roiling just beneath the surface. There had been demonstrations, such as the one staged by the woman from Homer, and the "liberation" of 12 otters from holding pens in Valdez on the night of July 12. Greenpeace staged events, but most of the local people felt that they were essentially media spectacles that had little to do with their needs. A regatta, or mock raid, organized by Kelly Weaverling and Riki Ott for the Port of Valdez in mid-September 1989 served to solidify feeling among the participants in the waning days of the oil spill, but fewer boats came than expected and the event made no more than a ripple in the national coverage. There were moments, especially in the early days of the spill, when it would have taken very little to galvanize the activists of the left and right and the independent-minded fishermen into action, such as a blockade of the channel, or sabotage. Indeed, to the end of 1989 and through the following year, successful fishermen with families and mortgages continued to speak of a blockade of the tankers as a reasonable line of action. During the spring and early summer, it had been a near thing. The ingredients were there, an unnecessary disaster, inept and paralyzed authorities, a powerful and organized body of victims, such as fishing people, to lend spine to the diffuse activism of the left, and articulate ideological leadership.

But it didn't happen. One reason was that the fishermen had made some progress working inside the channel—with, for example, the improved Alyeska contingency plan. Another was the divisive effect of money. A third reason was that although the battle was being fought at a critical link in the oil delivery system, the Port of Valdez was still a remote outpost. There had been a string of spills elsewhere that seemed intended to remind the nation of the condition of the delivery system,*

---

* Among them were three spills within 12 hours on June 23 and 24, 1989. A Greek tanker ran aground in Narragansett Bay near Newport, Rhode Island, spilling 420,000 gallons of

but support from the outside came mainly in the form of lip service as opposed, say, to a selective petroleum boycott. Ultimately, the people of south-central Alaska recognized that they could not (and cannot) fight Alyeska or Exxon alone.

On that day in July, however, Mavis Mueller's tiny cabin happened to be a hot point in insurrectionist feeling. The talk swirled around the room that smelled strongly of fish. People shifted here and there, jockeying for standing room. There was an air of existential anticipation, of something momentous about to occur that might carry everyone with it, although just what that thing was remained unclear. In fact, their moment had already passed.

Mavis and I found ourselves next to each other in front of an Edward Abbey–Monkey Wrench Gang poster. Mavis told me about the *Orca II*. "It's a spirit vessel. It's used as a sanctuary," she said. "A support vessel for wildlife. It's a vehicle for creative response."

Just past noon on September 25, ten days after the official deadline for the pullout of Exxon's cleanup forces, the *Orca II* pulled out of the Cordova harbor. It stopped at the fuel dock to tank up on gasoline, then went on northeasterly along Orca Inlet past the Chugach Corporation Fisheries and veered outward to the center of the channel in order to avoid the logs that had broken loose from a raft in the storm that had passed through during the last few days. The logs lay low in the water and were visible only at close range. The three of us—David, Lynn Schooler, and myself—were in the wheelhouse, looking out intently.

The stray logs occasioned a brief, grim exchange between Lynn and David. Lynn is from Juneau in southeastern Alaska, where there is strong feeling over timber cutting in the Tongass National Forest. Federal subsidies for logging and a guaranteed profit contract held by the Alaska Pulp Corporation and Louisiana Pacific have made the Tongass one of the biggest money-losing national forests in the country. In the meantime, watersheds are being despoiled and the slopes clearcut down to the water. The destruction to wildlife in southeastern Alaska from logging will probably far exceed that of the oil spill in Prince William Sound.

The immediate subject of discussion between Lynn and David was the logs that are cabled together in huge rafts along the banks of southeast

---

fuel oil; a Panamanian freighter collided with an oil-carrying barge in the Houston Ship Channel, spilling 250,000 gallons of heavy crude oil into Galveston Bay; and a Uruguayan tanker hit a rock in the Delaware River near Claymont, Delaware, spilling 310,000 gallons of fuel oil.

waters and that sometimes break loose and become a menace to boats. "It's a fact of life down there," Lynn said. In Prince William Sound, loose logs are much less common because of the so far comparatively low level of cutting, but here, just outside Cordova, storms regularly break up the rafts. One log could rip a boat apart, particularly a fast-moving gill-netter. It's a sore point that raises the larger, smoldering issue of logging in the sound, and of the questionable financial practices attached to it. The issue had receded from attention during the oil spill but bracketed it in time. From the perspective of fishermen, the eroding silt loads caused by logging on the slopes adjacent to marine habitats and spawning streams present a serious threat to their livelihoods.

Prince William Sound, the Kenai Peninsula, and the Kodiak archipelago can be viewed as the northernmost extreme of a vast temperate rain forest that begins in northern California. The further north the forest reaches, the narrower is the band it makes between the sea and inland regions, and—because of harsh conditions—the more marginal it is in economic terms as a timber resource. With reduced harvests in Oregon and Washington, however, south-central Alaskan timber had become increasingly lucrative, mainly through export to Asia. While we were on the *Orca II*, the new Chugach Native Corporation mill was nearing completion over in Seward, and logs barged from as far away as 300 miles were being stockpiled there. The mill was being built at a cost of over $20 million, 25 percent over original estimates. Previously, the corporation had sold off coal and timber stocks in order to generate tax losses, then sold the paper losses off to profitable companies, such as General Mills, that were in search of tax writeoffs. The strategy created problems for the Chugach Corporation with the IRS, but the by now highly leveraged Chugach Corporation still controls approximately one billion board feet of timber in the sound and elsewhere.

The Chugach Corporation is the dominant Native corporation in this region. It and various village corporations are in the process of selling off their timber rights. The corporations, including the village corporations of Tatitlek, Seldovia,* and the Eyak Corporation in Cordova, had contracted for harvests of about 14,000 acres of timber in Prince William Sound, the Kenai, and the Kodiak archipelago during the next year. The wished-for result of the 1971 American Native Claims Settlement Act, engineered by the late Senator Henry Jackson of Washington, had been

---

* In the 1990 legislative session a proposal for the state to buy back the timber rights to 24,000 acres off Kachemak Bay, the culmination of 12 years of complicated land-trade negotiations, died on a 20–20 tie vote in the Alaskan House.

to bring Native Alaskan lands into development, to capitalize those lands. It was happening. Because of their losses, often over the protests of Native shareholders, and quite at odds with the traditional Native view of ownership and boundaries, the Native corporations had found themselves the vehicles by which outside capital could enter the reserves.

The *Orca II* moved on at a speed of about seven knots. The loose-log conversation fell away as we neared the bend in the inlet that would take us out into Orca Bay and thence to the sound itself. The tailings of the storm that had delayed our departure for two days were still with us— great gray billows of clouds before us and off portside swelling up from behind the hump of Hawkins Island. The water was dark. The wooden double-ender moved lightly through the water, and down in the hold the Chrysler V-8 rumbled steadily. Originally, the boat had been a troller, and was converted by extending the cabin to the stern. We passed by several otters. They lay on their backs, eating, or cradling their pups, and scarcely gave us notice. Our main destination was Knight Island. We would spend several days there, then head up to Columbia Glacier and come back across the channel to visit Jon Rush and Sylvia Gill.

I had discovered both David Grimes and the *Orca II* to be rather different from what the heady atmosphere of the meeting in Mavis's cabin had led me to expect. The boat did have its fanciful aspect—the banners that fluttered from its masts, and inside the mementoes and photographs. The three of us stood in the wheelhouse. Next to the radar screen was a liquor bottle with a bouquet of dried weeds, and hanging from the ceiling two penny whistles, a mobile, and two dried dragonflies suspended by threads. Just above the windscreen was the *Time* magazine photograph of Joseph Hazelwood, whom David referred to as the "patron saint of the sound." He said, "Hazelwood had the reputation of being the best skipper in the company, and it was because of his intimate understanding of the sea. He was a rebel. He didn't like Exxon's policy of operation by imagery. He kept the appointment for the company. I'd like to get a message out to him that we don't blame him."

David himself was far less a person who had bought into a New Age agenda than one who was struggling to emerge whole from the firestorm that began with the spill and his part in the ad hoc advisory committee along with the other Cordovans, and then went on through the making of his oil spill video, *Voices of the Sound*, the purchase of the *Orca II*, animal rescue, and "spiritual cleanup." Despite the fact that he'd been at the very heart of the turmoil, he said, "Even while my efforts were directed toward salvaging something here, I had the sense that it wasn't Prince William Sound that was at risk. More, it was L.A. and New York and the Great Lakes."

He is from Springfield, Missouri, studied natural history in college, and has been coming up to Prince William Sound since 1974. He skippered a salmon boat for a time, but then turned to herring fishing. Like John Oliver, David cultivated his peripheral vision. "I am a fisherman," he said, "but I'm always on the outer edge of the curve. I have an ambivalence toward it. I'll see a pod of killer whales, or a mountain on Knight Island I'd like to climb. I've never been a competitive fisherman."

Lynn Schooler said that David was a changed man. Lynn himself was from Texas originally, but had grown up in Anchorage, homesteaded on the sound, and fished for a time out of Seward. He was expert with boats. A Vietnam veteran, he'd been watching people for evidence of delayed stress syndrome while we were in Cordova and had seen it.

For my part, I had felt an increasing disquiet over the enlarging gap between the spill as a heavily moneyed political and legal event and the spill as fact. I wished—perhaps oddly, but as it would turn out, rightly—to return to the scene of destruction in hopes it would act as a restorative. I didn't seek a survey (by then I understood that another survey would be self-defeating), but an intense address to the facts as they chose to present themselves.

By four o'clock, Knowles Head, the point of mainland at the outer, northern verge of Orca Bay, had become visible off our starboard side. Two tankers, small in the distance, were there, awaiting permission to enter the Valdez Arm. We altered our course southerly, swinging in the direction of Johnstone Point on Hinchinbrook Island. The tanker channel lay directly ahead. Since we remained in the lee of Hinchinbrook Island, the swells were low. Before us, the sky was dotted with broken clouds, but at our backs the clouds were thick and vertical swatches of rain reached down to the water.

Just before five, we passed Johnstone Point and came out into the channel north of the Hinchinbrook Entrance. There were three- to four-foot swells, what David referred to as "the ghost of the storm." They let me pilot the boat, and as we went into the swells at an angle slightly less than 90 degrees, the boat pitched to and fro like a canoe. The light shone on the water. Mixed with milky sediment, the green and blue water changed color as the sunlight passed in and out from behind the clouds. Behind us stood a double rainbow. Before us, a flock of sandhill cranes cut a long V-shaped pattern high in the sky. Their bodies looked thin, like the thin knife of their pattern. They were heading out for southern

California or Mexico. "They had to wait for the storm to pass, too," David said. Over the radio, we heard the announcement: "The bodies of two crewmen from the tug *Steadfast* have been found 20 miles northwest of Cape Saint Elias. . . ."

A quiet fell over the wheelhouse. Lynn and David grew watchful. Two more crewmen, according to the report, were either drowned or out at sea somewhere. Lynn theorized that if they were in a liferaft it might well drift up to where we were. Though Cape Saint Elias was 70 miles away, the prevailing currents might well carry them around the rim of land to the Hinchinbrook Entrance. Lynn knew the boat and said it was based in southeast. It had been a cleanup vessel. The crewmen had been headed home with their riches. The irony of that, the irony native to the hazard the sea always set against its riches, and the specific irony of this hazard driven against the lucre of the cleanup, carried with it a heavy freight of gloom. The two crewmen were never found.

Three Dall's porpoises appeared off our portside. They left small roost-ertails of spray in their wake and rapidly overtook us. They rode our bow wave, dove from one side, reappeared on the other, and then dove again. I climbed out onto the deck and leaned over the bow. They swam double-loops. Each would ride the wave on the surface at one side of the bow, then surf the surge of the wave underwater and hang there for a moment, and roll, then dart across the vacuum just beneath the bow. It came out on the other side, surfed the surge, rose to the surface, and swam out and across the front of the boat in a wide loop, glided back, and started in again. All three did this at once, making an intricate coun-terpoint out of their motion. They were black and white, concisely col-ored. They had the white ovals on their bellies and up their sides, and white at the tips of their dorsal and tail fins. The blue- and green- and cream-colored water rippled around them as they passed through and rolled. It shuddered against their whiteness and blackness, making them seem to shimmer. They were playing.

By eight o'clock, the clouds had begun to stitch back together in a mass. Green Island came into view off our portside. Knight Island ap-peared before us. Through an opening in the clouds, a short stretch of ragged mountain peaks appeared, raking the sky. The sky darkened and the clouds closed up. The lower slopes on the island were at first a chalky blue. As we approached, as night fell, the color deepened to a black obscurity. We entered Snug Harbor, a large bay not far above the southern end of the island. Shaped like a sideways s, its broad mouth tipped northeasterly so that it directly faced Bligh Reef up at the other corner of the sound. It had been among the hardest-hit places: oil in two-foot pools, and hundreds of large animals, birds, otters, deer, floating around in the tidepools and trapped between the rocks. This was one of the first places that Kelly Weaverling and members of the animal rescue crew had come to. It also became one of the most heavily intruded-upon sites, subjected to all manner of cleanup exercises.

A line of beaches along its southern side had been selected by the EPA's Office of Research and Development (ORD) as test sites for bioremediation. Through the agreement between ORD and Exxon, six separate, adjacent beaches had been isolated. The six beaches fell roughly into two types—sand and gravel beaches, and cobblestone beaches. One of each type was used as a control. The remaining beaches received two types of fertilization to enhance the activity of oil-eating microorganisms. The experiment, the first of its kind in the field, provided the basis for Exxon's use of bioremediation through the following year and summer of 1990 and for the use of a similar process in the June 1990 *Mega Borg* spill in the Gulf of Mexico.

It was quiet as we entered Snug Harbor, and dark, the darkness of midnight made more profound by the nearness of the island. David slowly picked his way inside the harbor, scrutinizing the depth finder and radar for obstructions. We set anchor and switched off the engine. The quiet abruptly deepened. There was only the light breeze snapping the boat's banners and the water lapping against the hull. At a call from David, Lynn and I clambered out to the deck. An aurora borealis spanned the sky. Tensile like a huge rubber band, it expanded and retracted, intensifying in brightness as it stretched. It flashed against the clouds and glinted on the spruce trees near the shore, the rocks, the dark water.

At seven in the morning, the three of us took the Zodiac to shore. David was in charge, and we scarcely noted the shoreline but immediately began to hike up a steep slope to a lake. A flood, probably caused by the rupturing of an ice dam years before, had leveled a stretch of woods, and the going was rough. We clambered over tree after tree and tight-roped the trunks, jumped into holes between the stumps, and clambered up again, clinging to old limbs. Amongst the fallen trees and out of their capsized root systems new trees and a dense bush had sprung up. Eventually, we came clear of the deadfall and made our way along a bear trail to a lake and stood on the rock outcropping along its shore. Not far away, a bare, glaciated mountain peak rose into the sky. The sky was bright and blue.

The lake was absolutely clear. It was perhaps 40 yards across. The reflection of the rocks and trees on the far side was perfect, but toward the center the stirring of the breeze upon the surface of the water obscured the reflection ever so slightly. The colors were there—gray rock, green spruce, the pale trunks of the hemlocks and the leaves turning to red and yellow—and the shapes remained quite recognizable, but the image was diffuse, like a Monet. It was visually exquisite, and pure, and conceptually arresting because of the interplay of elements—shoreline, water, and wind.

We took a different course back down through the deadfall, the chaos of destruction, and by then the inescapable question had come to me: In the course of things, what was the difference between this and the destruction of oil on the water? The immediate answer was simple: a deadfall was not toxic and it didn't keep walking all over itself, and the regeneration, the tangle of new growth coming up in the wealth of decay, was as wanton as the destruction. The second answer—which might be cast in the perspective of the passage of geologic time, and consider mutation as one among the forms of regeneration, and even the human role in the late twentieth century as an agent of nature's proclivity for weird catastrophe and regrowth—was far more difficult to grasp. I knew what I believed and would act on, but ultimately I did not know that answer.

We came out of the deadfall into a muskeg meadow. The ground cover was richly colored: little pools of water like dark eyes, coated with mud and organic scum, the green vine, licopodium, and the delicate lichens that came in gray, green, cream, yellow, and red, and russula mushrooms, inedible but extraordinary in their coloration, the dots of them in silver, violet, pink, the color of fish in the water.

Back down at Snug Harbor, we paused long enough to see that there was evidence of oil, a darkening between stones. When dug into, the fine gravel revealed more oil beneath the surface. My guess was it was another beach that had been cleaned with high-pressure hoses. In a streambed, transects had been set up—wires laid out in a grid and buried beneath the gravel, hooked up to something—a plate, or diodes—then run to a battery that was strapped to a tree at the edge of the stream. The battery clicked every few seconds, a signal that it was working. This was somebody's research project. I suspected that it had something to do with salmon, but I had no idea. Something was being counted. I stood and looked at the wires that entered the stream and resisted a strong urge to kick them loose.

We set out in the Orca II, passing the six test sites on the southern shore. They bled oil and the two different kinds of fertilizer into the water. We entered Montague Strait and passed Hogan Bay, which even from a distance remained visibly oiled. We turned around Point Helen at the southern extreme of Knight Island. To the south were Latouche, Evans, Elrington, and Bainbridge islands. We were in the same hard-hit territory the *Alpha Helix* had come through. We passed Little Bay. A tug appeared, pulling a barge loaded to the gills with equipment—containers, small machinery, boom, and cranes. It was a straggler of the pullout. We were struck by the fact that it was the first boat we'd seen since the evening before.

There was a bench in the wheelhouse, a stool, and then the skipper's chair. David was at the wheel and Lynn and I otherwise spread ourselves out. A pod of killer whales, their dorsal fins erect above the surface, appeared, and we chased them for a few minutes, then let them go. In the distance off our portside, a lone humpback dove. Its flukes swung up and caught the sun, then disappeared.

David began to talk about how he, Riki Ott, Rick Steiner, and Jack Lamb had ended up in Valdez back in March and found themselves at the center of what he called "the power grid." There was the tension among the three principal figures, particularly between Dennis Kelso and Frank Iarossi. According to David, it was "very difficult to tell when they were speaking out of their own sense of despair and truth and when they were speaking for their constituencies." He continued, "At one of the meetings Kelso was trying to get Exxon off the leadership role. Iarossi said, 'If you do that, we're out of here.' Kelso said, 'And if you do that, we'll take out ads showing you promising that Exxon will clean it up.' "

What David was describing was the moment in the history of the spill when the outward signs were confusion, inaction, and rancor over what method to use, while the slick sat on the water, awaiting the first, and then the second storm. At that same moment, the pitched battle was being waged between the state of Alaska and Exxon over who, first, was in charge, and who, second, was responsible. They were not the same thing, neither was easily resolved, and the confusion would persist for days and then for weeks and months after the spill, well into the next year. At an April 6 hearing before the U.S. Senate Committee on Commerce, Science, and Transportation, Senator Richard Bryan of Nevada, seeking the answers to the same questions, would finally show his exasperation to Samuel Skinner, secretary of the Department of Transportation, and William Reilly, the head of the EPA, by saying, "I am not trying to be critical of you or the President [Bush]. I am just trying to find out in the vernacular of the street who the hell is calling the shots."

Secretary Skinner replied that the Coast Guard was in charge, although, of course, this had never quite been the case. "One of the best sources of information on what was going to happen to this crude," he said, "was from the fishermen who have been in that area forty years watching the flow. . . . They were part of the group that we met with." This was where David, Steiner, Ott, Lamb, and the others had come in. The glibness with which Secretary Skinner alluded to their participation hardly accounted for the actual difficulties they first encountered in getting someone to listen to them about the need first of all to protect the hatcheries.

"We were over there in Valdez," David said. "It dawned on us that there wasn't much going on. We had to do something. What happens is you think somebody's in control and so you give up your day-to-day decision making, and we all were lulled. Somehow we had the illusion that there was this one great big not-for-profit oil company, which isn't true at all. You get this infra-structure that allows you to think that way. Our first couple days in Valdez were spent working through the cobwebs of that illusion. We were waiting for somebody to do something, and then finally it hit us that it was our home and nobody was there. All the things we'd been taking for granted were gone.

"But those of us in Valdez weren't used to speaking with authority, and so first, we had to learn what authority was about. It's doing the best you can with what you know. So far as speaking for the sound was concerned, we were the ones who showed up, that's all. When the first storm hit, Exxon had to admit the whole thing was out of control. We advised them on currents and winds, the hatchery system, fish biology. They were like kids, getting the story. We created the planning committee. It was like we'd created our own government. We had to give ourselves over to it."

Early in the afternoon, we pulled into Lucky Bay and set anchor. Because of its position in the center of the southern end of Knight Island and its shape—broad at its base, then narrow and twisting—the bay had been but lightly oiled. David set store in its name—Lucky. As we'd come into the bay, he said, "For those who know Knight Island, all you need to say is Lucky Bay." There was evidence of oil visible along the banks, at the bottoms of the rock faces. Above the rocks was the thick growth of bush, fern, and tree. In the water, two otters lay on their backs, feeding. A pup climbed up onto its mother's belly.

It was high tide as we headed up the slender bay in the Zodiac, and barely passed through a narrow channel bounded by rocks. We came around a bend into a pool and a dozen Canadian geese fled our presence, sending out fans of water as they beat against it. They swept around the bend in the bay by which we'd just entered and disappeared. Lynn switched off the outboard. We sat still as the Zodiac twisted ever so slowly in the pool. No one spoke except to draw attention to this thing or that. Surf scoters and common mergansers had paddled away from us near to the shore but otherwise seemed unalarmed. Down in a corner of the pool, a belted kingfisher sat on a hemlock limb that overhung the water. It was gray and had the white band around its neck, the long, silvery beak, and the odd, hydrocephalic-looking head. It dropped like a stone into the water and caught a fish.

The Zodiac drifted. There was no evidence of oil on the surface of the water. Very little was visible along the banks, and it didn't appear that this inner bay had been mechanically cleaned. All along the banks was the tumult of growth, fern, bush, lichen, and tree. The sun was out and everything reflected crazily in the water. A stream came softly into the pool at the top of the bay and high above it was a waterfall, a dense band of plummeting white against the dark mountain slope. Over the edge of the Zodiac, one saw, first, the reflection of one's own face, and beneath that the kelp, and almost indiscernible, and yet there, a line of differentiation between the lense of fresh water that floated on top of the salt water. Salt water came in with the tide. Fresh water flowed from the streams. White jellyfish, what David called "moon jellyfish," floated in the water. They looked like big, slightly disarrayed bouquets, floating, amorphous, the frilly white oral arms and tentacles hanging loosely from the body as they awaited the arrival of prey to be stung and absorbed. A bald eagle passed overhead and veered away. The Zodiac twisted slowly. The kingfisher returned to its perch. Everywhere, there was the sense of life layered upon itself.

To see this place, so near to the heart of the calamity and yet so unlike the ghettolike shores of Snug Harbor, was a restorative. It was clear that this was what David had hoped to find here. He burned sage in honor of the place. We drifted out of the pool, and in order to maintain our sense of quiet, rowed back to the *Orca II*. We left Lucky Bay and headed for the southwestern corner of Knight Island, then turned into a narrow, inside passage, Long Channel. Off our portside was Squire Island. On our starboard side was Deer Cove. An ebbing tide slowed the *Orca II*'s pace as it labored against the power of the water. Swollen with water, the channel seemed beguilingly benign, too. The rocks and nearby islands gave the sense of our being in an immense bathtub. We passed Echo Rock and stuck our heads out the windows of the wheelhouse and shouted at it. Echoes bounced back in a fine, exact facsimile. The channel was narrow and on either side all along the shorelines were heaps of dead popweed.

David slowed down further as he negotiated the rocks off the head of

Mummy Island. We swung back out toward Knight Island Passage again, a more open waterway which here ran north and south. Chenega Island came into view. At six in the evening, we passed the notorious Herring Bay. Small worksheds were still visible along the shoreline and a Zodiac loaded with three persons in orange float jackets sped across it. The human presence was nothing compared to what it had been. David said, "Back in Valdez, when the feds came in, they told us, whatever you need, we'll get it and Exxon will pay the cost.

"They gave us free rein, whatever we could think of. There was a brilliant redneck engineer who came down from the North Slope. We were trying to think up ways to clean up the oil. The skimmers they had certainly were not working. If the Soviet skimmer had been here, it probably could have got a lot of the oil. The engineer wanted to know if we could use the supersuckers he had up on the North Slope, so we talked about that, and he said, 'Look, are you guys going to be with me on this? It's going to cost me a million dollars.' We said, yeah, we'll back you up. It was crazy. Who were we? A bunch of fishermen, but for a while, it was like we were all generals.

"The next day we started to talk about alternative things, and we broke it to them then, the supersuckers. Iarossi was there and he kind of woke up and said, 'How many can we get?' That was when I started to see how Iarossi got to where he was. It was his ability to make decisions. We sent for the supersuckers, and in the meantime they were lightering the ship and all the Exxon people were kind of white. You could see they were living right on the edge.

"We spent entire days on the phone and hardly got any sleep. Nobody knew who to call for anything, or what to do, where to work, where the planes were, where the oil spill tech people were. When we talked to Cordova, we said, 'Do what you have to do.' They ordered their own boom for Port San Juan. PWSAC and the city of Cordova all went way out on a limb with their budgets, and that was the real message of the whole thing. There was enormous parallel work going on, but if you didn't do it, it might not get done. It was a perfect mirror of the world.

"Exxon was really trying to mobilize equipment from all over the world, and they were trying to control the situation in several different ways, but you just couldn't depend on Exxon to cover the bases. They had to pay for it, so they wanted to be as sure as they could that things were needed. It was a tremendous peacetime mobilization. They were grabbing barges and planes from everywhere. The pilots were maxed out on hours. It was just what you'd have if you had a war. The volume had been turned up, but you couldn't really figure out where the knob was to get it turned back down. There were press people. You'd try to sleep, do four interviews, and talk to Australian TV, and fly out with the press, or go look at boom, or write up something, a contingency plan, a supersucker, or why dispersants were a nonissue, or make the video. You were developing relationships with all these people, most of whom had an ego problem. You were trying to figure out who was a player, who had to get up, who would never get up to speed, and nobody knew who everybody was or what or where all the information was, and yet information was inherent in everything. If you wanted to do the work, you had to know what it took to do it. It was that simple."

A storm was approaching. We'd come up the western flank of Knight Island. Just before dark, the *Orca II* crept through a narrow slot to a bay that occupied the heart of Disk Island, a small island located between the northern end of Knight and Ingot islands—one of the sites of horror I'd seen with the *Alpha Helix* crew. The bay, so far as the three of us could make out, had no name. It was almost completely encircled by Disk Island. On a map, Disk Island looked like a ragged Pac-Man head with a small, open mouth. We ducked into the eastern edge of the bay, as deep into the shelter as possible, and set anchor. Rain drummed against the roof of the cabin, and David and I talked until one o'clock.

At sunrise, the storm continued to blow and we decided to stay put. The rain filtered down. Where we were the water was nearly calm, but through the narrow slot at the west end of the bay, looking out into Lower Passage between Ingot Island and the northern end of Knight Island, whitecapped waves were raging by. That was not a place we wanted to be. During the night, two other boats, the *Monde Uni*, a seiner from Cordova, and a DEC boat had also sought refuge in the bay. From our position, the *Monde Uni* was visible to the left of the slot. The DEC boat was near to shore on our right. I spent time out in the open at the stern of the *Orca II*. The gray Zodiac swung slowly on its tether, folding back against the *Orca II*, then stretching out again. The *Orca II* itself swung on its anchor. The *Monde Uni* and the DEC boat swung, aligning themselves variously in the shifting wind. A man appeared on the deck of the *Monde Uni*, holding a cup of coffee. The bay was encircled by a line of oil, the bathtub ring.

Back in the galley, we ate breakfast, then moved to the wheelhouse. Lynn talked about accidents, about people he had known who died at sea. He knew of a boat from Seward with a crew of ten caught out in a winter storm. The crew no doubt left the boat because it was icing up and they were afraid it would sink. Later, the boat was found afloat, but there was no trace of the crew. David told us of premonitions he'd had of people who were going to die. A close friend of his had been killed some time ago. Another friend had died this year. Two people who had been on the *Orca II* just this summer had died. It was the storm and this bay, which not long before had been a place of death, and perhaps the boat gently twisting on its anchor, that brought on such talk. We had a mooring in a place of refuge, almost as if we'd found the calm in the eye of the storm. David said a man had contacted Rick Steiner back in the early days of the oil spill and claimed he had a device that could turn oil to water. At first, Rick had thought it was another snake oil joke, but then he and David began to wonder what would have happened if the guy could actually do it.

After his work with the citizens' advisory group in Valdez, after he'd made the oil spill video, David and Rick Steiner had gone to the Shetland Islands. That was in May. By that time, Chuck Hamel had given him some advice about Exxon. "Don't kid yourself about playing the game on their terms because they've got the heavyweights in town now," Chuck had said. Nevertheless, David had felt a compelling need to continue to do something. He said he asked himself why he was still talking to the cameras, that he needed to be able to make decisions. "The bureaucracies got left behind," he said, "and for the time being the power had returned to the people if they wanted to use it. It was hard work and you had to watch out, or everything would set up again. The oil companies were trying to reclaim the ground they'd lost. It was like something got loose and we had to try to figure out a way to keep it alive. It was a matter of dreams and hopes."

So far as the *Orca II* was concerned, spirituality came, I gathered, to have to do with bringing sometimes unlikely people into convergence on the water. As the three of us sat in the wheelhouse and tried to discuss the metaphysical, transcendental matters, we found it difficult to speak clearly. We believed that they were the bedrock of all questions posed by the oil spill. It was best, perhaps, to come in from the sides and always look to the peripheries, to the Shetland Islands; to Juneau, where there'd been a boat that had, according to David, "something of right livelihood moving through its history"; to the timber question (he would soon join forces with Rick Steiner in an attempt to get Exxon settlements set against the purchase of timber rights in the sound).

David was a voluptuary in the sense that William Carlos Williams described Daniel Boone as one. He recognized the difficulties as being neither strictly "material nor political" but "purely moral and aesthetic." It was expressed in his conduct—his ability to fish, to speak to people like Frank Iarossi, and to remain independent. Through his love of the wild and his inclination to affirm that "wild logic," he was able to locate the potency of a place like Lucky Bay, and to understand that potency did not mean mastery, but alignment. He was singular, but among those who answered the call of the oil spill, and struggled with it, and even made their mistakes with it, he was not alone in the possession of such qualities.

It rained throughout the day and we decided to spend another night at Disk Island. There was an otter in the bay, who dived, then came up on the other side of the bay. Another otter appeared back where the first one had been, but then I couldn't find the first one. Perhaps it was just one otter. Bill Black and Kenny Carlson came over in their Zodiac from the *Monde Uni* to talk. They were out picking up oiled popweeds. Bill Black said he didn't know what he was going to do with them—maybe take them to Valdez and let them figure it out. He would do that. It would be in the newspapers, and Exxon would figure it out. Naturally, a program would be initiated for the retrieval of oiled popweed. Bill and David got out the charts and marked the places where there were rocks in the channel that should be avoided.

Bill Black said he'd heard that Billy Webber (an admired Cordova fisherman) had the idea of tying fishing boats to the anchors of the tankers waiting off Knowles Head. At this the wheelhouse of the *Orca II* swirled with a spirited, half-jocular conversation about the possible methods of blocking tanker traffic and the technical challenges presented by each. It was as if the men were seeking the story that might feasibly be acted out. The methods ran the gamut from violent to nonviolent, or nearly so—loading up the narrows with fishing vessels, casting seine nets that would jam the tankers' propellers. The beauty of Webber's idea was its simplicity, its stillness, and its accentuation of a tanker's vulnerability to its own conspicuous size. Once a fishing boat tied on to a tanker's anchor and observers were on the scene, the tanker would not move for fear of capsizing the fishing boat. A few fishing boats might interrupt the entire Alaskan oil trade.

After Bill Black and Kenny Carlson left, David went on talking about Billy Webber. He said that Webber could catch four times as many fish as anybody else and it never seemed to take much effort. He'd do strange things, David said, like hang back and watch while everybody else was desperately fishing, even during a short opening. Then he'd take yet more time to motor off somewhere else and find all the fish he needed where no one thought they'd be. As David spoke, Webber took on a legendary aspect. It kept raining and time grew indeterminate.

David said he'd had a vision on the Colorado River. He'd realized there how beautiful the world was, but then he'd felt a wave of despair and inadequacy over his inability to express it. "The despair," he said, "was the sense of never being able to capture the essence of the world. I picked up the guitar and played a melody and suddenly it all broke over me. I felt Bach saying, 'Do you think it was different for me? Do you think I didn't feel helpless?' " He remembered David LaChapelle, who during his first sojourn on the *Orca II* had had a vision of all the animals killed by the oil spill hovering above the sound in a gray mist. They were the ghosts, watching what was to follow. We three now occupied the ghost territory.

After a time, I stepped out to take a leak off the stern of the boat. I saw one otter and then the other. There were two, after all. They were oblivious to the storm that raged outside the bay. One would dive and then the other, each head popping up whimsically in one place or another. Geese floated in the water. They paddled slowly as a group, but their bodies, long necks, and heads seemed still. A black bear appeared from behind the ridge at the edge of the bay and descended the short, steep bank nearly to the water. I studied the circular bay, the rim of oil around it, and above that the rocky bank. The bear investigated the shoreline. The three boats twisted slowly on their anchors. The *Orca*'s Zodiac swung on its line, folded up against the hull of the *Orca*, then swung back. The *Monde Uni* swung our way. The DEC boat swung farther away. Through the slot in the bay, the jagged whitecaps could be seen sliding by.

The black bear moved sinuously, almost catlike, stepping adeptly from rock to rock and passing over and under the fallen timber. He disappeared into a dense stand of bush. The occasional trembling of outer branches marked his progress. The otters dove one at a time, then reappeared. The bear emerged from the bush. He had a way of walking with the front feet going out sideways a bit, reaching out there. He looked agile and powerful and balanced, and there was absolutely no waste in his motion.

Conclusion

THE BUBBLE NET

Some would argue that the damage left by the oil spill from the Exxon *Valdez* is moderate, particularly if the spill is compared to the human effects of other recent manmade disasters—Bhopal, Chernobyl, the continuing disaster at Britain's Sellafield, or at our own Hanford Nuclear Reservation. In Bhopal, some 2,000 people are known to have died as a direct result of the release of methyl isocyanate from the Union Carbide installation. At Chernobyl, the number of deaths is put at 37, with an additional 240 or so cases of acute radiation sickness, although the veracity of those figures is shrouded first by, shall we say, the guarded attitude the Russian government had toward information, and secondly by the unknown longterm effects of the radiation plume, particularly in Russia and Europe. Thousands more, it is likely, will develop cancers, and a vast expanse of Russian land has been permanently contaminated. The chronic destruction at Britain's Sellafield installation, where large numbers of Britons have had their lives endangered by nuclear waste from the world's largest commercial producer of plutonium, is well described in Marilynne Robinson's recent book, *Mother Country: Britain, the Welfare State and Nuclear Pollution*. There, too, the British government, which operates the plant, has displayed a curious attitude toward presenting its people with the truth about radiation. In the United

States, after years of questions and rising cancer rates in nearby farming communities and on the Yakima Reservation, shocking information is just now coming out about radiation plumes released during the forties and fifties from the Hanford Nuclear Reservation in Washington State.

None of these disasters is quite the same as another, except that they all involved the release of toxic substances and occurred in association with big money. No human is known to have died as a direct consequence of the Exxon *Valdez* oil spill itself. Numerous people, however, including the crew members of the *Valdez*, government representatives, technicians and workers who were early on the scene, and residents of the villages of Ellamar and Tatitlek, were imperiled by the effect of fumes upon their respiratory systems. Exxon has noted that during the cleanup only two of the 11,000 persons employed died on the job—one of those a heart attack casualty, and the other crushed by a ship's dumbwaiter—and that the injury rate was 30 percent lower than the national average for heavy construction projects. Cindy Coe, area director for the Anchorage office of the Occupational Safety and Health Administration (OSHA), confirmed the mortality rate but added that Exxon put out the injury rate figures (in December 1989) before the company had enough data to support the claims.

This is the disturbing attitude toward information, and toward language as nothing more than a means for manipulating perception. Beginning with the first days of the spill, Exxon repeatedly offered unconfirmed, incomplete, and misleading accounts. In July 1990, the *Valdez*, repaired at a cost of $30 million, was renamed the Exxon *Mediterranean* and reassigned to the Persian Gulf. Exxon officials explained that because of the decline of Alaskan oil production, the ship was no longer needed on the West Coast, and that giving ships names appropriate to the region they served was normal practice. Considering Exxon's approach to language, however, it's more likely that the company hoped the new name and assignment would wipe out the ship's former identity. Among the interested parties, too, Exxon has been the most adamant about protecting the confidentiality of research findings.

Nonetheless, according to Cindy Coe, the final numbers are likely to show that the cleanup effort was quite effective so far as provisions for worker safety were concerned. It's fair to add that the work conditions were hazardous, mainly due to oil-slickened rocks, tricky weather, rough seas, and water so cold that to fall into it meant almost certain death. In December, Exxon's health and safety manager, Fred Brown, said to me, "My goal was to not kill anyone. I was surprised by the hazards associated with the slippery conditions, but my biggest fear was of losing a boat with forty or fifty people on it."

It must be granted that the safety record was excellent, just as the "zero tolerance" pollution standard applied to cleanup vessels was exemplary, and that there were measures of good in the opportunities taken to research ways of responding to future spills and in the willingness, at least, of Exxon to devote its considerable resources to cleanup. At the same time, however, to see a hundred workers filing up from Valdez docks, after several days of safe but often meaningless labor, to consider the damage in much of the cleanup exercise, the wasted money, or the effect of the spill of money—it all became another conquest of nature and of the imagination.

During the year, the principal cleanup subcontractor, Bill Allen's Veco International, jumped from the fifth largest Alaska-based company to the largest. Mainly through its nonunion and union construction and maintenance subsidiaries (Veco, Inc., and Norcon), the parent company grossed $960 million, nearly nine times its revenues of $110 million the previous year. Of that gross, $800 million came from Exxon, and $32 million of it showed as profits from its 4 percent cost-plus cleanup contract. The profits, according to Allen, would be plowed into the newly purchased *Anchorage Times*. The company's other new subsidiary, Veco Environmental and Professional Services, Inc., created to provide technical support to Veco, Inc., and Norcon, had been called in to work on the Moroccan spill and the British Petroleum spill off Huntington Beach, California. By such arrangements, a part of the old adversarial relationship between conscientious environmental activists and the industries of extraction is subsumed beneath the corporate umbrella. The first requirement of a business devoted to environmental cleanup is a steady supply of environmental catastrophes.

Even the cleanup sites become capitalized. Research, such as that devoted to dispersants and bioremediation, was conducted by Exxon in cooperation with the EPA to the exclusion at times of other promising formulations by independent parties. Because of its hold on patents, Exxon will eventually benefit. This touches upon the question that comes up no matter where one looks in the petroleum industry: Are these matters of public or private domain? Historically, the oil industry has at times pleaded its free enterprise interests, by which it is allowed to go to the extremes of forming trusts, of fixing prices, of keeping secret matters that bear upon public concern, and at times of forming its own foreign policy. At other times, it pleads ties to national security, by which it is easily the largest single recipient of government welfarism, including the mustering of troops to protect its interests. To my mind, the question has become not so much whether or not Exxon put forth a good faith effort as where the company places its faith. The ultimate answer, I fear, is in the reluctance of the American people to penetrate the loop of power that exists between the oil interests and the government, and in the people's willingness to put up with almost anything to keep their gas tanks full.

The American consumer, as we have allowed ourselves to be called, makes up the most dangerous influence in the country—dangerous in the sense that our insatiable appetite for raw materials causes continuous and destructive change in the world. We seem unable to attend to the effects of our habits. Our heedlessness has become systemic, like an organism that learns to live out its time with a case of worms. There are statistics to confirm our role in the world—the fact that we use two and a half times more energy per capita than the citizens of Japan and western Europe, or that we use almost 40 times as much energy per capita as do citizens of, say, Nigeria and India, or that in little over ten years since the OPEC embargo and the shortage scare, and despite efficiency measures, we have allowed our consumption of petroleum products to creep back nearly to the record 1978 levels. These, and even more troubling statistics that tell of our part in the worldwide effects of pollution, are rolled out for public viewing regularly, but we seem unable to come to grips with them. While opinion polls suggest that we want environmental measures to be taken, we seem to lean toward action only fleetingly, when faced with an industrial or ecological calamity. Then, as the incident in Prince William Sound would seem to suggest, the nation flagellates itself, the press and broadcast news feed our frenzy with half-assimilated information, and we fasten on symbols in order to allay our disturbing sense of ignorance and guilt.

In this case one symbol was Exxon, what many came to regard as an evil empire, though it is in fact us. Another was the otter, the newfound Bambi that we sought to redeem, and so to redeem ourselves. The first is part of one of our controlling myths, the myth of endless resource and endless consumption. As late as the early twentieth century, it was a myth of hope and adventure, but now it has become a myth saturated with invidious and violent greed and by a vision of ourselves as an international privileged class. The second symbol, the otter, conjured up the myth of the lost garden. From this springs our melancholy regard for Alaska as the last wilderness on American soil. This is what triggered the remarkable but often sentimental response, and hence quickly exhausted the outpouring of concern over the spill. The two contradictory myths have converged to make a psychic loop from which we cannot seem to free ourselves, or hope to be freed, except by widespread catastrophe, or perhaps war. We have entrapped ourselves inside the paralyzing loop as if to find shelter from the wider loop of big business and government.

The otter itself is a keystone predator, a species rather like us in that its voracious appetite for shellfish is capable of causing precipitous change in a habitat. Left alone, it will increase its numbers beyond the capacity of a habitat to support it and then will die off or migrate. The animal is tangled up in the history of the fur trade and in wildlife legislation. Some of its specialized features made it vulnerable to an oil spill—its proclivity to shoreline mining (large numbers of shellfish concentrate along the shore) and the loss of insulating capabilities it suffers when its fur is coated with oil. Otter rescue became complicated, too, because of jockeying for power among the rescue centers, and disputes over whether otters should be rescued at all, and whether or not placing them in captivity actually increases their susceptibility to disease. As in so many instances with the response to the oil spill, the confused remedies mirrored the confusion of the incident—not necessarily a bad thing. It meant that the perturbed reality out there had also perturbed the mind. What was bad was when remedies became entrenched in their own system.

In the rescue centers, there was a distemper scare and a herpes scare (later, according to Randall Davis, otters were found to have herpes in the wild). The scares caused some to argue that the otters should not be released into waters where they might infect other otters. There was a controversy during the spring of 1990 over an otter die-off. Forty dead otters were discovered in Prince William Sound during a five-week period preceding mid-April, an unusually high number, according to Nancy Lethcoe, the Valdez coordinator of the state's winter cleanup effort. The question arose as to whether or not those otters had been contaminated by oil over the winter. There was another die-off among otters released with implanted radio transmitters, which raised questions as to whether or not captivity had weakened the animals. The otter carcasses were taken by the Department of Fish and Wildlife, and so the answers to questions, or partial answers (since there is no baseline for otter populations in Prince William Sound), vanished into the secret world of litigation, denying the public the necessary access to the confusion, and so to the hard choices that must be made.

It is estimated that some 2,000 to 3,000 otters died in the spill, as did some 90,000 to 300,000 birds.* This says nothing of the damage to other life forms and to habitats. Because of the lack of baseline studies and harsh conditions, which made retrieval difficult, losses are difficult to track with precision. During the summer of 1989, 994 otter carcasses were found, 71 percent of them in Prince William Sound and 29 percent off the Kenai Peninsula. A total of 26, 499 bird carcasses from 74 different species were recovered, the vast majority of these in the Gulf of Alaska. Provided there are no unexpected sublethal effects, the otter population is expected to rebound fairly quickly. With some bird species, recovery may take between 20 and 75 years. The hardest hit species were the murres and coast birds, such as loons, sea ducks, and grebes. Eighty-seven yellow-billed loons were found dead. This represents, the Department of Fish and Wildlife estimates, between 10 and 30 percent of the total yellow-billed loons killed by the oil spill, or over 250 individuals of an already rare species that numbers between two and five thousand.

A total of 338 otters were brought into the otter rescue centers. Of these, 114 died, 28 were placed in aquariums, and 196 were released. A total of 1,589 birds were received in the bird centers; 792 died and 797 were released. The expense for each rehabilitated otter was over $90,000 and for each rehabilitated bird, over $25,000. A small number of eagles were captured, rehabilitated, and released, at a cost of $42,000 each. The total cost of wildlife rescue and rehabilitation to Exxon was $41 million. All these figures are probably low. They obviously invite comparative applications. The price of one rescued otter, some would argue, is about the same as the cost of four low-cost dwellings for homeless families, but Exxon money, of course, was not being used to build low-cost dwellings for the homeless in Seward, Seldovia, and Valdez.

Also, such comparative applications of statistics fly in the face of individual commiseration with the plight of one oiled otter or bird. Brought face to face with injury or death, most everyone understands that this vulnerability is also one's own. What is troubling is the refusal to keep this understanding in play. Instead, we revert either to sentimentality, which tames the horrifying, or to indifference, which denies the wonder of life. What part of the imagination is awakened and what part closes down when the hunting animal breaks for its prey? What part closes down when it ceases even to hunt and merely allows its victims to pile up on the beaches, or on the shoulders of highways, or on the grates of

---

* Although this is the highest mortality rate for any oil spill in history, it is merely part of the overall picture. The high seas gillnet fleet, for example, traps and kills an estimated 700,000 seabirds annually.

city streets? In the case of the Exxon *Valdez* spill, the precondition for regarding the damage as moderate is not to take seriously the lives of animals. The next step in this mind-set (common to psychopaths) is to treat humans (the poor, the powerless, the enemy horde) as if they were animals.

During the 1990 spring session, the Alaska legislature passed a major bill requiring the oil industry to stockpile enough equipment in Alaska to respond to a 300,000-barrel spill (12.6 million gallons) and to be prepared to import equipment to combat larger spills within 72 hours.* The bill included provisions for reimbursing victims of spills and for increased state monitoring of vessel traffic and inspection of tankers and pipelines. Another bill, which would have substantially increased the penalties for oil spills, failed to pass due to intense pressure from the oil lobby. The Alaska legislature also passed bills that increased criminal penalties for the reckless operation of oil carriers.

In August of 1990, the U.S. Congress passed legislation inspired by the *Valdez* spill which increased the liability by shippers for up to $1,200 per gross ton instead of the previous ceiling of $150 per gross ton. It also mandated the creation of a $1 billion oil spill response and cleanup fund with the money coming from a five-cent-a-barrel fee on both domestic and imported oil. The law requires that all new tankers have double hulls and that existing tankers be retrofitted with double hulls or taken out of service over the next 20 years. It calls for the formation of regional response teams within the Coast Guard to deal with oil spills and a national response center where computers will hold lists of personnel and equipment that can be called upon. In what may be its most significant feature, politically speaking, it recognizes the primacy of state regulations. President Bush has signed the legislation. The provisions of the law are certainly vulnerable to revision through the pressure of powerful industry forces in government. Its effectiveness depends upon strict enforcement.

Contrary to its wishes, Exxon did resume cleanup, with a reduced force (about 1,000 workers), during the summer of 1990. Emphasis was placed upon bioremediation and the use of dispersants, even on shorelines. Throughout the summer, Exxon and the state of Alaska were in

---

* The oil industry itself is also instituting a response program that will include storage and deployment sites on both American coasts. Any improvement in response methods and any reduction in damage from spills would be welcome. As noted in the preceding pages, however, the likelihood of a response to a catastrophic spill actually working remains speculative at best.

dispute over chemical applications, the effects of excavation, and just what "environmentally stable" meant. Generally speaking, the state was in favor of more aggressive mechanical cleanup methods and more stringent standards, and more opposed to the use of chemical dispersants. Purity had clearly become unattainable. Gradually, the positions held by Exxon and federal representatives gained sway over the state's position. At midsummer, a group of Moss Landing Institute scientists (Michael Foster, a faculty member, and two graduate students, John Tarpley and Susan Dearn) published an article that argued that "most shoreline cleanup methods will increase immediate ecological damage and delay recovery." The three had served on Shoreline Cleanup Advisory Teams during the summer of 1989.

They point out that evidence concerning the ecological effect of various cleanup procedures is sketchy, but that water flushing, excavation, and the trampling of beaches certainly destroyed many oiled organisms that were still alive. This is basically the same observation that the *Alpha Helix* crew had made. Foster, Tarpley, and Dearn also note that dispersant use near shorelines introduces more toxic elements into delicate water columns. Concerning the use of dispersants generally, they repeat the doubts of other scientists concerning their effectiveness and risks and recommend site-by-site and the circumspect use of manual collection by, for example, vacuum pumps and skimmers. They argue that oil will degrade on beaches strongly affected by tides, currents, and waves (high-energy beaches) in a period of a few months to a few years and on protected beaches in periods on the order of ten years. They are not saying that oil that remains on the beaches isn't damaging, but simply that most available cleanup methods are more damaging than leaving the oil alone. Nor do they address the question of sublethal effects, or of longterm benthic pollution. (According to the Alaska Department of Fish and Game and the National Marine Fisheries Service—and based on their observations of the deformation of rockfish and herring fingerlings—this has occurred, although to what degree has been kept secret.)

Steve Provant of the Alaska DEC, among others, has objected strenuously to Foster, Tarpley, and Dearn's observations. Certainly, sensitive habitats, such as spawning estuaries, should be addressed with great sensitivity, but in my judgment the three Moss Landing scientists are basically on target. This means that much of the cleanup was both destructive and unnecessary and that the state, the federal agencies, and Exxon have sustained the destruction and expense of the cleanup for two years.

It is utterly clear that the primary emphasis should be placed upon preventing further spills in Prince William Sound and elsewhere. Coast Guard records indicate that on average an oil tanker in U.S. waters catches fire, explodes, hits a dock or another ship, breaks apart, experiences mechanical failure, runs aground, or ends up in some kind of accident two of every three days.* It is equally clear that a drastic reduction in the number of spills (including pipeline leaks and refinery explosions) is well within the industry's capabilities, and that the only way industry will become accountable is for it to be too expensive for it not to be so. This means that legislative loopholes need to be closed, inspections vigorously conducted, regulations strictly enforced, heavy fines imposed, and shipping systems shut down when they are operated unsafely. It also means that the industry needs to create a deeper cushion between standard operating procedures and operating at peak capacity, and that it needs to be less driven by supplying low-cost fuel to the American public. In turn, the public should be prepared to accept higher prices, shortfalls, and conservation measures. It should support alternative energy sources and be prepared to require that public officials face the facts, perhaps communicating its seriousness through a boycott.

As I write, U.S. forces are building up in the Mideast in response to Iraq's invasion of Kuwait. The world shudders and, in order to account for its voracity and ancient hatred, much of it assures itself that the president of Iraq, Saddam Hussein, is a devil. There is no telling where this will lead. One has to read very deeply into the newspapers to find serious discussion of the fact that the U.S. response is about protecting Western oil interests, that existing Arab boundaries were drawn by the Western alliance with oil resources in mind, that the oil-producing state upon which we most rely, Saudi Arabia, is a feudal kingdom, as is (or was) Kuwait, and that much of Hussein's support comes from vast numbers of disenfranchised Arabs outside Iraq. Arabia is but another, if very large oil ghetto. The policy of the petroleum companies, American foreign relations, and now the Arabian national companies, such as Saudi Aramco, have converged to make a ring of power near the site of the biblical Garden of Eden, a desert rich with the chemical detritus of dead

---

* It should be observed that only about 6 percent of the petroleum in marine waters comes from accidental sources. By far the majority of such pollution (84 percent) comes from land-based industry and failures in waste management. For example, 31 percent of petroleum pollution enters the oceans in the form of runoff from cities and river systems, 30 percent from the *normal* conduct of marine transportation (bilge bunkering, dry docking, and so on), and 10 percent from the atmosphere. Also, natural seeps are the source of another 10 percent. Since the oil carried by tankers is not weathered, however, and since it is precipitously released in quantity, it is much more toxic and immediately devastating than oil from most other sources.

fecundity. President Bush has said one reason for our military presence is the need to protect the "American way of life."

To protect this *way*, we require stability at the wellhead so that we may bend to it and drink deeply of the dark stuff while all around its edges the garden erupts with fire. To preserve the illusion of a clean conscience, we buy into the sacred imagery of innocent hostages, the exalted symbology of machines, ships of all descriptions, planes, tanks, armaments, food, water tanks, endless lists of equipment, the young and guileless soldiers, the expenditure of billions. As forbidding and compelling as the immediate issues of the wisdom of this action, or what, strategically speaking, is to come next, the real question runs hard like a riptide in the deep, bearing down upon what William Carlos Williams called our "agonized spirit," the "idiot" that "governs with its great muscles, babbling in a text of the dead years."

In December 1989, Exxon, Alyeska, and other oil industry codefendants cited in over 150 private and public lawsuits filed papers in the state of Alaska's Anchorage Superior Court requesting a sweeping order that all evidence gathered prior to trial be kept secret. Taken together, the bits of information could create a mosaic of Exxon operations that would betray trade secrets. Alyeska spokesman George Jurkowich described the motion as "a broad request to protect information gained in a very wide-ranging discovery process. What that means," he said, "is if there is information out there about Alyeska, you can come and ask Alyeska about it, and we'll make a judgment about whether to release it." The motion provoked strong protests from the state and other plaintiffs, particularly since many of the suits are not expected to even go to trial for ten years. Macon Cowles, a lead attorney for environmental groups, said that "Exxon's basic proposal is to put all this information in a black box."

On February 27, 1990, a federal grand jury in Anchorage indicted the Exxon Corporation and its shipping subsidiary on five criminal counts (two felony charges under the 1972 Ports and Waterways Safety Act and the Dangerous Cargo Act, and three misdemeanors under the Clean Water Act, the Refuse Act, and the Migratory Bird Act). Guilty verdicts on all counts could result in fines of upwards of a billion dollars. Again, resolution of these charges, if the cases are tried, will not come for years—20 years, 30 years, or more. As the information is released, it will spin within the judicial system, driving its bits ever deeper as if into a black hole.

Prior to the February 27 indictment, the U.S. Justice Department had attempted to hammer out a plea bargain agreement that would have assessed about $200 million in criminal fines and required Exxon to contribute up to $550 million to a fund for environmental restoration. The plea bargain arrangement was abandoned due to a last-minute protest from the state of Alaska because a part of the agreement stipulated that the federal government would delay filing a civil suit for at least four years. Alaska said this would have cast it and all other plaintiffs adrift without any federal support as they pursued their damages.

Rick Steiner had been involved in the collapse of the plea bargain agreement. In a conversation with Frank Iarossi, the head of Exxon Shipping, Steiner learned that in any event Exxon preferred putting money into a restitution fund, which it could then deduct as expenses. Fines are not deductible. Steiner also learned that Exxon and the Justice Department were about to sign the agreement. He reported this to Alaska Attorney General Doug Baily and then, according to Steiner, "the shit hit the fan."

Steiner and others, including David Grimes, had already been working on establishing a restitution fund. The upshot was the July 1990 proposal by The Coastal Coalition for a comprehensive settlement. It sought to bring together state, environmental, and Native plaintiffs and to have all resource damages resolved in one stroke by having Exxon pay $2 billion to establish a nonprofit corporation, the Alaska Restoration Fund. Moneys from the fund would be used to support research, education, sustainable economic development, and for continuing restoration of resources damaged by the spill (reestablishing herring runs, for example) as provided by the Comprehensive Environmental Response, Compensation, and Liability Act (CERCLA, otherwise known as the Superfund). Also, the fund would be used to acquire resources equivalent to those that were lost. "Contingent valuation" served as one of the means for arriving at the $2 billion figure—an amount that is probably well under the total of what Exxon would pay otherwise in fines, penalties, claims, and legal fees.

This is the same weird, but perhaps justifiable, statistically driven system by which value is attached to the dead and to hazily perceived potentials, such as how much a forest will be worth 50 years from now. It is weird because it attaches the language of positivism to the clearly unmeasurable, such as "existence value"—the benefit gained by the public from simply knowing that, say, a forest or a healthy yellow-billed loon population exists. The system is defensible precisely because it does seek to give real weight to the unquantifiable in a society that seems to have forgotten how to honor mere existence or how to grant the force of spiritual values in any form other than a demagogic one, such as the tawdry political trade in the flag, school prayer, abortion, and the drug problem.

The Coastal Coalition's proposal argues, most reasonably, that "research should be driven by fundamental scientific interest in the behavior and response of this ecosystem . . . not by the need to collect evidence for litigation." As justifications for its legal solution, the proposal covers several areas, notably the economic need to maintain the viability of the fisheries and the interconnected biological need to protect existing natural diversity. Among its recommendations for the use of the fund is the purchase of timber rights in the sound and on the Kenai Peninsula. This is a tricky course to chart because those who own the timberlands—largely Native corporations—needed to be brought in on the arrangement and to develop some other longterm basis for their own economic well-being, and because a portion of the timber rights have already been sold. The proposal sought to reel back what was already in progress. As of late July, it had gained the support of several Native corporations.

Implicit in the proposal is the need for human alignment with the natural world, of seeing the world as inalienable rather than endlessly alienable. It observes, for example, the necessary role of what are known as terpenes, the biogenic hydrocarbons—oil—that drip from spruce trees. Terpenes are one type of the aromatic hydrocarbons that occur naturally and are ubiquitous in the world. They are what we smell in a coniferous forest. They are the cause of the explosive nature of forest fires. They are washed from the ground into streams and then into coastal waters. They float. They are driven by currents and collect in varying densities in various places. They may play a role in the so-far-mysterious olfactory memory of anadromous fishes—salmon. They are also the natural sustenance for the very hydrocarbon-metabolizing bacteria that were the essential element in the most promising oil spill restoration technology—bioremediation. To cut the forests would therefore increase the susceptibility of marine habitats to the damaging effects of oil. This is one very discrete, though telling example taken from a forest filled with such interconnections of alive and dead things—trees, bush, lichen, mammal, bird, insect, fish. The forest also happens to be relatively intact and of marginal value on the timber market.

Rick Steiner and I had met in southeastern Alaska in June 1990 to discuss the then forthcoming Coastal Coalition proposal. Rick understood very well the ironies of the proposal, the gaps in the science, and the difficulties he would have in succeeding, but he was proceeding. "In order to restore the sound," he said, "we have to know what existed beforehand, but that baseline doesn't exist. Besides the fact that a lot of the oil spill research is useless, we'll never come to a consensus on the damage to resources. But timber preservation or restoration has everything to do with the oil spill. First, because any increased stress delays recovery, and Exxon restitution should be used to enhance recovery. Furthermore," he said, "because of the conditions here—the cold and the recently glaciated soil—the forest takes one to two hundred years to recover. The jobs the logging industry creates will eventually create hard times. What we need is a different way of economic thinking other than boom and bust economy, and a way of redirecting economy to a self-sustaining basis."

Capable of being earthy at one moment and cerebral the next, or funny and then composed, Rick was admired by other activists for his ability to engage the upper echelons of the industry and political power structure and to survive the sometimes intense scrutiny of the press without losing his sense of balance. I also admired in him what I had admired in many others—the capacity to absorb the powerfully conflicting forces of the oil spill and yet to continue to look up, to see what else was out there along the edges, and to take tough action, even when the action might seem outrageous, such as proposing a comprehensive legal settlement and carrying it directly to New York and Washington, D.C.

Part of my conversation with Rick occurred in Sitka Sound on a boat which was following two humpback whales at some distance. The whales swam in the shadows near the shoreline, scouting a herring school. Their long, dark backs were visible to us. Periodically, they dove one after another, lifting their flukes to the air. Their method of capture was to swim upward in circles from the deep, beginning beneath the fish. As they circled, they released air, creating a curtain of bubbles called a "bubble net." It was an original form of seining, actually, although the net was an illusion. The herring apparently considered themselves trapped, and their impulse was to swim higher and higher to try to get over the top, but of course the bubbles that made the net also rose to the surface.

From the boat, what we saw was the dark whales cruising the surface, then turning down. Their flukes hung for an instant as the animals gathered themselves for the dive. Then there was a quietude, nothing at all on the surface, and then a white circle of bubbles appeared on the water, sometimes a good distance away from where the whales had dived. In another moment, the herring suddenly appeared, scores of them desperately breaking the surface inside the ring. They were frantic. They looked like knives cutting repeatedly through the surface as they tried to fly straight up into the air. Finally, one of the whales (they took turns at this) breached the water with its huge jaws agape, the inside of its mouth white against its dark body, the dark water, and dark shore as it gulped the fish. The whale settled back into the water and blew white vapor. They did this repeatedly.

After a time, our boat passed a mill owned by a Japanese company, the Alaska Pulp Corporation. The trees that supplied the mill were cut from the notoriously administrated Tongass National Forest. The water churned up in the boat's wake turned a dark brown as a result of discharged waste. Along the shoreline, huge rafts of logs were cabled up in coves and on the leeside of bluffs. We'd been talking admiringly of the whales, and then of pollution and whales. Our conversation turned naturally to clear-cutting, and to habitat fragmentation, that is, the breaking up of a habitat that is caused by logging, development, by the noise of machines, the trampling of humans, and by oil spills. Fragmentation damages the most critical element of any habitat—its genetic diversity, or its exquisitely balanced chaos, and it occurred to me once again that the trick was to enter the chaos, not to control it, nor to wipe it out with one form of monomania or another, and yet at the same time to hold fast to a sense of right conduct, to keep looking outward, and not to get trapped inside an illusory net. I thought of Bruce Martin's description of the dimensions of the world, the four of them always simultaneously present, and of the indivisibility of the so-called real and the spiritual. The effect of this way of thinking was to make one spiritually accountable. It did not fragment the world.

NOTES

A NOTE ON THE SOURCES

The principal sources for this book have been, first, the experience as told to me by the residents of south-central Alaska, and second, the accounts of those in official capacities with federal, state, and local governments, and with the Exxon Corporation. In addition, beginning on the day of the oil spill, government agencies and private and public institutions have generated vast quantities of written material in the form of press or public information releases and memoranda. When such documents contained significant information, my approach was to check them one against another and whenever possible to speak directly to people in the institutions. These sources have been cited in the text.

Certain documents, articles, and books proved central. Among the documents are the National Transportation Safety Board (NTSB) hearings *The Grounding of the U.S. Tankship Exxon Valdez*; the Alaska Superior Court transcripts of the trial of Joseph Hazelwood; the Alaska Oil Spill Commission's four-volume publication *Spill: The Wreck of the Exxon Valdez*; Engineering Computer Optecnomics' *An Assessment of Tanker Transportation Systems in Cook Inlet and Prince William Sound*; the National Oceanic and Atmospheric Administration's daily overflight charts of the course of the oil spill; and the *State and Federal Natural Resource Damage Assessment Plan for the Exxon Valdez Oil Spill*.

The books and articles I consulted fell into two general categories. Some provided scientific and technical information. Among the most useful of these were the National Academy of Science's *Oil in the Sea: Inputs, Fates, and Effects* and *Using Oil Dispersants on the Sea*; Lou and Nancy Barr's *Under Alaskan Seas*; Pete Mickelson's *Natural History of Alaska's Prince William Sound*; D. K. Button's work on terpenes; and James Payne and Daniel McNabb, Jr.'s work on oil in the marine environment. Other works provided a sense of historical and intellectual context. Among these, I was especially attentive to Thomas Berger's *Village Journey: The Report of the Alaska Native Review Commission*; Robert Engler's *The Brotherhood of Oil* and *The Politics of Oil*; Morgan Sherwood's *Exploration of Alaska: 1865–1900*; Susan Sontag's *On Photography*; Walter Mead's *Mortal Splendor: The American Empire in Transition*; and William Carlos Williams's *In the American Grain*.

Following the oil spill, there was intense and often overlapping newspaper coverage in and out of Alaska. I regularly read the newspapers listed in the bibliography, but have cited them as sources only when the material is explicit and critical. Finally, it should be mentioned that since Art Davidson's *In the Wake of the Exxon Valdez: The Devastating Impact of the Alaska Oil Spill* was published before my work was completed, I was given the opportunity to consult his findings. The references that follow, named by author, or sometimes by title and date in the case of periodicals and documents, are to works listed in the bibliography.

Chapter 1. INTRUDERS

The naming of Bligh Island, whether by Cook or Vancouver, is variously reported. See Pethick, p. 178. Cook first gave the name Sandwich to the sound, then King William Sound. Subsequently the name was changed to Prince William Sound. See Cook (ed. Price), p. 228.

Chapter 2. THE SCREENS ON THE STAGE

For the account of Fidalgo's exploration and the naming of the port after him, see Lethcoe, p. 34. Early history of settlement and development is derived from Naske and Slotnick, passim. For an account of ANCSA and its effects see Berger, passim, and for subsistence see Berger, Stratton and Chisum, and Stanek, passim. For the death of Cook, see Cook (ed. Price), p. 255 ff., and for the personal history of Joseph Hazelwood, see *Time*, July 24, 1989. Background material on the oil industry was derived largely from Engler (both books), passim. For somewhat different perspectives, see also Adelman, Turner, and Sampson. Oil earnings figures are derived from industry accounts and Horton, p. 57. Production figures are taken from R. Smith, pp. 4–5. For accounts of Alyeska's troubles with pollution regulations and mechanical breakdowns, see the hearings of the National Transportation Safety Board, passim; LaResche, "Appendix C"; *Anchorage Daily News* (Epler) October 22, 1989 and October 29, 1989; Horton, p. 58 ff.; *Wall Street Journal* (McCoy) July 6, 1989; and Davidson, p. 79, passim. For quoted material from Eward, Woodle, Blake, Lawn, and Tom McCarty, see *Wall Street Journal* (McCoy) July 6, 1989; for quoted material from LaResche and Lawn, see Davidson, p. 94, and p. 83 ff.; for quoted material from Purtell, see Luoma. The material on the Thompson Pass spill is reported in Davidson, pp. 5–7 and corroborated in conversation with Charles Hamel. For information on the Alaskan tankerage fleet, see Luoma, passim, and Bell, passim. Material regarding Ott's experience is derived from interviews with her and from her "O.C., Inc.," passim.

Chapter 3. THE CHANNEL

My own observation of Prince William Sound was augmented by Dold and Soucie, and Mickelson, passim.

Chapter 4. THE IMAGINARY JOURNEY OF CAPTAIN JOSEPH HAZELWOOD

For events pursuant to the grounding of the Exxon *Valdez*, see the Superior Court transcripts of the Joseph Hazelwood trial, the NTSB hearings, and LaResche, all passim. When the accounts vary the court transcripts are given precedence. For the misidentified blood samples and 1990 Coast Guard hearings, see *Anchorage Daily News* (Deutsch and Campbell) July 26, 1990. For Hazelwood's personal history see *Time*, July 24, 1989. For the results of the Coast Guard study, see Bell, passim.

Chapter 5. CITY LIFE

Here and elsewhere, the chronology of the spill and response is derived from Lethcoe and Nurnberger, pp. 1–4, and from *Spill: The Wreck of the Exxon Valdez*, vol. 4, passim. For material on the Alyeska response, see the 1987 *Alyeska Oil Spill Contingency Plan*. Many of the pertinent facts within the *Plan* are also widely reported in books and articles. For specific Alyeska failures according to the *Plan*, see Davidson, passim; Horton, p. 57 ff.; *Wall Street Journal* (McCoy) July 6, 1989; *New York Times* April 3, 1989; and *Anchorage Daily News* (Epler) October 22, 1989 and October 29, 1989. For quoted material from Ott, see Davidson, p. 26; for the account of Steiner's observation flight, see Sims, p. 12; and for quoted material from Brennan, see Horton, p. 58. The attempts to use dispersants are recounted in testimony before the National Transportation Safety Board (especially Iarossi, Kelso, and McCall). See also Davidson, p. 29 ff. For the Exxon suit against the state of Alaska, see *Anchorage Daily News* (Toomey) October 24, 1989. For information on the regulations applying to the use of dispersants in Prince William Sound and on the nature of dispersants, see 1987 *Oil Spill Contingency Plan*, pp. 3–51ff.; Lethcoe and Nurnberger, pp. 38–53; and Butler, passim. For material quoted from Butler, see p. 249.

Chapter 6. CORDOVA

Material from Kumins is as cited in the text. My conversations with Cordovans are augmented by the account in Sims, and in Ott, "O.C., Inc.," passim. The quotation from Steiner concerning logistical support is drawn from Davidson, p. 110. Regarding Copeland's efforts, see Davidson, p. 109. Weaverling's account, as told to me, is augmented by information in Davidson, p. 134 ff. For salmon spawning, see Netboy, p. 32 ff.

Chapter 7. SHOWTIME

Don Moore's statement is recorded in the video, *Voices of the Sound*. Bill Allen's personal history and information regarding Veco International are drawn from various newspaper accounts, including *Anchorage Daily News* November 21, 1989

(Mauer), an internal memo from Veco's marketing division by Todd Bureau, and from *Alaska Business Monthly* October 1990 (Tyson). For a complete account of Veco and Allen's role in the gray whale rescue operation, see Rose. For the quoted material from Yost, see Davidson, p. 124.

Chapter 8. THE TEARS OF SCIENCE

For atmospheric and marine conditions, see *Spill: The Wreck of the Exxon Valdez*, vol. 2, pp. ii–1 ff. For the chemistry and behavior of oil, see Payne and McNabb, passim, Butler, passim, and Lethcoe and Nurnberger (Ott), pp. 30–37.

Chapter 9. THE RAPTURE OF MACHINES

For supplementary data on marine life, see Barr, passim. The test beach controversy was presented in the *Anchorage Daily News* on February 20, 1990 (Wohlforth) and March 2, 1990 (Maki). The quotations by Yost and Robbins are from Davidson, pp. 124, 190.

Chapter 11. GUESTS

For comparative data on the Sullom Voe and Alyeska Contingency Plans, see Lethcoe and Nurnberger (Ott), pp. 102–3.

Chapter 12. THE VALUE OF THE DEAD

Supplementary information on the response of Kenai Peninsula people, including the "bird burning" and Gore Point material, has been derived from the *Homer News*, March–July 1989. For quoted material from Flagg, see Davidson, p. 257. As noted in the text, for "contingency valuation" see Krutilla, and Freeman and Kopp, passim.

Chapter 13. SELDOVIA

Again, supplementary information is derived from accounts in the *Homer News*. For the response from Kenai Fjords National Park, also see Davidson, p. 240 ff.

Chapter 14. THE TRUTH ABOUT OIL

For background information on crude oil, see Payne and McNabb, Gourlay, Steele, Butler, Neff, and Baker, all passim. See also Lethcoe and Nurnberger (Ott), pp. 30–35.

Chapter 15. CRAPS

Passages from the text of Meganack's address are drawn from Frost, pp. 6–8. McMullen's remarks are reported in the *Anchorage Daily News*, June 19, 1989. For Engler's description, see Engler, "Portrait of an Oil Spill."

Chapter 16. MASKS

For *Alaska* magazine background material, see Davidson, p. 207.

Chapter 17. NO ROAD

Some of the late 1989 and early 1990 accounts are drawn from the *Cordova Times*.

Conclusion. THE BUBBLE NET

Wildlife mortality figures have been widely reported, including *Anchorage Daily News*, October 8, 1989. For financial information on Veco International and its subsidiaries, see *Alaska Business Monthly*, October 1990. Oil pollution statistics are drawn from Hyland, p. 493, and are 1976 estimates. Rehabilitation costs are derived from Exxon press material. For cleanup assessment, see Foster, passim. For the quotation by Cowles, see *Anchorage Daily News*, December 28, 1989. For terpenes, see Button and Button and Jüttner, passim. For The Coastal Coalition's proposal, see Steiner, passim.

SELECTED BIBLIOGRAPHY

BOOKS

Adelman, M. A. The World Petroleum Market. Baltimore: Johns Hopkins University Press, 1972.

The Alaska Almanac. 1989 ed. Edmonds and Anchorage: Alaska Northwest Books, 1989.

Alvarez, A. Offshore: A North Sea Journey. Boston: Houghton Mifflin Co., 1986.

Armstrong, Robert H. Guide to the Birds of Alaska. Anchorage: Alaska Northwest Publishing Co., 1983.

Arvidson, Rose C. Cordova, The First 75 Years, a Photographic History. Cordova: Fathom Publishing Co., 1984.

Barr, Lou, and Nancy Barr. Under Alaska Seas. Anchorage: Alaska Northwest Publishing Co., 1983.

Berger, Thomas R. Village Journey: The Report of the Alaska Native Review Commission. New York: Hill and Wang, 1985.

Brody, Hugh. Maps and Dreams. New York: Pantheon Books, 1982.

Brundtland, Gro Harlem, et al. Our Common Future: World Commission on Environment and Development. Oxford and New York: Oxford University Press, 1987.

Butler, James N., et al. National Research Council. Using Oil Spill Dispersants on the Sea. Washington, D.C.: National Academy Press, 1989.

Cook, James. The Journals of Captain James Cook on His Voyages of Discovery. Edited by J. C. Beaglehole. Vols. 1–4. Cambridge: Hakluyt Society, 1955–67.

Cook, James. *The Explorations of Captain James Cook in the Pacific as Told by Selections of his Own Journals 1768–1779.* Edited by A. Grenfell Price. New York: Dover, 1971.

Darwin, Charles. *The Origin of Species.* New York: NAL Penguin, 1958.

Davidson, Art. *In the Wake of the Exxon Valdez: The Devastating Impact of the Alaska Oil Spill.* San Francisco: Sierra Club Books, 1990.

Dumond, Don E. *The Eskimos and Aleuts.* Rev. ed. New York: Thames and Hudson, 1987.

Engler, Robert. *The Brotherhood of Oil.* Chicago: U. of Chicago Press, 1977.

———. *The Politics of Oil.* New York: Macmillan, 1961.

Gourlay, K. A. *Poisoners of the Seas.* London and Atlantic Highlands, N.J.: Zed Books, Ltd., 1988.

Greene, William N. *Strategies of the Major Oil Companies.* Ann Arbor, Mich.: UMI Research Press, 1982.

Klein, Janet. *A History of Kachemak Bay: The Country, The Communities.* Homer, Alaska: Homer Society of Natural History, 1987.

Kundera, Milan. *The Art of the Novel.* Translated by Linda Asher. New York: Grove Press, 1986.

Langdon, Steve J. *The Native People of Alaska.* Anchorage: Greatland Graphics, 1987.

Lethcoe, Jim, and Nancy R. Lethcoe. *Cruising Guide to Prince William Sound.* Valdez: Prince William Sound Books, 1985.

Lethcoe, Nancy R., and Lisa Nurnberger. *Prince William Sound Environmental Reader 1989—T/V Exxon Valdez Oil Spill.* Valdez: Prince William Sound Conservation Alliance, 1989.

Mangusso, Mary Childers, and Stephen W. Haycox, eds. *Interpreting Alaska's History: An Anthology.* Anchorage: Alaska Pacific University Press, 1989.

Mickelson, Pete. *Natural History of Alaska's Prince William Sound.* Cordova: Alaska Wild Wings, 1989.

Muir, John. *Travels in Alaska.* San Francisco: Sierra Club Books, 1988.

Naske, Claus-M., and Herman E. Slotnick. *Alaska, A History of the 49th State.* 2nd ed. Norman and London: University of Oklahoma Press, 1987.

Nelson, Richard K. *Hunters of the Northern Forest.* Chicago: U. of Chicago Press, 1986.

Netboy, Anthony. *Salmon: The World's Most Harassed Fish.* Tulsa: Winchester Press, 1980.

O'Donoghue, Brian. *Black Tides: The Alaska Oil Spill.* Anchorage: Alaska Natural History Association, 1989.

Pethick, Derek. *First Approaches to the Northwest Coast.* Seattle: U. of Washington Press, 1979.

Repetto, Robert, ed. *The Global Possible: Resources, Development, and the New Century.* New Haven and London: Yale University Press, 1985.

Robinson, Marilynne. *Mother Country: Britain, the Welfare State and Nuclear Pollution.* New York: Farrar, Straus, and Giroux, 1989.

Rose, Tom. *Freeing the Whales: How the Media Created the World's Greatest Non-Event.* New York: Carol Publishing, 1989.

Sampson, Anthony. *The Seven Sisters: The Great Oil Companies and the World They Shaped.* New York: Viking Press, 1975.

Sherwood, Morgan B. *Exploration of Alaska: 1865–1900.* New Haven and London: Yale University Press, 1965.

Sontag, Susan. *On Photography.* New York: Farrar, Straus, and Giroux, 1977.

Steele, John H., et al. *Oil in the Sea, Inputs, Fates, and Effects.* Washington, D.C.: National Academy Press, 1985.

Turner, Louis. *Oil Companies in the International System.* London: The Royal Institute of International Affairs/George Allen and Unwin, 1978.

Whitaker, John O., Jr. *The Audubon Society Field Guide to North American Mammals.* New York: Alfred A. Knopf, 1980.

Williams, William Carlos. *In the American Grain.* New York: New Directions Books, 1925, 1956.

ARTICLES, OFFPRINTS, PAMPHLETS

Baker, J. M., R. B. Clark, P. F. Kingston, and R. H. Jenkins. "Natural Recovery of Cold Water Marine Environments After an Oil Spill." Paper presented at the Thirteenth Annual Arctic and Marine Oilspill Program Technical Seminar, June 1990.

Button, D. K. "Evidence for a Terpene-Based Food Chain in the Gulf of Alaska." *Applied and Environmental Microbiology* (1984):1003–10.

Button, D. K., and F. Jüttner. "Terpenes in Alaskan Waters: Concentrations, Sources, and the Microbial Kinetics Used in Their Prediction." *Marine Chemistry* 26 (1989):57–66.

Cernetig, Vladimiro, Jr. "Black Waters." *Equinox* 46 (July/August 1989): 40–48.

Dold, Catherine A., and Gary Soucie. "Just the Facts: Prince William Sound." *Audubon Magazine* 91, no. 5 (September 1989): 80.

Foster, M. S., J. A. Tarpley, and S. Dearn. "To Clean or Not to Clean: The Rationale, Methods, and Consequences of Removing Oil from Temperate Shores." *Northwest Environmental Journal* 6 (1990):105–20.

Freeman, A. Myrick III, and Raymond J. Kopp. "Assessing Damages from the Valdez Oil Spill." *Economist* (Summer 1989): 5–7.

Gilliland, Jennifer R. "Moving Alaskan Crude: Who's in Charge?" *Audubon Magazine* 91, no. 5 (September 1989): 87.

Hodgson, Bryan. "Alaska's Big Spill." *National Geographic*, January 1990, pp. 5–42.

Horton, Tom. "Paradise Lost." *Rolling Stone*, December 14–28, 1989.

Hyland, Jeffrey L., and Eric D. Schneider. "Petroleum Hydrocarbons and Their Effects on Marine Organisms, Populations, Communities, and Ecosystems." Paper prepared for symposium, Sources, Effects and Sinks of Hydrocarbons in the Aquatic Environment, American University, 1976.

Krutilla, John V. "Conservation Reconsidered." *American Economic Review* 57 (Summer 1967): 777–86.

Laycock, George. "The Baptism of Prince William Sound." *Audubon Magazine* 91, no. 5 (September 1989).

Luoma, Jon R. "Alaska's Aging Tanker Fleet." *Audubon Magazine* 91, no. 5 (September 1989): 77–91.

Manville, Albert M. II. "Oiled Aftermath." *Defenders* 64, no. 4 (July/August 1989): 13–17.

Neff, J. M. "Water Quality in Prince William Sound." Batelle Duxbury Operations, Duxbury, Mass., April 1990.

Nickerson, Sheila, ed. "Exxon Valdez Oil Spill." Special oil spill issue, *Alaska Fish and Game* 21, no. 4 (1989).

Ott, Riki (Fredericka). "O.C., Inc." Unpublished manuscript.

———. "Oil in the Marine Environment: An Update." Anchorage: Oil Reform Alliance, 1990.

Payne, James R., and G. Daniel McNabb, Jr. "Weathering of Petroleum in the Marine Environment." *Marine Technology Society Journal* 18, no. 3 (1984), 24–42.

Sims, Grant. "A Clot in the Heart of the Earth." *Outside*, June 1989.

DOCUMENTS

"Alaskan Oil Spill Bioremediation Project." Publication of the United States Environmental Protection Agency. Document number EPA/600/8–89/073. August 1989.

Albert, Tom. "Trip Report: (1) Joint U.S./Canadian Meeting in Seattle, Wa., to Review Hydrocarbon Developments in the Beaufort Sea; (2) Meeting in Anchorage of National Research Council Panel to Review Environmental Studies Program of the Minerals Management Service; and (3) Meeting in Anchorage with Soviet Scientists Regarding Cooperative Marine Mammal Study this Summer in Soviet Far East." Memorandum to Ben Nageak, Director, North Slope Borough, Department of Wildlife Management, Barrow, Alaska, May 1989.

Alyeska Oil Spill Contingency Plan, 1987.

An Assessment of Tanker Transportation Systems in Cook Inlet and Prince William Sound, Engineering Computer Optecnomics, Inc., Annapolis, Maryland, Nov. 4, 1989.

Bell, H. H. (rear admiral and chairman, Coast Guard Safety Study Group) et al. "Report of the Tanker Safety Study Group." October 1989.

Collingsworth, D. W., W. Stieglitz, M. A. Barton, and S. Pennoyer (members of the federal and state Trustee Council following the Exxon *Valdez* spill). *State/Federal Natural Resource Damage Assessment Plan for the Exxon Valdez Oil Spill, August 1989, Public Review Draft*. Juneau, 1989.

———. *The 1990 State/Federal Natural Resource Damage Assessment and Restoration Plan for the Exxon Valdez Oil Spill*. Vols. 1 and 2. Juneau, 1990.

Deakin, Edward B. "Oil Industry Profitability in Alaska: 1969 through 1987." Report prepared for the State of Alaska Department of Revenue. March 1989.

Exxon Corporation 1989 Annual Report. Exxon Corporation. New York, 1990.

Hearing Before the Committee on Commerce, Science, and Transportation, United States Senate, One Hundred First Congress, First Session on Exxon Valdez Oil Spill and Its Environmental and Maritime Implications. Washington, D.C.: U.S. Government Printing Office. April 6, 1989.

Holland, J. S. FRED 1988 *Annual Report to the Alaska State Legislature* 89. Division of Fisheries Rehabilitation, Enhancement and Development. Juneau, 1989.

Kodiak Island Area Local Fish and Game Resource Guide. Kodiak Area Native Association with Assistance from the Alaska Department of Fish and Game, Division of Subsistence, December 1983.

Kumins, Lawrence C. "CRS Report for Congress: The Alaskan Oil Spill and Gasoline Prices." Congressional Research Service, Library of Congress. April 17, 1989.

LaResche, Robert E. (oil spill coordinator, State of Alaska). *Before the National Transportation Safety Board, Washington, D.C.: Proposed Probable Cause, Findings and Recommendations of the State of Alaska.* Juneau, July 1989.

Lee, Martin R. "The Exxon Valdez Spill." Environment and Natural Resources Policy Division, Congressional Research Service, Library of Congress. September 5, 1989.

―――. "Oil Pollution Liability and Compensation Legislation After the Exxon *Valdez* Spill." Environment and Natural Resources Policy Division, Congressional Research Service, Library of Congress. September 5, 1989.

Logan, Sid, et al. *Cook Inlet Regional Salmon Enhancement Plan, 1981–2000.* Cook Inlet Regional Planning Team, 1982.

Parker, Walter B. et al. *Spill: The Wreck of the Exxon Valdez, Implications for Safe Marine Transportation.* Report of the Alaska Oil Spill Commission, Executive Summary and Appendices. Vols. 1–4. Anchorage, 1990.

Preliminary 1988/89 Herring Season Catch Summary. Alaska Department of Fish and Game, 1989.

Preliminary Review of the 1989 Alaska Commercial Salmon Fisheries. Alaska Department of Fish and Game, 1989.

Restoration Following the Exxon Valdez Oil Spill. Proceedings of the Public Symposium Held in Anchorage, Alaska, March 26–27, 1990. Restoration Planning Work Group, July 1990.

Savikko, Herman. *1988 Preliminary Alaska Commercial Fisheries Harvests and Values.* Regional Information Report No. 5J89-03. Alaska Department of Fish and Game. Juneau, 1989.

Smith, Rodney. "1989 Review of Hydrocarbon Development in the Beaufort Sea: Highlights of U.S. Oil and Gas Activities." Marine Management Service (included as an attachment to Tom Albert's North Slope Borough Memo).

Spill: The Wreck of the Exxon Valdez. Appendix. Vols. 1–4. Alaska Oil Spill Commission, Juneau, 1990.

Stanek, Ronald T. *Patterns of Wild Resource Use in English Bay and Port Graham, Alaska.* Technical Paper No. 104. Alaska Department of Fish and Game, Division of Subsistence, 1985.

State of Alaska (Plaintiff) v. Joseph Hazelwood (Defendant). State of Alaska, Third Judicial District. Transcript of Proceedings Before the Honorable Judge Karl S. Johnstone. Vols. 1–30. Anchorage, 1990.

Steiner, Rick. "Draft Proposal for a Comprehensive Settlement of Natural Resource Damages from the 'Exxon Valdez' Oil Spill." *Coastal Coalition,* July 1990.

Stratton, Lee, and Evelyn B. Chisum. *Resource Use Patterns in Chenega, Western Prince William Sound: Chenega in the 1960s and Chenega Bay 1984–1986,* Technical Paper No. 139, Alaska Department of Fish and Game, Division of Subsistence, December 1986.

VIDEOS

Voices of the Sound. Film Center for the Environment, 1989.

NEWSPAPERS AND MAGAZINES

Alaska Business Monthly, Alaska Fish and Game, Anchorage Daily News, Anchorage Times, Cordova Times, Homer News, Los Angeles Times, The Nation, National Fisherman, Newsweek, New York Times, Seattle Times, Spokane Spokesman Review, Time, Valdez Vanguard, Wall Street Journal

INDEX